UTILITARIANISM AND THE ETHICS OF WAR

This book offers a detailed utilitarian analysis of the ethical issues involved in war.

Utilitarianism and the Ethics of War addresses the two basic ethical questions posed by war: when, if ever, are we morally justified in waging war; and if recourse to arms is warranted, how are we permitted to fight the wars we wage? In addition, it deals with the challenge that realism and relativism raise for the ethical discussion of war, and with the duties of military personnel and the moral challenges they can face. In tackling these matters, the book covers a wide range of topics—from pacifism to armed humanitarian intervention, from the right of national defense to preemptive or preventive war, from civilian immunity to the tenets of just war theory and the moral underpinnings of the rules of war. But, what is distinctive about this book is that it provides a consistent and thorough-going utilitarian or consequentialist treatment of the fundamental normative issues that war occasions. Although it goes against the tide of recent work in the field, a utilitarian approach to the ethics of war illuminates old questions in new ways by showing how a concern for well-being and the consequences of our actions and policies shape the moral constraints to which states and other actors must adhere.

This book will be of much interest to students of the ethics of war, just war theory, moral philosophy, war and conflict studies, and IR.

William H. Shaw is Professor of Philosophy at San Jose State University, USA. He is the author/editor of numerous books.

'William H. Shaw's *Utilitarianism and the Ethics of War* is a terrific book that will enlighten readers interested in moral problems about warfare as well as friends and foes of utilitarian moral theory.'

Stephen Nathanson, Emeritus Professor, Northeastern University, USA

'In this important new work, Professor Shaw reflects not simply upon what states and their leaders actually consider or how they actually reason when declaring and conducting armed conflict, he offers convincing arguments regarding what they are also obliged to consider, and how they ought to reason about war and its consequences in terms of its overall impact on the welfare of their citizens and of society at large. While such utilitarian considerations traditionally infuse "just war" reasoning unsystematically, Shaw's is the first explicitly systematic treatment by an eminent utilitarian moral philosopher of just exactly how considerations of well-being and the common good offer the most useful and advantageous analysis of war's likely impact and permissibility. This is a significant revision and clarification of just war reasoning generally that ought to be read by every serious scholar or student of political theory, international relations, or moral philosophy.'

George Lucas, Emeritus Professor, U.S. Naval Academy

'William Shaw provides a cogent, compelling, and comprehensive account of the ethics of war, arguing persuasively that utilitarianism provides the most satisfactory basis for answering questions both about the justification of going to war, and about the ethical limits of conduct in war. This book provides a much-needed counterpoint to the deontological approaches that dominate contemporary discussion of military ethics.'

Alastair Norcross, University of Colorado, USA

'Shaw's *Utilitarianism and the Ethics of War* masterfully develops utilitarian prescriptions about when wars should be fought and about what are the rules that commanders and lower-ranked military personnel should follow in wars. Especially impressive are Shaw's explanations of how utilitarianism underwrites the principles of just war theory. This is a very wise book.'

Brad Hooker, University of Reading, UK

War, Conflict and Ethics

Series Editors:
Michael L. Gross
University of Haifa
and
James Pattison
University of Manchester

Founding Editor:
Daniel Rothbart
George Mason University

This new book series focuses on the morality of decisions by military and political leaders to engage in violence and the normative underpinnings of military strategy and tactics in the prosecution of war.

Civilians and Modern War
Armed conflict and the ideology of violence
Edited by Daniel Rothbart, Karina Korostelina and Mohammed Cherkaoui

Ethics, Norms and the Narratives of War
Creating and encountering the enemy other
Pamela Creed

Armed Drones and the Ethics of War
Military virtue in a post-heroic age
Christian Enemark

The Ethics of Nuclear Weapons Dissemination
Moral dilemmas of aspiration, avoidance, and prevention
Thomas E. Doyle, II

Chinese Just War Ethics
Origin, development, and dissent
Edited by Ping-cheung Lo and Sumner B. Twiss

Utilitarianism and the Ethics of War
William H. Shaw

UTILITARIANISM AND THE ETHICS OF WAR

William H. Shaw

Routledge
Taylor & Francis Group

LONDON AND NEW YORK

First published 2016
by Routledge
2 Park Square, Milton Park, Abingdon, Oxon OX14 4RN

and by Routledge
711 Third Avenue, New York, NY 10017

Routledge is an imprint of the Taylor & Francis Group, an informa business

British Library Cataloguing-in-Publication Data
A catalogue record for this book is available from the British Library

Library of Congress Cataloging-in-Publication Data
Names: Shaw, William H., 1948- author.Title: Utilitarianism and the
ethics of war / William H. Shaw.Description: Abingdon, Oxon ; New
York, NY : Routledge is an imprint of the Taylor & Francis Group, an
Informa Business, [2016] | Series: War, conflict and ethics | Includes
bibliographical references and index.Identifiers: LCCN 2015032121 |
ISBN 9780415825801 (hardback) | ISBN 9781138998964 (pbk.) |
ISBN 9780203538333 (ebook)Subjects: LCSH: War--Moral and ethical
aspects. | Military ethics. | Utilitarianism.Classification: LCC U21.2 .
S5236 2016 | DDC 172/.42--dc23LC record available at http://lccn.loc.
gov/2015032121

ISBN: 978-0-415-82580-1 (hbk)
ISBN: 978-1-138-99896-4 (pbk)
ISBN: 978-0-203-53833-3 (ebk)

Typeset in Bembo
by GreenGate Publishing Services, Tonbridge, Kent

CONTENTS

PREFACE

This book addresses the two basic ethical questions posed by war: When, if ever, are we morally justified in waging war; and, if recourse to arms is warranted, how are we permitted to fight the wars we wage? It also deals with the challenge that realism and relativism raise for the ethical discussion of war and with the duties of military personnel and the moral challenges they can face. In tackling these matters, *Utilitarianism and the Ethics of War* covers a wide range of topics—from pacifism to armed humanitarian intervention, from the right of national defense to preemptive or preventive war, from civilian immunity to the tenets of just war theory, and from the role responsibilities of military officers to the moral underpinnings of the rules of war. Other authors have, of course, dealt with these and many other topics I discuss. What is distinctive about this book, however, is that it provides a consistent and, I believe, broadly compelling utilitarian or consequentialist treatment of the fundamental normative issues that war occasions.

The utilitarian tradition in ethics is venerable, and today utilitarianism continues to be a vital current in theoretical and applied ethics. Nevertheless, contemporary utilitarians have had relatively little to say about war despite the enormous impact that war and the threat of war have had on human well-being. Few philosophers who write on any of the various ethical issues raised by war take an explicitly utilitarian approach, and there is no systematic or comprehensive treatment of the basic questions of war and peace from a utilitarian or consequentialist perspective. This book remedies that shortfall. In pursuing a utilitarian approach to those questions, it provides answers to them that are, I think, morally attractive and philosophically credible. It tries also to show the plausibility of that approach, both intrinsically and in application to particular issues, and to enrich our understanding of utilitarianism by applying it to this important normative domain. Forcing utilitarianism to address the ethical problems of war requires developing and elaborating the theory, especially the different ways in which rules, rights, and motives figure into utilitarian assessment of armed conflict. On the other hand, a utilitarian approach to the ethics of war illuminates old questions in new ways by showing how a concern for well-being and the consequences of our actions and policies shape the moral constraints to which states and other actors must adhere.

Working out what a nuanced utilitarian approach implies about when and how wars may be waged is a valuable project because it suggests fresh, consistent, and cogent answers to some pressing moral questions, or so I shall argue. Normative ethics is a rich and contested terrain, however, and there are a number of rival theories of right and wrong, each with able defenders. Although this book makes a case for utilitarianism, especially in connection to questions of war, it does not purport to prove to everyone's satisfaction that utilitarianism or some other form of consequentialism is the correct or one and only satisfactory account of moral rightness. That task is beyond the scope of this book. Indeed, when it comes to something as foundational as this, strict proof is probably impossible. The project's significance is not, however, limited to those who already favor some sort of consequentialism in ethics or who are persuaded by what I have to say on behalf of utilitarianism. As I shall argue, utilitarianism may provide the best way of thinking about the ethics of war even if, contrary to what I believe, it is not the best overall theory of right and wrong, and much of my argument retains its force even if one abandons or modifies certain aspects of utilitarianism. Moreover, because almost all ethical theories join commonsense morality in placing moral weight on preserving and promoting well-being and in considering consequences to be relevant to the moral assessment of actions and policies, understanding exactly what can be said about warfare from a strictly utilitarian perspective is something that anyone interested in the ethics of war should find pertinent and instructive.

Many doubt, however, that ethics can be meaningfully applied to war. Chapter 1 takes up this challenge. Against so-called realism, it argues for the coherence and necessity of treating war in ethical terms. It goes on to rebut ethical relativism and to raise some doubts about the adequacy of conventional just war theory, thus opening the door to a utilitarian approach. Chapter 2 outlines that approach, laying the theoretical foundations for the book. It elaborates and defends an open-ended, indirect form of utilitarianism that retains the act-utilitarian criterion of right while emphasizing the importance of rules, rights, and character traits. It contrasts utilitarianism with other normative approaches, both consequentialist and non-consequentialist, and explains the enduring appeal of the theory.

After tracing what the classical utilitarians had to say about war, Chapter 3 explicates the basic utilitarian criterion for assessing the morality of waging war—the Utilitarian War Principle (UWP)—defending that principle against various objections and suggesting why even non-utilitarians may find it attractive. Although UWP provides the basic criterion of when it is right to fight, applying it can be tricky because of empirical complexities and uncertainty about the future. In practice one may need to rely on some easier-to-follow rule or set of rules. After arguing that anti-war pacifism cannot play this role, Chapter 4 explicates the *jus ad bellum* principles of traditional just war theory and contends that utilitarians should view them as pragmatic guidelines, which help to determine whether it is right to wage war.

Although self-defense against armed attack is the one universally accepted moral basis for war, the meaning, justification, and limits of the right of national defense are contested matters. Chapter 5 explicates and defends this right from a utilitarian perspective. It then goes on to probe its contours and boundaries. In particular, it examines whether the right of national defense encompasses preventive war, whether it rules out armed humanitarian intervention, and whether national liberation movements or other non-state entities can be said to have an analogous right.

Chapters 6 turns to the moral constraints on military operations once war has broken out. After explicating what I call the received rules of war, it explains why utilitarianism endorses them and argues, against Michael Walzer (2006b) and others, that it provides the most plausible and coherent grounding for them. It contrasts the utilitarian perspective with conventionalism and rebuts the charge that a utilitarian approach fails to capture the "deep morality of war." Chapter 7 continues this analysis, probing more closely the status of combatants and non-combatants. It contends that combatants must follow the same rules whether or not their side is in the right, spells out what they must do to protect civilians, and argues that utilitarianism underpins these duties more firmly and cogently than do rival normative approaches.

Chapter 8 rounds out the book's consequentialist exploration of the ethics of war by examining the value of standing armies, the role responsibilities of military personnel, the virtues it is desirable for them to have, and the moral quandaries that military service can give rise to—including the obligations of servicemen and women when confronted with immoral orders or when they believe that their country is fighting an unjust war.

In developing a utilitarian approach to the basic ethical issues of war, this book breaks fresh and, I believe, important ground. However, it swims against the current of contemporary ethical theorizing about war, which is largely non-consequentialist in temper. Not only does the utilitarian approach to war that I develop challenge certain things that other philosophers say, but it also makes some of the problems that exercise them disappear and renders others purely scholastic. As a result, I fear that some readers or potential readers will have antecedent theoretical commitments that dispose them to resist or even dismiss out of hand the ideas presented here. I can only suggest that considering the ethics of war in a different normative light may illuminate things they truly care about. On the other hand, some readers of a more practical bent may wish that the book said less about theoretical matters and more about specific historical cases or about various contemporary conflicts, such as those roiling the Middle East today, or perhaps that it dealt with the ethics of modern military technology or addressed in a more nuts-and-bolts way the situation-specific moral challenges that military personnel can face. To these readers, I can only stress the importance of establishing, as this book endeavors to do, a satisfactory perspective from which to examine the moral questions that war poses and of outlining its implications for the most important of these. Thus, I focus largely on wars between states and on the duties of their soldiers, believing that it is important to get these central matters straight before exploring other issues and others sorts of armed conflict. For this reason, then, it bears emphasizing that this book is not intended to be the final word on utilitarianism and the ethics of war, still less to settle all the moral issues to which armed conflict can give rise.

★★★★★

Utilitarianism and the Ethics of War reflects my long engagement with utilitarian and consequentialist ethical thought as well as my more recent thinking about the ethics of war, stimulated by a year I spent as a Stockdale Fellow at the U.S. Naval Academy in Annapolis, Maryland. I am grateful to the Stockdale Center for Ethical Leadership for its financial support and to my colleagues there, in particular Ed Barrett, George Lucas, and Valerie Morkevicius, for their encouragement, intellectual stimulation, and good fellowship. Vuko Andrić, Ben Eggleston, Bernward Gesang, Michael Gross, Steve Nathanson, James Pattison, and Helge Rückert provided helpful, often very extensive, comments on the manuscript, for which I thank them. I thank Helge, in addition, for having arranged for me to teach a special, three-week seminar on utilitarianism and the ethics of war at the University of Mannheim. I have also benefitted from discussions with Uwe Steinhoff. San Jose State University, too, deserves my thanks for the research leave that enabled me to complete this book. Finally, I acknowledge my great debt to my wife and life partner, Carolyn Martin Shaw, whose generosity made this project possible and whose sage counsel and good spirits helped keep it afloat.

1

BEYOND REALISM
AND RELATIVISM

War has always plagued human society. Indeed, armed conflict between organized groups has been so common and its impact so manifold and profound that the violent strife of war might seem to constitute history's central refrain. In the past, some militarists have celebrated this strife, glorifying the test of human will that war represents, extolling the valor and other martial virtues it produces, or lauding the domination of the weak by the strong that war makes possible. Nowadays, such attitudes seem antiquated if not downright barbaric. War in the modern world has largely lost whatever romance it may once have had. Still, even today the perceived glories of war can entice young men to take up arms, and at times whole nations can, it seems, be caught up in an atavistic fervor for war (Fiala 2008; Hedges 2002). Nevertheless, when reflecting on the matter coolly, few doubt that war is an evil even if sometimes a necessary one; that humankind would be better off if we could reduce, if not eliminate altogether, its incidence; and that we should strive to see that war, if and when it does break out, is waged as humanely as possible. And there is good reason for this. War entails death and destruction; even when waged in the noblest of causes, it spells mayhem, misery, and massacre.

Like almost every human activity, however, war has always been a rule-bound or norm-governed enterprise (Roberts and Guelff 2000: 3), and throughout history people have, sometimes and to some extent, thought about it in moral terms.[1] In many different societies, people have believed that sometimes states lack a morally sufficient reason for waging war; that is, that it would be wrong, ignominious, or irreligious, not merely unwise, inexpedient, or imprudent, for a given country, say, to attack a peaceful neighbor. Similarly, the warriors of many, perhaps most, cultures have accepted some restrictions on the conduct of warfare. Varying with the time and place, certain weapons, certain tactics, or certain ways of fighting have been considered dishonorable or even taboo.[2] In line with this, the commonsense morality of most people today condemns some wars, such as those of national aggrandizement, as wicked and immoral, while deeming others, such as wars of national defense, to be morally permissible or at least necessary evils, and it unambiguously repudiates certain ways of fighting, for example, the systematic use of rape or the butchering of civilians as a military tactic.

It seems, then, to make perfect sense to try to determine exactly when, if ever, it really is morally permissible to wage war and precisely how morality allows us to fight the wars, if any, that it is right for us to fight. This book addresses those issues in a utilitarian spirit, one that puts normative priority on the promotion of well-being. In a nutshell, it argues that a state or other political entity may permissibly wage war when and only when no alternative course of action would have greater net benefit, taking into account the interests of all, and that when it does wage war, it should do so in accordance with those rules the endorsement, promulgation, and anticipated adherence to which will produce better results than any other set of rules or no rules at all. Unpacking, illustrating, and defending these theses will take some time, and along the way my argument will probe alternatives to, and acknowledge some gaps and unresolved problems in, the utilitarian approach.

Before proceeding, however, we must grapple with *realism*, the contention that morality does not apply to war—that somehow war is beyond or outside morality, not subject to its concepts, principles, or strictures.[3] Under the label of realism, however, different ideas and different theses are often jumbled up. These need to be distinguished, delineated, and assessed separately. To begin with, we can divide realism into two branches, *realism about recourse to war* and *realism about the conduct of war*, each of which can be understood or elaborated in different ways. The two branches deal with conceptually distinct issues, so in principle one could be a realist in one domain without being a realist in the other.

Realism in its different guises has been perennially attractive. All its variants have found adherents over the years, and ordinary people sometimes express realist sentiments. Nor is it surprising that the violence inherent in combat and the deadly, destructive, and inhumane character of war itself should lead people to doubt that ethics can have anything to do with it. War seems by its very nature to signify the absence of morality. Realism thus poses a challenge to any attempt to think about war in moral terms, not merely the attempt to do so from a utilitarian point of view. As realism is probed more closely, however, it loses whatever surface plausibility it may have.

Realism about recourse to war

This first branch of realism avers that war among states is neither right nor wrong; it is outside morality altogether. When it comes to war, in particular, and to relations between states, in general, moral concepts and principles have no application, and moral analysis is irrelevant. Morality's remit, it is urged, does not extend to questions of war and peace. Realists do not necessarily deny that morality exists—they need not be moral nihilists—or that it appropriately governs other areas of our lives and other decisions we make. Rather, they allege that it is a misapplication of morality, a kind of category error, to believe that whether a state should go to war is a moral question at all. Call this *metaethical amoralism about recourse to war*.

The glaring problem with this stance is that morality seems to apply to all spheres of human endeavor; all our actions, policies, and institutions appear open to moral assessment. Why should war be an exception? It is true, of course, that the cruel, savage violence of combat and the death and devastation wrought by war seem to mock our ordinary moral values. But, if anything, this suggests that war is wrong or often wrong, not that war is somehow beyond morality and, thus, neither right nor wrong.

In his famous history of the Peloponnesian war, Thucydides presents one version of metaethical amoralism about war (Thucydides 1996: 350–7). He pictures the Athenians in dialogue with the leaders of Melos, threatening the island with destruction if it does not subordinate itself to Athens and ally with it against Sparta. When the Melians begin to raise moral objections, the Athenians reply curtly that morality applies only to those who are equal in power, that the Melians are not their equals, and that, therefore, their relationship is not governed by morality. If states are sufficiently unequal in their power that one of them can coerce the other to do what it wants, then morality is inapplicable. Only if the states are roughly balanced, the Athenians imply, with neither able to dominate the other, do justice and rights then enter the picture. This suggests, along the lines of Glaucon in Plato's *Republic* (358e–359b), that morality among states is, at best, a kind of contract among equals, but, if so, it is not much of a contract because it becomes void as soon as the situation changes and one party can get away with breaking it.

Closely related to the Athenian stance is that of Hobbes, who, as it happened, translated Thucydides' great work into English. Hobbes's political philosophy implies that states have no moral obligations to one another because there is no ruler above them that can enforce such obligations. Although individuals can escape the amoral anarchy of the state of nature by conceding all power to a sovereign—Hobbes's famous Leviathan—the sovereigns of different nations find themselves in a morality-free war of all against all because there is no higher power able to impose law and morality on them. In a related vein, John Austin, the influential nineteenth-century expounder of legal positivism, held that, absent a world sovereign able to enforce rules, there can be no true law among nations. What is called international law is not, in his view, genuine law at all (Austin 1995: 20). Austin is almost certainly wrong about this even if one agrees with the central tenets of positivism (Hart 1994: 213–37), but one can feel the attraction of his position. In any event, though, Austin's view does not entail, nor did he believe, that there is no morality where there is no law. To the contrary, we are all bound, he thought, by the commands of God, whose rules are intended to promote our long-term well-being.

The basic problem with the Hobbesian or Athenian view is that, if we believe that morality exists at all, then it is implausible to accept that it ceases to apply when an individual or a state can get away with ignoring it. There are simply no credible, let alone compelling, grounds for supposing that morality fails to extend to international relations and, more specifically, to the decisions that states make about war and peace. For one thing, as utilitarians in particular will be quick to urge, these are decisions that typically affect large numbers of human beings and that have an enormous impact, for good or ill, on their lives. How could morality not concern itself with them?

Realists tend to be students of war and international relations, not philosophers. Rarely are they interested in pursuing questions about the nature of morality or mounting a serious philosophical case for metaethical amoralism about recourse to war. In fact, they frequently slide from that position to the distinct idea that, as a matter of fact, states or the leaders of states never decide questions of war and peace on moral grounds. Morality may, at least in theory, apply to war—contrary to metaethical amoralism—but in practice it is inert and, hence, irrelevant. These realists are struck by the fact, or apparent fact, that states seem almost always to have gone to war for self-interested reasons and (as shall be discussed below) to have fought those wars in whatever way seemed conducive to victory. To these realists, it seems naïve to look at war and, more generally, at relations among nations through the prism of morality because morality is irrelevant to what nations do or do not do. Call this *practical amoralism about recourse to war*.

Those who endorse this thesis do not lament the putative irrelevance of morality to the conduct of states, nor do they try to spur states to decide questions of war and peace on a moral basis. Human nature being what it is and the nature of states and the environment in which they act being what they are, encouraging states to act morally would be, in the view of these realists, a futile undertaking. That states inevitably behave amorally is simply a fact that we must accept and in light of which, and with our eyes wide open, we must act. As the Athenians tell the Melians, insofar as it is in their power to do so, states will inevitably pursue their interests without regard to morality.

Practical amoralism about recourse to war has a grown-up, this-is-the-way-the-world-works air about it. But is it true that states are always entirely egoistic in their conduct? I think not. It is easy to find examples of states or the leaders of states waging war, not as a result of calculated self-interest, but in pursuit of some moral, religious, or ideological ideal, for which they are willing to incommode themselves and expend their country's human and material treasure. Moreover, states can have mixed motives just as individuals can, and in both cases doing what is right can sometimes—perhaps often—coincide with doing what is in one's interest. Perhaps states rarely act in line with moral principle if doing so would seriously harm their interests. That seems plausible. On the other hand, it seems equally plausible that states sometimes act in ways that they clearly would not have, had they not been in the grip of some ideal or felt bound by some moral principle.

Still, one may continue to be struck by the fact that the conduct of states, if not entirely free of morality, tends overall to be self-serving, with each state pursuing its own interests as best it can with little or no intrinsic regard for the interests of other nations. Such egoism might, in fact, be far-sighted and enlightened, with an appreciation of the benefits of international peace and cooperation; it need not dictate duplicitous or aggressive behavior. That will depend on what a state deems its interests to be and what it believes to be the most efficacious means of advancing those interests. To be sure, national leaders routinely defend their conduct in moral terms, and ordinary people frequently judge the conduct of nations as right or wrong. It is open to the realist, however, to contend that these facts are misleading: Scrape away the façade and you will find that states act only on their interests. Like its counterpart, the sophomoric thesis that individual human beings are motivated only by self-interest, this contention is hard to refute. Examples of apparently moral, altruistic, or even self-sacrificial behavior will be met with the response that if one digs deeper, one will find some kind of self-interested rationale for the conduct in question. However, the explanatory plausibility of egoism at either level seems threadbare; the motivations of human beings, whether private citizens or national leaders, are not so simple.

Suppose, nevertheless, that realism of the sort I have been discussing is broadly correct and that states seldom act against their interests or that, lip service to morality aside, statesmen rarely feel constrained by it in deciding whether to wage war. Still, this is a point about the motives of states or the people who lead them and about what inclines them to act one way rather than another. It tells us that to be successful in dealing with them we should be prepared to appeal to their interests. Because states are rarely motivated by intrinsic regard for morality or for the interests of other states and other peoples, if we are to get them to act rightly or in a way that promotes the collective interests of humanity, then we must develop structures and provide incentives that induce them to so act. This may be salutary advice. But it does not show that war is somehow beyond morality or that the decision to wage it cannot be subject to moral assessment.

Some realists affirm not only that states tend to look at war only from the perspective of national interest, but also that this is how they should view it. They contend, on the one hand, that the only duty of political leaders is to promote the interests of the state or its citizens and, on the other, that if nations and their leaders think about international affairs in moralistic terms, then they are bound to be led astray, fighting religious, ideological, or idealistic wars—for example, wars to make the world safe for democracy or to free other nations from tyranny—that it would have been better for them not to have fought. Indeed, the whole world would be better off, these realists urge, if instead of undertaking crusades or waging wars to make the world more just or more democratic, states concerned themselves only with prudently pursuing their national interests. We can call this thesis *prescriptive amoralism about recourse to war* because it involves a normative stance: It tells us how states ought to act. Prescriptive amoralism does not say merely, and trivially, that from the point of view of national interest, it is appropriate that states attend only to their national interest. Implicitly, prescriptive amoralism makes a broader claim than this, namely, that states should act—that is, that it is right or morally desirable for them to act—only on a non-moral basis because when a state acts otherwise, it tends to cause mischief, producing more harm than good for everyone. If states would only stick to their interests and mind their own business, then the world would be a better place—safer, more secure, and more peaceful.

Realists who affirm this position—that the world is better off to the extent that states act amorally—probably enjoy its paradoxical flair. The thesis, however, sits uneasily within the general realist perspective precisely because of its normative character. If morality does not apply to questions of war and peace, then it seems odd or even inconsistent to say that it is wrong for states to decide such questions in some particular way. But be that as it may, one can still ask, and it is certainly a question that utilitarians will want to ask, whether it is true that the world would be a better place if states acted only on the basis of national interest. Of course, one immediately wants to know what is meant by "better" and by "national interest." By the former, let us assume, as I did above, that the prescriptive amoralist is thinking in terms of such uncontroversial considerations as security, prosperity, and the well-being of a state's citizens. "National interest" is trickier. To ensure that the prescriptive amoralist's thesis avoids triviality and advances an interesting claim, then national interest cannot include adherence to certain moral values or the promulgation of certain moral ideals. Nor, if the realist thesis is to be at all plausible, can it include such things as unbridled territorial expansion, control of foreign resources, the enslavement of alien populations, or military hegemony over other states because it is improbable, to say the least, that it would make the world a better place for all states actively and amorally to pursue such interests.

Let us assume, then, that the prescriptive amoralist has in mind national interest as understood by a basically pacific, non-ideological, and commercially minded democratic society. The claim, then, is that if such a nation acts in matters of foreign policy on the basis of considerations other than national interest, in particular, if it acts on the basis of moral principle, then it will almost always (a) end up worse off in terms of its national interest and (b) make other states and other peoples worse off, too.

To begin with (a), it might seem circular or tautological to affirm that a state will be worse off in terms of its national interest if it does not act on the basis of national interest (whatever a state takes its national interests to be). But this is incorrect for three reasons. First, if a state acts on the basis of national interest, then inevitably it is acting on the basis of its leaders' perception of national interest, and perceived national interest can deviate from actual national interest. Second, just as constantly seeking happiness may not be the best way for an individual to achieve a happy life, so constantly seeking to promote national interest might not be the best way to promote national interest. Whether it is or not is an open question. Third, as mentioned earlier, in acting on the basis of moral principle, a state does not necessarily act contrary to its own interests. Proposition (a), therefore, is not tautological, but is it true? Suppose for the sake of argument that it is and, thus, that it usually goes against national interest for a state to adhere to a morally based foreign policy. Even if this were so, however, anyone not already wedded to moral egoism will deny that it is always or necessarily wrong for a state to put aside its interests in order to do the right thing, any more than it is always or necessarily wrong for an individual to do so.

This is where contention (b) comes in. The prescriptive amoralist could concede that it is not necessarily wrong for a country to act for moral reasons when this runs contrary to its own interests. But he or she will nevertheless urge that when states do act for what they take to be moral reasons—say, by waging war to unseat an unjust foreign regime—they tend to muck things up, with results that are bad not only for them but for others, too. That this can happen is undeniable. Moral crusades often go awry. But the law of unintended consequences applies equally to the pursuit of national interest, which, history shows, can be just as benighted, ill-informed, or counterproductive as any example the realist can muster of a misguided moral quest. The prescriptive amoralist needs to show that when states act on the basis of moral principle, they blunder so frequently and so badly that we would all be better off if they never attempted to do so. This seems implausible. The examples that the realist adduces of states wreaking havoc in the name of morality, if indeed they are examples of attempted moral reasoning at all, are invariably examples of poor, ill-informed moral reasoning, based on implausible principles, faulty factual assumptions, or dubious conjectures about the future. This stacks the deck by implicitly contrasting moral thought and action at its worst with prudential conduct at its best, that is, by juxtaposing morally motivated but naïve, stupid, or self-deluded conduct with thoughtful, prudent, and judicious self-interested conduct.

Contrary to the prescriptive realist, states do sometimes bring about good results when they act for moral or other non-self-interested reasons. A shining example is Britain's suppression of the international slave trade in the nineteenth century. In response to such cases, the realist might contend that such conduct really was in the interest of the state in question but, even if that were true, it will not help the realist if the state was acting on what it took to be moral principle. The realist can also respond that he is making a generalization, which is not undermined by a few counterexamples. But there is little reason to believe that in general when states try to act rightly they will in fact act wrongly or that they are less likely to act wrongly if they are unconcerned with acting rightly.

Realism about the conduct of war

This second branch of realism contends that there are no moral restrictions on what combatants do during war. In other words, the categories *right* and *wrong* do not apply to warfare, that is, to the way war is fought. As the ancient maxim puts it, "when arms are raised, the laws fall silent." We can call this *metaethical amoralism about the conduct of war*. This sort of realism is often attributed to General William T. Sherman, who notoriously pronounced that "war is hell" and that "war is cruelty and you cannot refine it" and whose actions during the American Civil War (burning Atlanta to the ground and intentionally laying waste to the countryside in his subsequent march to Savannah) seem to have reflected those sentiments (Walzer 2006b: 32). Although Sherman's memorable remarks are open to different interpretations, in saying that war is hell, he may implicitly have been endorsing a thesis like this: If hell is beyond morality, then once one enters the devil's realm—the realm of war—trying to distinguish between right and wrong is senseless. Whether a state or other political collectivity acts rightly or wrongly in resorting to arms— and Sherman certainly thought that the North had right on its side and the South did not—once war has broken out, morality has no place. The second quotation from Sherman tallies with this. In implying that war cannot be softened, it suggests that the very nature of armed conflict entails that right and wrong do not pertain to its conduct.

Imagine, though, soldiers who steal from civilians or rape women when they pass through a rural village in enemy territory or in a neutral country or, even, in a remote part of their own country.[4] Surely such conduct is not beyond moral assessment. Even if we were to grant, for the sake of argument, that when war is raging, theft and rape might be acceptable in the first case, surely they are not in the other two. At the very least, there are pertinent moral distinctions to be drawn among the cases. It seems implausible, to put it mildly, to contend that nothing that happens during war can be examined in moral terms. Although Sherman torched Atlanta without qualm, he would have swiftly repudiated, morally and not just strategically, the suggestion that its inhabitants be put to the sword.

When faced with this argument, a realist like Sherman would presumably retreat from the proposition that nothing combatants do is subject to moral assessment to the narrower thesis that combatants do no wrong if they act in a way they judge to be advantageous for prevailing in the conflict. This view, however, allows morality back into the picture for it implies that soldiers who rape or steal from civilians, who use exploding bullets, or who kill enemy prisoners act wrongly if such conduct serves no military purpose. Once a realist concedes that there are things it would be wrong for combatants to do, then war is not a completely amoral activity. Even if the rules that govern it differ or appear to differ from those that govern normal peacetime activity, to ask what they are—that is, to discuss what combatants may permissibly do or not do—is to enter the realm of normative discourse and debate. For example, does the combatant act rightly if he believes that killing prisoners is militarily useful, or must it actually be militarily useful? And how useful must it be? Is he morally permitted to kill ten prisoners if the only utility of doing so is that it gives his unit time to take a nap?

We can thus set aside metaethical amoralism about the conduct of war. Commonsense morality is correct to affirm that morality applies to the conduct of war and that combatants sometimes act immorally, for example, by intentionally bombing hospitals, destroying museums or churches, torturing prisoners of war, abusing civilians or stealing their property, or refusing to give quarter in combat. A realist might accept this point but respond that, in fact, neither combatants nor those who direct a nation's war effort allow moral considerations to affect their actions. This position can be called *practical amoralism about the conduct of war*. It is the thesis that morality is in fact irrelevant—not, perhaps, theoretically, but in practice—to how wars are fought. When push comes to shove, or so practical amoralism affirms, both combatants and the military and political leaders above them will do whatever they think is necessary to overcome the enemy, regardless of the morality of their actions.

This contention is false, however, or at least there are numerous exceptions to it. Throughout history, battlefield combatants have sometimes restrained their conduct because of moral considerations or from a sense of honor, eschewing, for example, perfidy in dealing with the enemy. War requires combatants to act in non-self-interested ways, in particular to risk themselves for their comrades or even to die for their country, so it seems odd to maintain that although moral considerations often govern their conduct, they never affect their behavior toward the enemy. On the other hand, those who direct wars and command armies sometimes refrain from actions that might be militarily efficacious on what are, at least to some extent, moral grounds—for example, because those actions would involve slaughtering civilians (as when the Americans decided against using nuclear weapons in the Vietnam War). Perhaps these are only rare exceptions—the Americans, after all, did bomb Hiroshima and Nagasaki—but they impugn the notion that moral considerations never affect how adversaries choose to fight.

Suppose, however, that even though practical amoralism is false and that moral notions can and sometimes do constrain the conduct of combatants, it is nevertheless unusual for morality to inhibit warfare and, further, that it is generally assumed that wars are fought without scruple. If so, then one might argue that it is unreasonable to expect combatants to act morally or to criticize them for failing to do so. Call this *apologetic amoralism about the conduct of war*. It seeks, not so much to justify conduct that is, in fact, immoral but, rather, to excuse it on the grounds that it is to be expected; that it is, indeed, almost inevitable that combatants act wrongly. Given their circumstances, the argument goes, we should not be surprised that they tend to act without regard to morality, nor blame them for so acting. The notorious My Lai massacre might seem to challenge this line of thought: Surely, one might think, we should condemn combatants for systematically and deliberately killing unarmed villagers. Yet at the time, many Americans found some sympathy for the soldiers who participated in the slaughter. They were not soulless psychopaths but, rather, ordinary men who had been taught to dehumanize the Vietnamese, the thinking went, by an army that was itself far from over-scrupulous in avoiding civilian casualties and tended not to distinguish too carefully between irregular guerilla forces and the civilians who supported them, and who were led to act as they did at My Lai by experiences and trauma that outsiders can only guess at (Glover 1999: 58–63).

Still, this sort of apologetic realism has its limits. Even if one has some empathy for the soldiers at My Lai, this hardly implies that they were blameless or should escape responsibility for their conduct. Indeed, these days almost all Western military organizations require their combatants to obey the laws of war even if ordered to violate them by an immediate superior, and they hold them accountable for failing to do so.[5] To this, the realist might respond that in war both sides understand that they are entering an arena where anything goes, that both are desperately trying to prevail, and that both know that the other is prepared to do whatever it takes to win. If so, the realist concludes, then it is not only unreasonable, but also unfair, to blame or rebuke either side for acting badly. The premises of this argument seem false to me, but perhaps in certain cases the conclusion is plausible anyway. If both sides use poison gas or torture captured prisoners for information, then how, one might ask, can we criticize combatants on either side for doing so? This would be unfair, however, only if we singled out only one side for criticism. We could perfectly well censure both sides for such conduct and hold them accountable for it. This is especially true when the combatants are injuring, not enemy troops, but innocent bystanders. War, after all, is not a game that affects only the players.

In response to this, some realists double down. They assert not only that it would be unreasonable or unfair, once the antagonists are locked in struggle, to expect either side to forego any action it deems to have military utility, but also that the combatants should not recognize any moral constraints on their actions because waging war without humanitarian or other restraint increases the likelihood that the struggle will be brought to a decisive conclusion and in a shorter time frame than would otherwise have been the case. Had Sherman behaved more humanely, the argument goes (an argument that Sherman himself can be surmised to have accepted), then the American Civil War would have dragged on longer, and the overall bloodshed and destruction would have been greater. Thus, paradoxically, waging war without scruple or moral compunction will reduce the wreckage and slaughter it breeds. Call this *prescriptive amoralism about the conduct of war*. It entails that the long international effort, starting with the St. Petersburg Declaration of 1857 and extending through the various Geneva Conventions, to make war somewhat less needlessly destructive has been not only idealistic or even naïve but also positively counterproductive.

This prescriptive realism hangs on a dubious factual premise, for it is extremely doubtful, to say the least, that the more cruelly and ruthlessly a war is fought, the less overall devastation there will be. It also ignores the extent to which it is in the collective interest of states to impose restrictions on the conduct of war and thus reduce needless carnage; if this were not so, then there would be no Geneva Convention. Adherence to the rules of war can also facilitate post-war reconciliation (Johnson 2000: 447). To be sure, the idea is sometimes expressed that it can be more humane for a state to employ overwhelming force to achieve swift and decisive victory than for it to wage war at a lower level of intensity for a longer period. It is better, the reasoning goes, to have the conflict resolved as quickly as possible, than for it to drag on indefinitely. One can see how this might be true in some circumstances especially if victory for one side is more or less inevitable, but even then it would spell a net humanitarian loss if the violence is excessive or employed with little discrimination. And if the two sides are more evenly matched—consider Iran and Iraq during their 1980–8 war—then urging them to commit themselves totally to the struggle, throwing all their resources into it, hardly appears to be a reliable way of reducing overall death and destruction.

In any case, total war does not entail total disregard for the morality of how one is fighting that war, but this is what the prescriptive thesis we are considering requires. A state could marshal all its human and material resources in titanic struggle and yet refrain on moral grounds from, for example, destroying civilian crops or shooting army medics. The commonly accepted rules of war may conceivably make achieving victory in some cases more difficult or more costly, but they are not so onerous that one side will prevail only if it ignores them. (Indeed, ignoring those rules is rarely likely to produce any significant or sustained military advantage.) Even if I am wrong about this, however, and it really were the case that adherence to the received rules of war would prevent a belligerent from achieving a victory that was within its grasp, we are still some distance from the proposition, which the prescriptive realist is urging, that there will be less overall violence and devastation if neither side acknowledges any moral constraints on its conduct. This is the prescriptive realist's key proposition: that war will be less horrific, overall and in the long run, if it is fought, not with the current rules or with a different and better set of rules, but without any rules at all. Some propositions that appear absurd turn out, when probed, to actually be absurd. This is one of them.

Against relativism

Realists are correct to remind us, if we need reminding, that states frequently act amorally and that combatants have often waged war with little or no concern for the morality of their actions. But realists have not shown that war is beyond the remit of morality or that it should be treated as if it were. To the contrary, moral concepts and principles can and should be applied to war, both to the question of whether and when a state or other collectivity should go to war and to the question of how it should fight the wars it wages. True, "wars are not conducted according to the desiccated deliberations of a philosophy seminar full of pursed-lipped old maids" (Burleigh 2011: 164), but sound moral thinking about war will be neither naïve nor homiletic, and it will take account of the complicated, sometimes obscure, and often treacherous environments in which real-world decisions about war must be made. To be sure, in a world of hard-bitten actors, moral criticism may sometimes seem futile, and keeping one's moral bearings when dealing with amoral or even evil agents can be challenging. Nevertheless, determining when and how it is morally permissible to fight is an essential project, one that is not just philosophically engaging but has profound practical implications as well.

If we put realism aside, then, what moral concepts and principles should guide the examination of war? Over the years, some have held that morality itself is relative, simply a function of what a particular society happens to believe. Known as *ethical* or *cultural relativism*, this thesis asserts that right and wrong are determined by what a given society or culture deems to be right and wrong. What is right in one place may be wrong in another because the only basis for distinguishing right from wrong, and thus for assessing the morality of actions, is the moral system of the society in which the act occurs. This proposition entails that if two societies have different moral ideas about when war may be waged or how it may be fought, then there is no way to adjudicate between them. Each set of ideas is correct—for the society that holds them.

In support of ethical relativism, its advocates point to the apparent diverseness of human values and the multiformity of moral codes across societies and through history. It is not difficult to identify societies, the moral systems of which have tolerated or even encouraged practices that may seem immoral or even depraved to us, such as polygamy, pedophilia, stealing, slavery, infanticide, or cannibalism. In light of this, the ethical relativist believes that there can be no non-ethno-centric standard by which to judge actions. Some have argued, to the contrary, that apparent differences in moral outlook between societies reflect only differing factual beliefs and divergent circumstances rather than fundamental differences in values. But suppose, as seems likely, that societies really have sometimes differed fundamentally in their moral outlooks, that is, in at least some of the basic moral principles they accept. Still, the relativist's conclusion does not follow. A difference of opinion among societies about right and wrong does not prove that none of the conflicting beliefs is erroneous or that none is better or more plausible than any of the others. Disagreement in ethical matters does not entail that all opinions are equally correct.

The ethical relativist is correct to emphasize that in viewing other cultures we should keep an open mind and not simply dismiss alien social practices on the basis of our own cultural prejudices. But the relativist's theory of morality is implausible. There is no good reason for maintaining that what a society thinks (or what a majority of that society thinks) about moral matters is automatically right, and the belief that it is automatically right has unpalatable implications.

To begin with, it undermines any moral criticism of the practices of other societies as long as their actions conform to their own standards. For example, in the seventeenth century, the Iroquois of Quebec apparently believed that torturing captured warriors from other tribes for amusement was morally permissible.[6] Ethical relativism prevents us from saying that they were mistaken. Relatedly, ethical relativism entails that there is no such thing as ethical progress. Although moralities may change, they cannot get better or worse. Thus, we cannot say that moral standards today are more enlightened than were the moral standards of, say, ancient Greece, where it was sometimes considered permissible to slaughter captured combatants or to enslave the citizens of a defeated city, especially if they were non-Greek. Finally, from the relativist's point of view, it makes no sense for people to criticize principles or practices accepted by their own society. People can be censured for not living up to their society's moral code, but that is all. The moral code itself cannot be criticized because whatever a society takes to be right really is right for it. Reformers who repudiate, say, the aggressive militarism of their society cannot be right unless or until the majority of the society comes to agree with them. The minority can never be right in moral matters; to be right it must become the majority.

As a normative theory, that is, as a general account of right and wrong, ethical relativism does not hold up, and philosophy instructors routinely strive to disabuse first-year students of it. Conceivably, however, one might advocate ethical relativism, not as a general account of right and wrong, but only as a limited normative thesis about war. The non-relativist affirms that there are some moral principles, the soundness of which do not hinge on a society's recognizing them, but he or she need not assert that morality is entirely invariant with respect to culture. To the contrary, the non-relativist might concede that certain aspects of morality—perhaps, for example, rules regarding one's obligations to kin—are relative to the given society because they concern practices that societies can organize in different ways without violating any fundamental, non-relative principles of morality. Could war be one of those areas? That seems almost inconceivable. For one thing, war can affect those who do not share the belief system of the society in question; it is not a closed cultural practice, an activity restricted to the like-minded. Moreover, and more importantly, because war potentially impacts human beings in such harmful and destructive ways—consider the Japanese invasion of Manchuria or the Rape of Nanking—it will almost certainly fall within the purview of whatever non-relative principle or principles one takes there to be.

To repudiate relativism and maintain that there are some non-relative moral standards, that is, some standards the cogency of which does not depend on their endorsement by one's society, does not, of course, tell us what those standards are. If society is not the final arbiter of right and wrong, either in general or when it comes to war, then what is? Utilitarianism provides a possible answer. By making happiness or well-being the moral standard, it provides an objective, non-relative guide to right and wrong, one that is independent of the particular moral code taught by the society in which we live. Because the importance of well-being is hard to deny—indeed, its value seems to require no argument (Shaver 2004)—utilitarianism supplies a basis for morality that appears truly universal. We can use that standard to critically assess the moral practices of other societies as well as the moral code taught by our own society. At the same time, utilitarianism acknowledges that the sources of human well-being are complex and that they can vary between cultures and over time as well as between different human beings. Because of this, actions that promote happiness in a particular society or in a specific cultural or historical context may differ from actions that promote it in another society or in another context. In this way, utilitarianism permits right and wrong to vary from society to society while still upholding a non-relative moral standard.

Because all societies can be presumed to acknowledge the importance of well-being, at least implicitly, normative critique can plausibly appeal to it in any, or almost any, actually existing society (Rachels 2003: 26–8). That is to say, whatever the social context, it is almost always germane to point out that a given rule, law, policy, institution, or action will result in less well-being overall than some alternative to it. True, societies will usually recognize other, possibly competing values, and they may fail to acknowledge that the well-being of certain classes of people matters. Even here, though, exploitative practices such as serfdom or the subordination of women that a certain society accepts may sometimes be in tension, acknowledged or unacknowledged, with other strands of that society's moral culture, including a recognition of the general desirability of people's lives going well for them; this was probably true, for example, of chattel slavery in the antebellum

American South. Furthermore, those practices will often reflect contestable empirical or partly empirical views about the well-being of excluded groups, views that are thought to justify those practices, such as Aristotle's belief that some human beings are natural slaves and thus better off with a master to guide them. In any case, the fact that happiness or well-being is such an attractive and widely shared value gives utilitarians an advantageous foothold from which to begin making their case, for it is difficult to dismiss well-being as a parochial value, of concern or relevance only to some societies.

Conventional just war thinking

If realism is misguided, then questions of armed conflict can and should be analyzed from an ethical point of view. And if we dismiss relativism, then to address those questions we must look beyond the norms that a given society happens to embrace. I have just claimed that utilitarianism may provide a plausible, non-relative perspective from which to assess norms, and Chapter 2 spells out the meaning and implications of utilitarianism and suggests some considerations in its favor. The rest of the book then uses that theory to supply answers to questions about the moral justifiability of war, the moral restraints on combat, and the professional responsibilities of military personnel. As I mentioned in the book's preface, however, one may find those answers cogent and convincing even if utilitarianism is not, contrary to what I believe, the most satisfactory overall moral theory.

At this point, though, I wish briefly to contrast utilitarianism with what most surveys of the ethics of war and peace identify as the two main approaches to the field, once realism has been put aside: namely, *anti-war pacifism* and *just war theory* (e.g., Lackey 1989; Orend 2005). I say more about anti-war pacifism in Chapter 4 and elsewhere, but it is the absolutist view that wars are immoral and that it is always wrong, always morally unjustifiable, for either nations or individuals to fight them. Although utilitarianism may incline one to a largely pacifist outlook, as it did Bentham, in principle the theory refrains from forbidding war across the board. Rather, it holds that whether we are morally justified in waging war hangs on the consequences of doing so. Like utilitarianism, just war theory contrasts with pacifism in maintaining that it may sometimes be morally permissible to wage war. Accordingly, just war theory specifies the principles that should guide us in determining when recourse to war is morally legitimate. This part of the theory is known as *jus ad bellum* (justice in going to war). In addition, the theory identifies the basic principles that should guide combatants when they do fight. This part of the theory is known as *jus in bello* (justice during war).

Originally shaped by Aquinas, Vitoria, Suarez, Grotius, and other great minds of the pre-modern period and with roots in earlier Roman and Christian thought, just war theory represents a rich intellectual tradition, one that has had enormous, well-deserved influence. It unquestionably constitutes the dominant approach to thinking about the morality of war.[7] Most contemporary writers on the ethics of war implicitly work within a just war framework, broadly understood, even when they challenge or revise some of its precepts. Although thinkers in this tradition differ on a variety of points, there is sufficient agreement among them that we can plausibly identify a standard or mainstream version of just war theory, which I shall be discussing at various points in the book. Some contemporary writers working in the just war tradition have extensive knowledge of its history, to which they seek to remain faithful (e.g., Johnson 1981, 2011), but most of them are analytically oriented moral philosophers, who find that the just war framework provides an intuitively attractive starting point for probing the issues that concern them, even if they end up revising or possibly abandoning some of its precepts.

George R. Lucas, Jr. (2013: 50) has rightly complained of the "methodological anarchy" of contemporary just war theory, for not only is there disagreement about its principles and their proper interpretation, but also there is no shared understanding of what undergirds them or on what basis they are to be defended or elaborated. For some writers, the principles of just war theory rest on tradition, reflect natural law, or embody the inherited moral wisdom of Western thought about war. For others, they are best seen as prima facie ethical principles grounded on moral intuition or moral common sense and which we must, when faced with specific decisions, try to balance and apply as best we can. Some contemporary philosophers writing on war, however, pursue a more ambitious approach. They seek to refine, emend, abandon, or supplement the inherited principles of just war theory so as to provide us with as coherent and attractive a set of principles as possible and to tease out the implications of those principles to resolve various ethical conundrums that war gives rise to. Largely unconcerned about first principles, these writers move back and forth between possible mid-level normative principles and our judgments about hypothetical cases, adjusting or altering both as necessary in order to reach an equilibrium in which their proposed principles square with "our" moral intuitions or considered moral judgments about particular cases.

Many contemporary philosophers find this a natural way to proceed, but reliance on our intuitive moral judgments has its limits. A familiar but important criticism is that because our moral intuitions are shaped by various contingent social and psychological factors, there is little reason to take them as having even initial credibility (Brandt 1979: 16–23). Reflecting the social norms we have imbibed, they cannot safely be viewed as having independent force when it comes to evaluating those norms or to determining what rules or policies it is desirable for us to follow (Kaplow and Shavell 2002: 80n). Even if those intuitions are revised and refined through a process of reflective equilibrium (Rawls 1971: 20), the end result still reflects its contingent starting points. There is more to ethics, it seems reasonable to contend, than just teasing out the implications of what we already think (Singer 2005: 345–6).

Furthermore, experimental psychology has discovered that our moral intuitions are subject to various framing effects and to distortion by cognitive and emotional factors that are quite arbitrary (Appiah 2008: 73–120), perhaps reflecting the imperfect heuristics that tend to govern human thought (Brink 2014: 680–8;

Green 2014). As a result, especially when confronting abstract, artificial, or stylized decision situations, our intuitions are less settled, less stable, and less consistent than philosophers have hitherto assumed (Norcross 2008: 66–8). Moreover, when it comes to war, we often feel tugged this way and that by different hypothetical scenarios because the ethical puzzles posed by war are so far from ordinary life. In working around this problem, many writers start with our intuitions about peacetime cases, using, for instance, simple imaginary scenarios about individuals who kill in self-defense or who save some people by acting in ways that cause others to die, and then reason by analogy from these to general principles about war. However, philosophers writing about war disagree about many of these peacetime cases (see, e.g., Frowe 2011: 15–18), and even if we have firm, shared intuitions about them, analogical reasoning may fail to capture how profoundly war differs from the everyday world that shaped our intuitions about right and wrong to begin with.

These days it is common for those working in the just war tradition to see the normative principles that govern war as ultimately based on human rights (Hartle 2004; Lee 2012; Orend 2006). Thus, wars may be fought justly only insofar as they are necessary to defend human rights, and they must be fought in a way that respects human rights. I will say more about rights in later chapters, but such an approach is less satisfying, normatively, than it sounds and fails to offer the theoretical unity that, as Lucas points out, seems missing from just war theory. For one thing, it is doubtful that all morally permissible wars are permissible because and only because they safeguard human rights or that all wrongful wars are best seen as wrong because they violate human rights. Nor, as we shall see, do human rights undergird all of the moral restrictions on the conduct of war.

Moreover, that we have certain human rights is often simply taken for granted; their content is treated as unproblematic, and they are only vaguely linked to the rights and duties of states. Indeed, couching the discussion in terms of human rights seems sometimes just to restate the author's initial judgments of right and wrong, rather than to explain or justify those judgments. For example, being told that it is wrong for combatants intentionally to slaughter innocent women and children because they have a human right not to be killed adds little or nothing to the judgment that it is wrong to kill them. Expressing that judgment in terms of rights obscures more than it clarifies for what is really wrong, what really bothers us morally, is that they have lost their lives for little or no reason, not that their rights have been violated. Likewise, it is unsatisfying to be told, as we sometimes are (Lee 2012: 146; McMahan 2009: 173–4), that when innocent civilians are sadly but permissibly killed as a foreseen but undesired side-effect of a morally justified military operation, then their right to life has been infringed but not violated or, alternatively, that it has been justifiably overridden even though it was neither forfeited nor waived. Such assertions seem only to be a fancy way of dressing up a moral trade-off that the author believes we should accept. That the victims had a right to life does little or nothing to explain why it is right to accept that trade-off.[8]

These last comments and the reflections of the previous few paragraphs are meant only to tempt the reader to consider, as an alternative to conventional just war theorizing, a utilitarian approach to the ethics of war—a possibility that the contemporary literature commonly overlooks or neglects to take seriously,[9] but which I shall be developing in this book. They are not intended to debunk the notion of human rights, which, as we shall see, utilitarians endorse, still less to disparage the contributions of the many fine scholars who approach the ethics of war within a just war framework. There is much to be learned from them. As we shall see in later chapters, utilitarianism finds value in the precepts of just war theory, but from a utilitarian perspective those precepts are not foundational; at best they are secondary principles, ultimately subordinate to the principle of utility. Although the precepts may provide useful guidance, they must be understood, interpreted, and perhaps revised from a broader consequentialist perspective.

Contemporary writers who take a just war approach tend to interpret their theory in a deontological way—Lango (2014: 33–4, 39) does so quite explicitly—and, as I have intimated, either ignore or express hostility to the utilitarian or consequentialist tradition in ethics. It is worth noting, though, that the classical just war theorists wrote before philosophers distinguished between consequentialism and non-consequentialism, and as we shall see in Chapter 4 and elsewhere, there are significant consequentialist strands within just war theory itself. Is utilitarianism, then, a rival to just war theory or simply an interpretation of it? If just war theorizing is understood to subsume all non-pacifist ethical discourse about war, then utilitarian thinking about war is a species of it. If, however, just war theory is understood as a free-standing normative framework, then utilitarianism is clearly a rival to it, even if it seeks to preserve some of its insights. Whichever way one looks at it, an advantage of approaching the ethics of war from a consequentialist or utilitarian perspective is that it allows one to resolve or, at least, sidestep many of the seemingly insoluble disputes among moral philosophers concerned with war. It provides a clear and, I believe, convincing way to tackle the fundamental questions of war and peace. Or so I shall be arguing in this book.

Notes

1 In this book, I use "moral" and "ethical" more or less interchangeably, and unless stated otherwise, by "right" or "permissible" I mean "morally right" and "morally permissible."
2 See Hanson (2009), Howard (1979), Howard et al. (1994), Merton (1993), and Whetham (2009).
3 The term *realism* is the standard label for this position. It comes from the discipline of international relations and is not to be confused with any of the various positions that philosophers sometimes call *realism*.
4 During the Hundred Years' War, French civilians suffered as much, if not more, from the depredations of French armies than they did from English armies (Merton 1993: 116–17, 128–9; see also Keegan 1998: 48).
5 In a meeting I attended with some officers in the U.S. Navy in 2010, a combat helicopter pilot said that if ordered to fire into a building containing civilians, he would refuse to do so. His colleagues at the meeting took this to be so obvious as to require no comment.
6 See Keegan (1998: 52) and the 1991 film *Black Robe* (dir. Bruce Beresford).

7 Thus, the lead essay of Walzer (2004) is aptly titled "The Triumph of Just War Theory."

8 There are puzzles, too, as mentioned in Chapter 6. If innocent civilians foresee that they are liable to be killed by an air raid, does not their right to life entitle them to shoot at the planes in self-defense? And if so, are the pilots (who are, ex hypothesi, fighting a just war) now justified in directly targeting them?

9 For example, of the fifty-eight thinkers represented in Reichberg et al. (2006), a comprehensive anthology on the ethics of war, the only utilitarian is John Stuart Mill, and the selections from him are not explicitly utilitarian in character.

2

UNDERSTANDING UTILITARIANISM

Utilitarianism represents an old and distinguished tradition in moral philosophy, the influence of which extends to law, economics, public policy, and other realms and is evident in much of our everyday moral thinking. Beginning with Jeremy Bentham and continuing down to the present day, many able philosophers have expounded, defended, and enriched utilitarian theory. Today the utilitarian tradition is as alive as ever, with critical analyses, fruitful elaborations, and proposed modifications of its core claims continuing to fill the leading professional journals. Few contemporary utilitarians, however, have had much to say about when, if ever, we may fight wars and (assuming they may sometimes be fought) how we are permitted to fight them.[1] This lack of interest is surprising, given that war and the threat of war wreak havoc with human well-being, and it contrasts with the concerns of the great nineteenth-century utilitarians—Bentham, James and John Stuart Mill, and Henry Sidgwick—all of whom wrote about war.

Before elaborating the utilitarian approach to war, however, it will help to discuss utilitarianism more generally in order to clarify the approach I adopt and to correct inaccurate or simplistic constructions of the theory, which have often led those writing on the ethics of war to reject prematurely a utilitarian approach to the subject. Accordingly, this chapter outlines the theory as I understand it, surveying its key features and endeavoring to show its coherence and plausibility and to rebut some common criticisms of it. But this sympathetic restatement of the theory cannot answer every question, address every reservation, or disarm every possible objection that one might have. Even if it were in my power, doing so is outside the compass of this book.[2] In any case, even without embracing utilitarianism as a comprehensive ethical doctrine, one may still find, I believe, that it offers a reasonable and illuminating way of thinking about the ethics of war or, at least, that it constitutes a necessary component of any satisfactory treatment of the various ethical issues surrounding war. On the other hand, if utilitarianism proves valuable in this realm, this would redound to the theory's credit, increasing its overall plausibility.

Consequentialism

Utilitarianism involves two fundamental ideas: first, that the results of our actions are the key to their moral evaluation; and, second, that one should assess and compare those results in terms of their impact on welfare, that is, on the well-being of people and other sentient creatures. This section and the next look at these aspects of utilitarianism: its consequentialism and its welfarism.

Utilitarianism is first and foremost a kind of consequentialism. Philosophers use the term *consequentialism* to identify a general way of thinking about right and wrong. Consequentialist ethical theories maintain that right and wrong are a function of the consequences of our actions—more precisely, that our actions are right or wrong because, and only because, of their consequences. The *only because* is important since almost all ethical theories take consequences into account when assessing actions, and almost all philosophers believe that the consequences of our actions at least sometimes affect their rightness or wrongness. What distinguishes consequentialist from non-consequentialist ethical theories is their insistence that when it comes to rightness or wrongness, at the end of the day nothing matters but the results of our actions.

When consequentialists affirm that the results or consequences of an action determine whether it is right or wrong, they have in mind, more specifically, the value of those results. That is, it is the goodness or badness of an action's consequences that determines its rightness or wrongness. Different consequentialist theories provide different accounts of what is good and bad, and they link the rightness or wrongness of actions to the goodness or badness of their results in different ways. The most common type of consequentialism, however, asserts that the morally right action for an agent to perform is the one that has the best consequences or that results in the most good. It is thus a maximizing doctrine. Unless stated otherwise, this is what I shall have in mind when discussing consequentialism. According to it, we are not merely permitted or encouraged, but morally required, to act so as to bring about as much good as we can. Consequentialists are interested in the consequences not only of one's acting in various positive ways, but also of one's refraining from acting. For example, if I ignore a panhandler's request for money, then one result of this may be that her children eat less well tonight. If so, then consequentialists will take this fact into account when assessing my conduct.

It could happen that two actions will have equally good results. In that case, there is no single best action and, hence, no uniquely right action. The agent acts rightly if he or she performs either of them. Another possibility is that an action might have bad consequences and yet be the right thing to do. This will be the case if all the alternatives have worse results. Finally, when consequentialists refer to the results or consequences of an action, they have in mind the entire upshot of the action, that is, its overall outcome. They are concerned with whether, and to what extent, the world is better or worse because the agent has elected a given course of conduct. Thus, consequentialists can take into account whatever value, if any, an action has in itself as well as the goodness or badness of its subsequent effects.

The good is agent-neutral and independent of the right

Consequentialism assumes that we can sometimes make objective, impartial, and agent-neutral judgments about the comparative goodness or badness of different states of affairs.[3] At least sometimes it will be the case that one outcome is better than another outcome—not better merely from some particular perspective but better, period. Thus, for example, it is a better outcome (all other things being equal) when eight people have headaches and two people die than when two people have headaches and eight people die. Most people believe this, as do most philosophers, including most non-consequentialists. However, some non-consequentialists contend that this idea makes no sense (e.g., Thomson 2001: 12–19, 41). A given state of affairs can be better for Fred or worse for Sarah than another state of affairs, they say, but it cannot be said to be just plain better. There is no such thing as being just plain better, only being better for someone, better from some perspective, or better along some particular dimension. Consequentialists disagree.

They take it for granted not only that the goodness or badness of an action's outcome is an objective, agent-neutral matter, but also that this is something that can be identified prior to, and independently of, the normative assessment of the action. The point, after all, of consequentialism is to use the goodness or badness of an action to determine its rightness or wrongness. And circularity would threaten the theory if our notions of right and wrong infect our assessment of consequences as good or bad. Consequentialism thus assumes that we can identify states of affairs as good or bad, better or worse, without reference to normative principles of right and wrong.

Probable consequences, not actual consequences, are what matter

According to consequentialism, then, an action is right if and only if nothing the agent could do would have better results. However, we rarely know ahead of time and for certain what the consequences will be of each of the possible actions we could perform. Consequentialism therefore says that we should choose the action, the expected value of which is at least as great as that of any other action open to us. The notion of expected value is mathematical in origin and conceptualized as follows. Every action that we might perform has a number of possible outcomes. The likelihood of those outcomes varies, but each can be assumed to have a certain probability of happening. In addition, each possible outcome of a given action has a certain value; that is, it is good or bad to some specified degree. Assume for the sake of discussion that we can assign numbers both to probabilities and to values. One would then calculate the expected value of action A, with (let us suppose) three possible outcomes, by multiplying the probability of each outcome by its value and summing the three figures. Suppose that the first possible outcome has a probability of 0.7 and a value of 3, the second outcome has a probability of 0.2 and a value of −1, and the third outcome a probability of 0.1 and value of 2. The expected value of A is thus $(3 \times 0.7) + (-1 \times 0.2) + (2 \times 0.1)$, which equals 2.1. Action A is the right one to perform if and only if no alternative action has a greater expected value than this.[4]

In reality, of course, we never have more than rough estimates of probabilities and values. Indeed, we are likely to be ignorant of some possible outcomes of an action or to misjudge their goodness or badness, and we may overlook altogether some possible courses of action. Nevertheless, the point being made is important. Consequentialism instructs the agent to do what is likely to have the best results as judged by what a reasonable and conscientious person in the agent's circumstances could be expected to know. It might turn out, however, that because of untoward circumstances, the action with the greatest expected value ends up producing poor results—worse results, in fact, than several other things the agent could have done instead. Assuming that the agent's original estimate of expected value was correct (or, at least, the most accurate estimate we could reasonably expect one to have arrived at in the circumstances), then this action remains the right thing to have done. Indeed, it is what the agent should do if he or she were to face the same situation again with the same probabilities as before. On the other hand, an agent might perform an action that has less expected value than several other actions the agent could have performed, and yet, through a fortuitous chain of circumstances, it turns out that the action had better results, brought more good into the world, than anything else the agent could have done. Nevertheless, the agent acted wrongly.

Some consequentialists disagree with this, adopting the rival view that the right action is the one that actually brings about the best results (or would in fact have brought about the best results, had it been performed) regardless of its expected value. How can it be right, they ask, to do what in fact had suboptimal results? Or wrong to do the thing that had the best results? Because these consequentialists still want the agent to act in whatever way is likely to maximize value, they draw a distinction between objective rightness and the action it would have been reasonable (or subjectively right) for the agent to perform. Comparing the actual results of what we did with what the actual results would have been, had we done something else instead, raises philosophical puzzles, given that science tells us that the universe is indeterministic and that the consequences of our actions stretch indefinitely into the future. However, the main reason for orienting consequentialism toward probable results rather than actual results is that the theory, like other ethical theories, is supposed to be prospective and action guiding.[5] In acting so as to maximize expected value, the agent is doing what the theory wants him to do, and he is not to be blamed, nor is he necessarily to modify his future conduct, if this action does not, in fact, maximize value. Accordingly, we should say, I believe, that this is not merely the reasonable, but also the morally right, way for the agent to act.

Welfarism

Consequentialism is not a complete ethical theory. It tells us to act so as to bring about as much expected good as we can but is silent about what the good is. Thus, depending on one's theory of value, there are different ways of filling out consequentialism and turning it into a complete ethical theory. Utilitarianism represents one way.

Utilitarianism takes happiness or, more broadly, well-being to be the only thing that is good in itself or valuable for its own sake. This is called *welfarism*, the value thesis that individual welfare or well-being is all that ultimately matters; it is the sole good, the only thing that is intrinsically valuable or worthwhile for its own sake. Things other than well-being that we hold to be good—friendship, say, or individual freedom—are good only indirectly. They are good because, and to the extent that, they are good for people, that is, contribute to their well-being or make their lives go better for them.

Bentham, Mill, and Sidgwick equated happiness with pleasure and unhappiness with pain, and they were concerned with happiness only because they implicitly identified it with well-being or what is good for people. Today, utilitarians acknowledge that happiness is not the only, and perhaps not the best, way to understand well-being. For convenience, however, I shall go on using "happiness," "well-being," and "welfare" interchangeably, but what really matters for utilitarianism is well-being—how well people's lives go for them—whether or not one understands well-being in terms of happiness. Contemporary philosophers have advanced different accounts of well-being; some believe that well-being consists in having certain sorts of mental states, others that it consists in having one's desires fulfilled, and still others that it consists in living a life that has certain objective characteristics, regardless of whether one likes or desires them. I shall not adjudicate among these and other competing conceptions of well-being. Doing so would take us too far afield and, in any case, despite conceptualizing well-being in different ways, philosophers (like ordinary people) largely agree on the things that typically promote it and the things that typically reduce it, although, no doubt, there is much yet to be learned from psychology and the other social sciences about these matters.

Utilitarianism holds, first, that a state of affairs is good or bad to some degree (and better or worse than some other state of affairs) only in virtue of the well-being of the lives of particular individuals. There is no good or bad above and beyond that, no good or bad above and beyond the happiness or unhappiness of individuals. Second, utilitarians believe that the good is additive, that is, that total or net happiness is the sum of the happiness or unhappiness of all the individuals we are considering. More happiness here counterbalances less happiness there. Underlying this, of course, is the assumption that in principle we can compare people's levels of happiness or well-being. But one should not interpret this assumption too strictly. Utilitarians have always granted that interpersonal comparisons of happiness or well-being are difficult, and they can even concede that some issues of comparison and addition may be irresolvable in principle. Utilitarians need affirm only that we can rank many states of affairs as better or worse. Finally, utilitarians believe that everyone's well-being is equally valuable so that his happiness or unhappiness, her pleasure or pain, carries the same weight as that of any other person. "Everybody to count for one, nobody for more than one," to quote the famous dictum Mill attributed to Bentham (Mill 1969c: 257).

For utilitarians, then, the standard of moral assessment is well-being, and the right course of action is the one with the greatest expected well-being. Non-utilitarian variants of consequentialism typically drop this exclusive commitment to well-being, seeing things other than or in addition to it as having intrinsic value. A utilitarian believes that the things we normally value—say, close personal bonds, knowledge, autonomy, or beauty—are valuable only because they typically lead, directly or indirectly, to enhanced well-being. Friendship, for instance, usually makes people happier, and human lives almost always go better with it than without it. By contrast, a non-utilitarian consequentialist might hold that the value of some things is at least partially independent of their impact on well-being—for example, that it is good that a person has autonomy or knowledge regardless of whether it makes the person's life better for him. A non-utilitarian consequentialist might conceivably go even further and maintain that a world with more equality or beauty or biological diversity is intrinsically better than a world with less even if no one is aware of the increased equality, beauty, or diversity and even if it makes no individual's life more valuable.

In addition to, or instead of, challenging the unique value placed on well-being, a non-utilitarian consequentialist might deviate from utilitarianism by declining to count equally the well-being of each. For example, the non-utilitarian might believe that enhancing the well-being of those whose current level of well-being is below average is more valuable than enhancing by an equal amount the well-being of those whose current level of well-being is above average. Or the non-utilitarian consequentialist might give up the belief that the good is additive and that the net value of an outcome is a straightforward function of various individuals' goods and bads. G.E. Moore (1968: 27–36), for example, famously urged that the value of a state of affairs bears no regular relation to the values of its constituent parts. Although the non-utilitarian consequentialist would, in these ways, be challenging the value theory of utilitarianism, he or she would remain committed to the proposition that one is always required to act so as to bring about as much good as possible.

The most common criticism of utilitarianism

Utilitarianism combines welfarism and consequentialism.[6] As we have seen, it is universalistic (because it takes everyone's interests into account equally), aggregative (because it sums the happiness or unhappiness of everyone to determine the overall value of an outcome), and maximizing (because it enjoins us to act so as to bring about as much well-being as possible). Although the theory can also be used to assess rules, laws, policies, and institutions as well as people's motivations and character traits (Kagan 2000; Pettit and Smith 2000), when it is applied to actions, it lays down the following criterion of rightness: An action is right if and only if no other action available to the agent has greater expected well-being; otherwise, it is wrong.

Critics of utilitarianism perennially point to the inevitable uncertainty of our knowledge of the future. We can never know all the consequences of the things we do, they remind us, still less the results of every possible action that we might have performed. The fact that the causal ramifications of actions extend indefinitely into the future compounds this problem, seeming to thwart any claim to know what course of conduct is best. Although, as previously mentioned, we do not need to know what the outcome of an action will be in order to estimate its expected value, in fact we are unlikely to know all the possible outcomes an action might have or to do more than guess at their comparative probabilities, and we are liable to overlook some alternative courses of action altogether. Furthermore, as previously noted, comparing people's levels of well-being is tricky and imprecise, and when many people are involved, the matter may seem hopelessly complex. Finally, even if we had all the relevant information and could perform the necessary calculations, there would rarely be time to do so before we must act. Critics of utilitarianism seize on these facts to argue that utilitarianism is an unworkable guide to action. This is the most common criticism of utilitarianism.

Utilitarians have several pertinent responses. To begin with, they can concede the above points and yet argue that they do not impugn the utilitarian goal of maximizing well-being. The correctness of that goal is not undermined by shortfalls in our knowledge of how best to attain it. Well-being is still what we should aim at, however difficult it may be to see the best way to bring it about. They can also point out that uncertainty about the future is a problem for other normative theories as well. Because almost all of them put some moral weight on the consequences of our actions, uncertainty about the future also affects their normative judgments.

Furthermore, utilitarians can stress that human beings are already well acquainted with the nature and typical causes of happiness and unhappiness. Despite our ignorance, we know many of the things that conduce to people's lives going well or that thwart their flourishing. Human beings have been around for a long while, and in reflecting on the possible consequences of an action, we do so with a wealth of experience behind us. Although by definition the specific situation in which one finds oneself is always unique, it is unlikely to be the first time human beings have pondered the results of performing an action of type A, B, or C in similar sorts of circumstances. In line with this, Mill's *Utilitarianism* ridicules people who talk

> as if, at the moment when some man feels tempted to meddle with the property or life of another, he had to begin considering for the first time whether murder and theft are injurious to human happiness ... It is truly a whimsical

> supposition that, if mankind were agreed in considering utility to be the test of morality, they would remain without any agreement as to what *is* useful ... There is no difficulty in proving any ethical standard whatever to work ill, if we suppose universal idiocy to be conjoined with it.
>
> (1969c: 224)

Mill's point also answers the complaint that "there is not time, previous to action, for calculating and weighing the effects of any line of conduct on the general happiness" (1969c: 224). In ordinary circumstances, we can and should follow certain well-established rules or guidelines that can generally be relied upon to produce the best results. We can, for example, make it a practice to tell the truth and keep our promises, rather than try to calculate possible pleasures and pains in every routine case, because we know that in general telling the truth and keeping promises result in more happiness than do lying and breaking promises. In this vein, Mill emphasized the necessity of "intermediate generalizations" or "corollaries from the principle of utility":

> To inform a traveler respecting the place of his ultimate destination is not to forbid the use of landmarks and direction-posts on the way. The proposition that happiness is the end and aim of morality does not mean that no road ought to be laid down to that goal ... Whatever we adopt as the fundamental principle of morality, we require subordinate principles to apply it by.
>
> (1969c: 224–5)

Relying on subordinate principles also alleviates another problem. Conscientious agents can make mistakes in their calculations, and bias can infect the reasoning of even a sincere utilitarian, especially when his or her own interests are at stake. In normal circumstances, however, one is less likely to err and more likely to promote well-being by sticking to certain settled guidelines than by trying to calculate from scratch the consequences of various courses of action.

A deeper objection to utilitarianism

Even if utilitarianism surmounts these practical objections, its critics allege that there is a deeper and more profound reason for rejecting the theory: namely, that it sometimes requires one to do immoral things.

According to the utilitarian principle, rightness and wrongness turn on the specific, comparative consequences of the various courses of action open to the agent. Without knowing something about the particular situation in which the agent must act, we cannot judge conclusively whether acting a certain way will be right or wrong. We cannot say absolutely or on the basis of *a priori* reasoning that actions of a certain type are always right or always wrong. Utilitarians see this flexibility as a strong point of their normative standard, but their critics view it as a fatal flaw: The utilitarian goal of maximizing well-being, they argue, can sometimes necessitate the agent's acting immorally. The critics concede that it generally conduces to net well-being for people to tell the truth, to keep their promises, and to refrain from injuring other people, from damaging their property, or from violating their rights. But there can be exceptions, they urge, and in unusual circumstances, promoting overall well-being might call for the agent to do something we normally consider quite wrong.

For this reason, the critics maintain that we must repudiate utilitarianism. To make their case, they often elaborate various imaginary scenarios or "counterexamples" in which circumstances conspire to require a welfare-maximizing agent to behave in some appalling way—to kill an innocent person, perhaps, or torture a young child, to frame a suspect for a crime he did not commit, or to support slavery or some other system of grievous social and economic inequality. Thus, for example, the critics might ask us to imagine an old and miserably depressed tramp, whose future will be one of continued unhappiness and who has no family or friends. If it can be done painlessly and without anyone noticing, and assuming that the killer would enjoy doing it or that he or others would benefit from the tramp's death in some way, then murdering the tramp would appear to be justified on utilitarian grounds. Yet surely, insist the critics, killing him would be foul and immoral, and because utilitarianism would condone it, one must reject the theory.

The utilitarian response

In reply to this sort of attack, utilitarians will begin by arguing that their theory does not mandate the conduct the critic says it does. They challenge the facts imagined in these cases, urging that it is preposterous to suppose that killing or torturing an innocent person, for example, could possibly be the single most effective thing one could do to promote long-term social well-being. Is there really absolutely nothing else that would have better results? The more dreadful the action or policy the critic envisions, the less believable it becomes that carrying it out would bring about more good than anything else one could do. Consider the allegation that a slave system might somehow maximize collective welfare and that therefore utilitarians would be obliged, shockingly, to support it. Given all that we know about human history, psychology, and social dynamics, how could it possibly promote "utility in the largest sense, grounded in the permanent interests of man as a progressive being" (Mill 1977: 224) for society to adopt slavery? Slaves inevitably suffer from their lot and chafe against their chains, and they can be terrorized by the threat of future punishment in a way that no animal can. Moreover, even otherwise decent people tend to exploit those over whom they have absolute power. If we keep in mind real people and the ways in which the world really works, it becomes utterly fantastic to suppose that slavery might promote the long-term collective well-being of humanity better than any alternative way of organizing society (Hare 1979: 119–21).

Assume, however, that the critic refuses to allow the utilitarian to challenge the hypothesized facts. He or she simply insists that they are as stipulated and that in the imagined case somehow or other conduct or policies we normally consider morally unacceptable really would maximize welfare. In response, of course, utilitarians must acknowledge that their principle entails that it is right to perform that action, whatever it is, that does in fact produce the greatest (expected) good overall and in the long run. But they deny that the imagined conflict with ordinary morality provides decisive grounds for rejecting utilitarianism.

To begin with, suppose that the critics asks us to imagine that it would maximize welfare to perform an action that, although normally considered wrongful, is not absolutely horrific—lying to an acquaintance, for instance, or breaking a promise, or hurting a small child. In these cases, the utilitarian will point out that, assuming the stakes are high enough—perhaps twisting the arm of a hysterical young girl is really the only way to make her quickly tell us where a psychopathic killer, whom she has mistakenly befriended, is hiding—then it is doubtful that ordinary, commonsense morality would condemn the action. Everyday morality is not absolutist; it recognizes that unusual circumstances can sometimes justify breaking the ordinary moral rules and that in rare cases it really can be right, all things considered, to tell a lie, break a promise, or cause an innocent person pain.

To this, however, the critic is likely to respond that although commonsense morality permits us to override its rules when the benefits of doing so are great, it does not license us to do so in order to obtain only a small increase in overall welfare—1,001 units of benefit from breaking a promise, say, as opposed to 1,000 units from keeping it (Hooker 2000: 145–6; Ross 1930: 35). It is dubious, of course, that one can give meaningful content to the hypothesis that breaking a promise produces one-tenth of a percent more good than keeping it, and even if the goodness of states of affairs could be ranked exactly as this, no one could claim to know these rankings with the imagined degree of precision. Nevertheless, suppose that, in the long run and all things considered (including the effect on one's reputation, the willingness of others to trust one, and potential damage to the general practice of promising), slightly more good would come from breaking a promise than from keeping it and that the agent knows this for a fact. The critic believes that this conflicts with our ordinary moral ideas, but when one colors in some realistic details—skipping my promised lunch with Gretchen when my day is extremely busy and I have arranged for her best friend Alice to show up at the restaurant in my stead—then it is far from clear that breaking the promise would be so patently immoral that any moral theory that permits or requires it can have no claim on one's allegiance. Moreover, utilitarians will argue that there is nothing sacrosanct about ordinary morality. If its rules sometimes conflict with utilitarianism, then we should adjust our ordinary moral thinking or at least have a greater appreciation of its limits of applicability.

To be sure, if the imagined welfare-maximizing action is truly horrific or unconscionable, such as torturing an innocent person, then it becomes harder to dismiss our ordinary moral instincts, which rebel against such conduct. Where the stakes are high, however, ordinary morality itself may be stumped: Would it be right or wrong to torture to death an innocent person if doing so will somehow magically stop a war in which tens of thousands will otherwise die? Questions like this are not ones that the rules of everyday morality were designed to answer. But if the welfare benefit of the terrible conduct is comparatively modest—killing a healthy hospital patient in order to use her organs to save the lives of three others—then doing so would undoubtedly contradict everyday moral thinking.

Here, though, utilitarianism can endorse our ordinary moral sentiments without abandoning its own standard of right. In other words, utilitarians can maintain that it's a good thing that doctors refuse to even entertain the idea of killing healthy patients, that ordinary people oppose slavery categorically and across the board, and that law enforcement officials never, ever, consider conspiring to frame someone for a crime he did not commit. The reason is simple. Although it is possible that performing some ghastly deed might be the best course of conduct in some far-fetched set of circumstances imagined by the critic of utilitarianism, these are not circumstances real people will encounter. In the world as it actually is, we do much better if people are dead set against doing atrocious things—if they recoil in horror at the prospect of supporting slavery, framing an innocent person, torturing a child, or killing a healthy patient for her organs, and reject out of hand the possibility that doing such things might be morally acceptable conduct. People who feel and act this way will, of course, do the non-utilitarian thing in the fanciful circumstances imagined by the critic of utilitarianism. But they will act the right way in the world they actually live in, a world in which such dreadful actions diminish net happiness. Indeed, the more strongly and categorically people oppose such conduct, the more likely they are to behave in happiness-promoting ways in the real world.

An example: the wrongfulness of killing

From a utilitarian perspective, the negative consequences of intentional homicide are obvious. In addition to whatever pain the victim suffers, killing someone deprives the person of future well-being, and it typically brings sorrow and grief to family and friends. Moreover, fear of being murdered can quickly and easily spread worry and insecurity throughout society. All societies firmly prohibit people from killing other people in the society, at least under ordinary circumstances, and there is a fully compelling utilitarian case for their doing so. Without such a prohibition, social existence would barely be possible.

Now, consider again the case of the old tramp, whose murder would, according to the critic of utilitarianism, optimally promote net well-being. Even if the supposed facts are exactly as the critic imagines—and that's a very big *if*—one is unlikely to know, or have compelling grounds for believing, that this is so, all things considered and in the long run. Furthermore, teaching people that it is permissible to kill others whenever they are firmly convinced that doing so is for the best would have disastrous social consequences. Here again John Stuart Mill is a valuable guide. "If it were thought allowable for any one to put to death at pleasure any human being whom he believes that the world would be well rid of," he writes, then "nobody's life would be safe" (1969b: 182). Moreover, a readiness to kill other people, even in the cause of promoting the good of all, represents a disposition that utilitarians would strive hard to discourage in favor of attitudes and sentiments (like a respect for life) that tend to promote welfare. Real utilitarians cannot love and assist others as they should and yet be as ready to kill people as the critic, in propounding the unhappy tramp case, imagines them to be.

Utilitarianism in practice

Utilitarianism's basic criterion of rightness is simple and straightforward. As we are beginning to see, however, in practice the theory's implications can be surprisingly subtle.

Praise and blame

For utilitarians, whether an agent acted wrongly is distinct from the question of whether he or she should be blamed or criticized for so acting (and, if so, how severely). Utilitarians apply their normative standard to questions of blame or praise just as they do to questions of rightness or wrongness. In particular, they will ask whether it will best promote expected well-being to criticize someone for failing to maximize expected well-being. Blame, criticism, and rebuke, although hurtful, can have good results by encouraging both the agent and other people to do better in the future, whereas neglecting to reproach misconduct increases the likelihood that the agent (or others) will act in the same unsatisfactory way the next time around. However, in some circumstances, to blame or criticize someone for acting wrongly would be pointless or even detrimental—for example, if the person did so accidentally, was innocently misinformed, or was suffering from emotional distress. In such circumstances, chastising the person for not living up to the utilitarian standard might do more harm than good.

Suppose that a well-intentioned agent acted in a welfare-promoting way, but that she could have produced even more good had she acted in some other way. Should utilitarians criticize her? Depending on the circumstances, the answer may well be no. Imagine that she acted spontaneously but in a way that was unselfish and showed regard for others, or suppose that she could have produced more happiness only by violating a generally accepted rule, the following of which usually produces good results. Or suppose that pursuing the other, even better course of conduct would have required a disregard for self-interest or for the interests of those who are near and dear to her that is more than we can normally or reasonably expect from human beings. In these cases, blame would seem to have little or no point. Indeed, if the agent brought about more good than most people do in similar situations, we may want to encourage others to follow her example. Praising an agent for an action that fails to live up to the utilitarian standard can sometimes be right. Utilitarians applaud instances of act-types they want to encourage, and they commend those motivations, dispositions, and character traits they want to reinforce.

Motives, dispositions, and character traits

Utilitarians take an instrumental approach to motives. Good motives are those that tend to produce right conduct whereas bad motives are those that conduce to wrongful conduct. And they assess habits, dispositions, attitudes, behavioral patterns, and character traits in the same instrumental way: One determines which ones are good, and how good they are, by looking at the actions they typically lead to. It does not follow from this, however, that a moral agent's only motivation or sole concern ought to be the impartial maximization of happiness. To the contrary, the utilitarian tradition has long urged that more good may come from people acting from other, more particular motivations, commitments, and dispositions—for instance, from the love of virtue for its own sake (Mill 1969c: 237) or out of devotion to friends and family (Sidgwick 1966: 432–4)—than from their acting only and always on a desire to promote the general good.

As we have seen, utilitarians should not try to compute, prior to acting, the probabilities of the possible outcomes of all the alternatives available to them. Even if this were humanly possible, it would be absurd and counterproductive. At least in minor matters and routine situations, stopping and calculating generally leads to poor results. One does better by acting from certain motives or habits or by doing what has usually proved right in similar situations. Thus, utilitarianism implies that one should not always reason as a utilitarian or, at least, that one should not always reason in a directly utilitarian way. Better results may come from our acting in accord with principles, procedures, or motives other than the basic utilitarian one. This last statement may sound paradoxical, but the utilitarian standard itself determines in what circumstances we should employ that standard as our direct guide to acting. The proper criterion for assessing actions is one matter; in what ways we should deliberate, reason, or otherwise decide what to do (so as to meet that criterion as best we can) is a separate issue.

Utilitarians will naturally want to guide their lives, make decisions, and base their actions on those principles, motives, and habits that produce the best results over the long run. Which principles, motives, and habits these are is a contingent matter, but many utilitarians, including in particular Mill, Sidgwick, and G.E. Moore, have maintained that one often does best to focus on the welfare of that limited number of human beings to whom one is closely connected. More generally, utilitarians approve of people's acting out of a concern for things other than the maximization of well-being insofar as their having this sort of motivational structure leads them to bring about more good in the long run (Railton 1988).

Reliance on rules

Although utilitarianism bases morality on one fundamental principle, it also stresses, as we have seen, the importance of following certain well-established rules or guidelines that can generally be relied upon to produce good results. We should, for instance, make it an instinctive practice to tell the truth and keep our promises because doing so produces better results than does case-by-case calculation. We are less likely to go wrong and more likely to promote good by cleaving to well-established secondary rules. Furthermore, when secondary rules are well known and generally followed, people know what others are going to do in certain routine and easily recognizable situations, and they can rely on this knowledge. This improves social coordination and makes society more stable and secure. "Any other plan," writes John Stuart Mill (1972a: 762), "would not only leave everybody uncertain what to expect, but would involve perpetual quarrelling: and hence general rules must be laid down for people's conduct to one another, or in other words, rights and obligations must … be recognised."

An analogy with traffic laws and regulations illuminates these points. Society's goal, let us assume, is that the overall flow of automotive traffic maximize benefit by getting everyone to his or her destination as safely and promptly as possible. Now imagine a traffic system with just one law or rule: Drive your vehicle so as to maximize benefit. It is easy to see that such a one-rule traffic system would be far from ideal and that we do much better with a variety of more specific traffic regulations. Without secondary rules telling them, for example, to drive on the right side of the road, to yield to traffic on the left, and to obey traffic signals, drivers would be left free to do whatever they thought best at any given moment depending on their interpretation of the traffic situation and their calculation of the probable results of alternative actions. The results of this would clearly be chaotic and deadly. Some philosophers seem to think that if people were smart enough and well informed enough, and if time and effort were no consideration, then secondary rules would be unnecessary. But this is a delusion because the optimal course of action for me depends on what I expect others to do, and vice-versa, and expectations can only be coordinated by a system of rules to which people routinely adhere without regard to consequences (Barry 1995: 220).

For the reasons just canvassed, utilitarians contend that to promote the good effectively, we should, much of the time, rely on and encourage others to rely on secondary rules, precepts, and guidelines. Furthermore, in many cases the full benefit of secondary rules can be reaped only when they are treated, not merely as guidelines or rules of thumb, but rather as moral rules—rules that, once internalized, one is strongly inclined to follow, to feel guilty about failing to adhere to, and to invoke when assessing the conduct of others. Having people strongly disposed, say, to tell the truth, keep their word, or refrain from interfering with other people's property can have enormous utility. Nor will utilitarians readily license people to override these moral rules. The reason is obvious, as Mill explains: "If one person may break through the rule on his own judgment, the same liberty cannot be refused to others; and since no one could rely on the rule's being observed, the rule would cease to exist" (1969b: 182).

Agents who genuinely embrace a rule as part of their personal moral code will not break it whenever they believe that doing so will marginally increase overall utility; indeed, in normal circumstances they will not even entertain the idea of doing so. For their part, utilitarians will be more concerned to instill in people a firm disposition to follow certain basic rules (the general utility of which has been established), than they will be desirous of harvesting the extra utility that might hypothetically come from people shrewdly deviating from those rules. Utilitarians will not criticize or blame a person for adhering to a moral rule endorsed by their theory in the rare case in which diverging from it would have had better results, even if the person was in a position to know this. Criticizing someone for misapplying a rule or disregarding a generally recognized exception to it makes sense. But it would be counterproductive to fault people for following, in the appropriate circumstances, the very moral rules fidelity to which one is seeking to inculcate in them.

The utilitarianism I have been sketching should not be confused with a hybrid theory known as *rule utilitarianism*. It maintains that the utilitarian standard should not be applied to individual actions but should be used instead only to determine the appropriate moral rules to follow. The rule utilitarian asks what set of rules society should adopt to maximize happiness. Those rules, in turn, provide the criterion of right and wrong. Actions are assessed not by their results but by whether they conform to the utility-derived rules: Actions are right if and only if they do. By contrast, the utilitarianism I favor (often called *act utilitarianism* to distinguish it from rule utilitarianism) retains the criterion for determining the rightness or wrongness of actions that was spelled out before—namely, that an action is right if and only if no rival action has greater expected well-being—while encouraging us to inculcate in ourselves and foster in others a set of intuitive moral principles, the following of which will generally produce the best long-term results.

An advantage of this position is that while it takes rules seriously, it allows us to appeal directly to utility when the rules conflict, when we are in exceptional circumstances, or when we face situations for which there are no applicable rules. The rationale for defining right, as rule utilitarians do, in terms of adherence to rules (rather than maximization of utility) is pragmatic: Doing so is believed to bring better long-term results.[7] However, once one distinguishes, to use the now standard terminology, between adopting the utilitarian standard as our *criterion* of right and using it as a *decision procedure*, that is, as a direct guide to how to act, then utilitarians can achieve these pragmatic benefits without revising or abandoning their fundamental normative principle. Traditionally, utilitarians have wanted to apply their standard to a wide range of objects—to the assessment of institutions, social policies, character traits, dispositions, and motivations, as well as to moral rules and, yes, individual actions. Sticking with the principle of utility as the ultimate moral gauge is more in keeping with this ambition.

Furthermore, even putting aside the difficulties of identifying the ideal set of rules for a society to adopt, to view morality as an entirely rule-governed affair seems too limited a perspective. A utilitarian can appreciate the importance of moral rules—indeed, endorse some of them as virtually absolute—and yet recognize that we probably cannot identify utility-maximizing rules to cover all conduct and all circumstances. G.E. Moore (1968: 162–4) made this point clearly, as did Mill when he distinguished situations in which there is … a necessity that some rule, of a nature simple enough to be easily understood and remembered, should not only be laid down for guidance, but universally observed, in order that the various persons concerned may know what they have to expect: the inconvenience of uncertainty on their part being a greater evil than that which may possibly arise, in a minority of cases, from the imperfect adaptation of the rule to those cases

from situations

in which there does not exist a necessity for a common rule, to be acknowledged and relied on as the basis of society life; where we are at liberty to inquire what is the most moral course under the particular circumstances of the case.

Mill concluded that in some cases "our conduct ought to conform itself to a prescribed rule; in others, it is to be guided by the best judgment which can be formed of the merits of the particular case" (1974: 1154–5).

The importance of rights

Talk of rights looms large in contemporary ethical discourse and, as mentioned in Chapter 1, moral theorists working within the just war tradition frequently frame the ethical issues of war in terms of rights. So it is worth expanding on how rights, including human rights, fit into the larger utilitarian perspective.

Broadly speaking, a *right* is an entitlement to act or to have others act in a certain way. Because different rights involve different clusters of permissions and constraints on people's actions, talk of rights is sometimes ambiguous. To assert that someone has a right to do something can mean that the person has no obligation not to do it, that others are obligated not to stop the person from doing it, or that others have a positive obligation to ensure that the person can have or do the thing he or she has a right to (Hare 1981: 149–50). Generally speaking, though, if a person has a right to do something or to be treated in a certain way, then someone else has a correlative duty to act or refrain from acting in some way.

Some rights depend on the rules, laws, and principles of a given legal system. In addition to legal rights and other rights defined and created by specific institutions, we can speak of moral rights. Some of these rights derive from the particular roles or relationships that people are in or from undertakings they have given or expectations they have created. Equally important are those moral rights that are independent of the agreements people make or the particular relationships they enter into. These human rights are, by definition, rights that all people enjoy, everywhere and at all times; they are not merely entitlements of a specific legal or political system or set of cultural understandings.

A widespread criticism of utilitarianism is that it does not take rights seriously. Generally speaking, rights take precedence over considerations of immediate utility. They limit or restrict direct appeals to welfare-maximization. For example, to have a right to free speech means that one is free to speak one's mind even if doing so will fail to maximize happiness because others dislike hearing what one has to say. If rights are moral claims that trump straightforward appeals to utility (Dworkin 1977: xi), then utilitarianism, the critics argue, cannot meaningfully respect rights because their theory subordinates them to the goal of advancing well-being. However, this criticism ignores the importance that utilitarianism places, as we have seen, on rules, principles, and norms other than welfare-maximization. To be sure, utilitarians look at rights in a different light than do moral theorists who see them as self-evident or as having an independent deontic status founded on non-utilitarian considerations. For utilitarians, rights are grounded in the promotion of welfare.

Jeremy Bentham was consistently hostile to the idea of natural rights, largely because he believed that those who invoked natural rights were only dressing up their moral prejudices in fancy rhetoric. In a similar vein, many utilitarians today believe that people are too quick to declare themselves possessors of all sorts of putative rights and that all too frequently these competing, often ill-defined, rights claims only obscure the important moral issues. But Bentham well understood the necessity, if we are to maximize well-being, of institutionalizing certain rights that protect an individual's person, property, and freedom of action from infringement by others, including the state. Indeed, it is difficult to see how a welfare-maximizing legal system or moral culture could fail to establish and uphold certain entitlements, such as the right to personal property or the right to be free from assault and other bodily invasions. Contrary to what their critics sometimes imply, utilitarians do not determine what rights people have in a direct, case-by-case way. Rather, they insist on the importance of society's entrenching certain sorts of claims, prerogatives, and entitlements. The task for utilitarians, of course, is to determine the exact set of rights, the acceptance and institutionalization of which will produce the most desirable results.

Having done this, though, it would then be counterproductive for utilitarians to disregard, override, or permit violations of those rights in an endeavor to boost well-being in particular cases. When institutionalized and generally acknowledged and respected, rights provide people with certain protections or a realm of choice that is not subject to direct calculation of utility. If you have a right to control access to your home, then you may admit and exclude whomever you wish; you do not have to allow homeless people to sleep in your living room even if doing so would be likely to increase net happiness. If we support a certain right on grounds of utility, then we must tolerate cases in which its exercise fails to maximize well-being. Practically speaking, it is impossible to institutionalize a right (and secure the benefits that this brings) and at the same time condemn its exercise or routinely license its violation in an effort to harvest greater utility.

Naturally, utilitarians will circumscribe the rights they endorse in various ways or build certain readily identifiable exceptions into them so as to maximize utility. The right to free speech does not permit one to defame others, and although homeowners have rights over their property, the law may legitimately prohibit them from storing toxic chemicals or restrict what they may build on their land. But once we have institutionalized a right that has already been specified and delimited so as to maximize well-being, there will be no feasible way to authorize violations of it simply on the ground that doing so would increase utility in that particular case (Hardin 1988: 102–3).

John Stuart Mill went beyond Bentham by unambiguously endorsing not just legal but also moral rights. Moral rights, he wrote, are "legitimate and authorized expectations," and for one to have a right to something is simply to have "a valid claim on society to protect him in the possession of it" (1969c: 220, 250). For Mill, utility determines when one has such a claim. There is nothing distinctively utilitarian about Mill's characterization of rights as entitlements or expectations that society should uphold. Whatever account one gives of moral rights—what rights we have, why we have them, and what is important about them—one will surely think that society ought to recognize and defend them. But even if the class of rights is coextensive with (or at least a subset of) the class of claims that society should uphold, different normative theories will understand or expand on this point in different ways. For Mill and subsequent utilitarians, a right is nothing other than a valid claim, and one has that claim because of the utility of society's protecting claims of that sort.

Utility thus determines what claims society should affirm and protect; these claims, then, constitute our rights. By contrast, non-consequentialist rights theorists reverse this explanatory order. Although affirming that if one has a right, then society should protect it, they identify the rights that people have independently of considerations of social utility. For example, they see rights as grounded in concepts such as dignity, respect, autonomy, or self-control or as reflecting the moral inviolability of persons (Nozick 1974: 32). For them, my right to x is the reason that society should protect me in the possession of x, whereas for the utilitarian or consequentialist that society should protect my claim to x is the reason I have a right to x in the first place.

Today, most utilitarians follow Mill in recognizing not just legal rights but also moral rights, including human rights. That is, they believe that there are certain claims or entitlements that it promotes social utility to recognize and protect, even if these rights are not legally formalized. They want people to acknowledge that others have rights and to be firmly minded to respect those rights, to refrain from violating them, and to push, where relevant and feasible, for their institutionalization. Although they adopt an instrumentalist approach to rights, utilitarians nevertheless desire to internalize in themselves and to inculcate and reinforce in others a firm, non-instrumental commitment to those rights and their corresponding norms. Only in this way, they believe, can we reap the full advantage of a system of rights (Brandt 1992: 179–212; Shaw 1999: 184–96).

The appeal of utilitarianism

Utilitarians approach issues of character and conduct from several distinct angles. First, about any action they can ask whether it was right in the sense of maximizing expected well-being. Second, they can ask whether it was an action the agent should have performed, knowing what she knew (or should have known) and feeling the obligation she should have felt to adhere to the rules and respect the rights that utilitarians would want people in her society to acknowledge and embrace. Third, if the action fell short in these respects, utilitarians can ask whether the agent should be criticized and, if so, how much. This will involve taking into account, among other things, how far the agent fell below the standard, whether there were extenuating factors, what the alternatives were, and what could reasonably have been expected from someone in the agent's shoes, as well as the likely effects of criticizing the agent (and others like her) for the conduct in question. Finally, utilitarians can ask whether the agent's motivations are ones that should be reinforced and strengthened, or weakened and discouraged, and they can ask this same question about the broader character traits of which these motivations are an aspect.

Looking at the matter from these various angles produces a nuanced, multidimensional moral assessment, one that seems true to the complexity of our moral lives. But even if one finds the utilitarian approach attractive, its superiority to other ethical theories cannot be conclusively demonstrated. To be sure, a few modern utilitarians have attempted to prove the theory in a rigorous manner—for example, R.M. Hare (1963, 1981) by arguing that it is entailed by the logic of moral language itself and John Harsanyi (1976, 1982) via rational-choice theory—but few view these efforts as logically decisive even if they do highlight considerations that lend support to utilitarianism. In this respect, however, utilitarianism is in no worse shape than its rivals, for attempts to establish non-utilitarian system of ethics all face serious objections. It seems plausible, in fact, to say that any normative theory is "necessarily grounded in intuitions of truth or value that cannot be objectively demonstrated or disproved" (Hardin 1988: 179).

For its part, utilitarianism rests on the conviction that individual well-being is what ultimately matters, that everyone's well-being matters equally, and that the goal of morality should be the impartial promotion of the interests of all. Some philosophers have thought that these premises were beyond challenge. Henry Sidgwick, for example, wrote that he perceived "as clearly as I see any axiom in Arithmetic or Geometry, that it is 'right' or 'reasonable' for me ... to do what I believe to be ultimately conducive to universal Good or Happiness" (1966: 507). Likewise, G.E. Moore (2005: 87, 94) and, for a time, Bertrand Russell (2009) thought that it was self-evident that the morally right action is the one with the best overall outcome. But these great thinkers were almost certainly mistaken. Even if utilitarianism's core convictions are plausible and attractive, they are not self-evident, nor are they beyond rational criticism.

Non-utilitarian approaches to ethics rest, of course, on other moral assumptions and appeal to different judgments and values. Utilitarians, however, believe that it counts in favor of their theory that it requires only a very small number of ethical assumptions, whereas its non-consequentialist rivals, such as the commonsense pluralism of Ross (1930), typically depend on a wide and diverse range of moral intuitions and ethical judgments. Moreover, the ethical assumptions on which utilitarians rely are not only few in number, but also very general in character, whereas non-consequentialist theorists typically appeal to a variety of more specific, lower-level normative intuitions. These intuitions—about specific cases, about the rightness or wrongness of various types of conduct, or about the correctness of certain normative rules—seem more likely to be distorted by the authority of cultural tradition and the influence of customary practice than are the more abstract, high-level intuitions upon which utilitarianism relies.

Furthermore, the ethical assumptions that utilitarians make correspond with the postulates that guide us in other areas of life. Their goal-oriented, maximizing approach to ethics coheres with what we implicitly believe to be rational conduct in other contexts. In particular, when seeking to advance our personal interests, we take for granted that practical rationality requires us to weigh, balance, and make trade-offs among the things we seek in order to maximize the net amount of good we obtain (Pettit 1991: 238). In contrast, deontological or non-consequentialist systems of morality hold that violating a given rule can be wrong, even when doing so would result in there being fewer overall violations of that very rule; utilitarians find this paradoxical or even irrational (Shaw 1993). They also argue that non-utilitarian moralists, when pressed to defend their rules, ultimately rely on the contention that there is sometimes a morally weighty distinction between one's doing x and one's letting x happen or that there is sometimes an important moral difference between one's intending x and one's foreseeing that x will happen as a result of what one does. Neither proposition, utilitarians maintain, can withstand critical scrutiny (Bennett 1995: 85–142; Kagan 1989: 83–182).[8]

These criticisms of rival approaches to ethics buttress the utilitarian conviction that conduct should be assessed in terms of its impact on how well people fare—more specifically, that the right action is the one with the greatest expected well-being. That conviction in turn rests, as I have suggested, on a cluster of closely connected ideas and values, which, even if they cannot be proved to be correct, are reasonable and attractive and less vulnerable to criticism, or so utilitarians believe, than are the ungrounded assumptions of rival theories. However, even if one finds the general utilitarian principle appealing, a further test is whether, when one examines utilitarianism closely and in various contexts, it provides a lucid and coherent normative system, an account of right and wrong and of how we ought to live that is both intellectually compelling and morally persuasive. By addressing some criticisms of the theory and by sketching the supple and often subtle ways it works in practice, this chapter has given some reasons for thinking that it does provide such a system.

In this book, however, I shall not pursue further utilitarianism's overall soundness as an ethical theory. Rather, I focus on its viability when applied to the topic of war. In doing so, my primary goal is to find plausible answers to the ethical problems war can pose, that is, to use utilitarianism to resolve or at least shed light on some vexed and unresolved issues in this area. There are different ways of understanding and developing utilitarianism, of course, and not all utilitarians will fully agree with my version of it. Nevertheless, almost everything I say about utilitarianism and war will hold true if one substitutes other variants of the theory and, indeed, with only modest adjustments, it will hold true, or largely true, if one substitutes many non-utilitarian forms of consequentialism as well. Even those who eschew consequentialism as a general normative outlook will, I hope, find that utilitarianism offers a sensible way of dealing with issues in the specific, limited domain that is my concern. In any case, because almost all non-consequentialists place value on well-being and affirm that consequences matter to the determination of right and wrong, assessing the ethical issues of war from the utilitarian perspective should capture at least part of what they care about.

Notes

1 Three noteworthy exceptions are Brandt (1972), Sinnott-Armstrong (2007), and Nathanson (2010).
2 I discuss utilitarianism in greater detail and depth in Shaw (1999).
3 Some non-standard variants of consequentialism permit agent-relative assessments of value (see Portmore 2001), but I focus on consequentialism as it is more usually understood.
4 The expected value of an act is a function of the probabilities of its possible outcomes and the value of those outcomes. But suppose those values are uncertain. If we can attach probabilities to the different values that an outcome might have, then entering them into the original calculation of an outcome's expec*ted* value would give us its expec*table* value. Expectable value is thus a function of the probabilities (a) of an action's possible outcomes and (b) of the possible values of those outcomes (Zimmerman 2008: 38–9). Hereafter I ignore this complication.
5 In this regard, a famous thought experiment by Frank Jackson poses a stumbling block for actual-results consequentialism. For a good discussion, see Andrić (2013). For a contrary but I think unpersuasive perspective, see Feldman (2006).
6 John Stuart Mill was explicit about this:

> That the morality of actions depends on the consequences which they tend to produce, is the doctrine of rational persons of all schools; that the good or evil of those consequences is measured solely by pleasure and pain, is all of the doctrine of the school of utility, which is peculiar to it.
>
> (1969a: 111)

7 Hooker (2000) is an exception. He defends rule consequentialism on non-consequentialist grounds.
8 There has been extensive, intricate philosophical discussion of these matters, which I cannot pursue here. Chapter 7 returns to the intending/foreseeing distinction. On doing vs. allowing harm, see Howard-Snyder (2011).

3

WHEN IS IT RIGHT TO FIGHT?

Chapter 1 criticized realism and relativism and argued that examining war in moral terms is not only a possible and coherent project but also an important undertaking. Chapter 2 outlined the utilitarian approach to ethics that I favor. Now it is time to begin applying that theory to war. I begin by reviewing what the great eighteenth- and nineteenth-century utilitarians had to say about war. Although largely ignored by theorists today, their views are often perceptive and instructive. Still, it must be said that they failed to answer with sufficient precision the central question of when, if ever, we are justified in waging war. Nor have contemporary utilitarians examined this issue with the care it deserves. This chapter redresses that dereliction. After identifying and clarifying what I call the Utilitarian War Principle, I advance some considerations in its favor and tackle some criticisms of it.

The early utilitarians on war

William Paley was an early expounder of the greatest happiness principle although, unlike Bentham and his successors, he embraced it on theological grounds. In his influential text, *The Principles of Moral and Political Philosophy*, Paley contrasted the principles of morality that apply to the affairs of nations and those that govern the private transactions of individuals. In the latter case, the good that might come from breaching a general rule, for example, the rule that we are to keep our promises, can never justify its violation: "The common happiness gains more by the preservation of the rule" whatever "inconveniency" this may produce in individual cases. In matters of state, however, this is not necessarily so. There, situations can arise in which "the general tendency [of the rule to promote utility] is outweighed by the enormity of the particular mischief." Adhering to a particular treaty, for example, could have such negative consequences that "the magnitude of the particular evil" would "call in question the obligation of the general rule." Still, it is risky to allow individual nations to decide for themselves "the comparison of particular and general consequences," especially given the precedent that might be set and the grave harm that would follow from a loss of respect for treaties. Moreover, this "loss, which affects *all*, will scarcely be made up to the common stock of happiness by any benefit that can be procured to a single nation" (2002: 457–8).

Taking for granted a division of labor in which, ideally, each state focuses on the well-being of its own citizens, *Principles* maintains that the "final view of all rational politics is to produce the greatest quantity of happiness in a given tract of land." National wealth, strength, and glory are valuable only insofar as they contribute to happiness—specifically, to the happiness of individuals for "the happiness of a people is made up of the happiness of single persons" (2002: 419). Turning to war, Paley distinguishes between "*justifying* causes of war" and "*insufficient* causes or *unjustifiable* motives of war." The former—the "objects of just war"—are "precaution, defence, or reparation" (2002: 461), but Paley does not explicitly connect these to broader utilitarian principles. Among the unjust grounds for war are internal disputes in other nations and the extension of territory or of trade. After elaborating on the negative consequences of enlarging territory by conquest, Paley admonishes princes (1) to seek instead to increase the happiness of their own land and (2) "never to pursue national *honour* as distinct from national *interest*" (2002: 464). *Principles* concludes with a defense of standing armies. Their benefits—standing armies are both more effective and more economical than militias—outweigh the dangers they pose, which wise policies can, in any case, mitigate (2002: 467–71).

Like Paley, Jeremy Bentham held that the end of the sovereign "ought to be the greatest happiness of the society concerned" (1843a: 537). The goal of international law, however, should be "the greatest happiness of all nations taken together." A dispassionate legislator of international law would regard as a crime not only "every proceeding—every arrangement, by which the given nation should do more evil to foreign nations taken together, whose interests might be affected, than it should do good to itself" but also the refusal of a nation "to render positive services to a foreign nation, when the rendering of them would produce more good to the last-mentioned nation, than it would evil to itself" (1843: 538).

Like his contemporary the utilitarian radical William Godwin (1971: 21–2, 210), Bentham disapproved of war more strongly than Paley appears to have done, and he sought its elimination. "All war is in its essence ruinous," Bentham wrote; "mischief upon the largest scale" (1843a: 544, 552). An anachronism in the modern world, war damages the interests of the masses, forcing them "to murder one another for the gratification of the avarice or pride of the few" (quoted in Conway 1989: 87). The few, in turn, rarely suffer the miseries brought about by the wars they direct. Bentham firmly rejected the idea that war benefits the national economy. It leads, rather, to higher taxation and increased executive power, and the colonies and trading privileges that are sometimes won by war do little or nothing to increase a nation's wealth. On the other hand, he believed that the frequency of war could be reduced by free trade, the development of international law, a foreign policy that was open to scrutiny and based upon non-interference with other nations, and by an effort to combat popular enthusiasm for war by debunking concepts such as national honor and martial glory.

Although a staunch critic of war, Bentham was not an out-and-out pacifist because he believed that genuinely defensive wars could be justified. "*Defence* is a fair ground for war," he wrote. "The Quaker's objection cannot stand. What a fine thing it would have been for Buonaparte to have had to do with Quaker nations!" (Bentham 1843b: 581). Noting in "Principles of International Law" that all states regard themselves as bound to protect their subjects against injuries from the subjects or governments of other states, he wrote that "the utility of the disposition to afford such protection is evident" (1843a: 544). In that essay, he goes on, in his characteristic, systematizing way, to catalogue various types of war, to review their typical causes or triggers, and to suggest some means for preventing them. For example, "homologation" of the unwritten laws of custom can remove uncertainties of interpretation that give rise to war, and defensive confederations can prevent wars resulting from fear of conquest. In the final section of "Principles," Bentham outlined "A Plan for an Universal and Perpetual Peace," based on two propositions: (1) reducing the armed forces that any European nation may possess—unlike Paley, he favored broadly based citizen militias as a means of combatting both foreign and domestic oppression (Conway 1989: 83)—and (2) emancipating all "distant dependencies." To promote its own welfare, he argued, Britain should give up its colonies and found no new ones. It should avoid all military alliances and any trade treaties intended to exclude other nations, and it should reduce its naval forces to the minimum necessary to defend its commerce against pirates.

Suppose that a state believes itself to have been aggrieved or finds its rights violated. Is it reasonable for it to go to war against its aggressor? That will depend in part on the "state of his [the aggressor's] mind with relation to the injury." If there is no bad faith (*mala fides*) on his part, then "it can never be for the advantage of the aggrieved state to have recourse to war, whether it be stronger or weaker than the aggressor" (Bentham 1843a: 545). Whatever the injury in question, the expense of war will always outweigh it. However unjust the aggression may appear, it is better, Bentham contends, to submit to it than to encounter the calamities of war. Even if the aggressor is acting in bad faith, whether recourse to war is worthwhile will depend on the circumstances. Unless the aggressive attack represents the first step toward national destruction, prudence may well dictate yielding.

Early in his career, James Mill—Bentham's disciple and the father of John Stuart Mill—seems not to have been particularly averse to war. At one point, he favored renewed hostilities against France and volunteered to defend the capital if an invasion came (Yasukawa 1991: 179–84). Over time, however, he grew increasingly opposed to war, coming to share many of Bentham's views—for instance, that war damages the national economy and brings suffering and ruin to the masses:

To what baneful quarter ... are we to look for the cause of the stagnation and misery which appear so general in human affairs? War! is the answer. There is no other cause. This is the pestilential wind which blasts the prosperity of nations. This is the devouring fiend which eats up the precious treasure of national economy, the foundation of national improvement, and of national happiness.

(Mill 1808: 119)

Wars occur, Mill contended, because they are in the interests of the rulers. It augments their power and provides opportunities for personal enrichment. They take advantage of the people's ignorance, misleading them with talk of national pride, glory, honor, and power (Yasukawa 1991: 189–91).

Despite his denunciation of war, James Mill joined Bentham in believing that wars of self-defense and possibly even preventive wars might be justified. Political reform, in particular the weakening of the power of the few, can help prevent unjustified wars. Utility is to be the guide:

When a nation has suffered, or only imagines that it has suffered injury, honour says, Go to war directly; revenge. When it has suffered real injury, and when there is no doubt about the matter, the principle of utility says, Consider whether the evil which you have suffered is likely to be compensated by war. If the evils of war are likely to outweigh the gains, it is better to abstain from war, and to pass by the injury. When the happiness of the people is the object in pursuit, this is the rule which will be followed.

(Quoted by Yasukawa 1991: 191)

In fact, Mill believed that avoiding war was not as difficult as generally thought because in the majority of cases, "both parties are to blame, and a little more wisdom on either side might have averted the calamity" (Mill 1808: 121).

In his essay "Law of Nations," James Mill argued for (1) developing a clear code for identifying the rights of nations and regulating their conduct with one another and (2) establishing an international tribunal for rendering decisions in conformity with that law, promptly and accurately. Although the tribunal would lack enforcement power, it would "operate as a great school of political morality." If the code were known and important deliberations of the tribunal were disseminated and even taught in school, "a moral sentiment would grow up, which would, in time, act as a powerful restraining force upon the injustice of nations" (Mill 1825: 32). In fact, the "approbation or disapprobation of mankind" is the "only power which can operate to sanction the laws of nations" (1825: 9).

In the world as it actually is, Mill thought, states are deterred from aggression not so much by the threat of legal sanction as by the threat of retaliation, and war is the principal "retributive sanction" (1825: 19). Nations should resort to it, however, only when some right of theirs, or something that ought to be treated as a right, has been violated. Moreover, for the extreme remedy of war to be justified, the violation must be serious and compensation must have been refused. Determining which rights are important enough that their violation warrants war is not easy. Some cases, of course, are clear-cut. A satisfactory code of international law would identify these and also spell out the sorts of injuries that might or might not justify war depending on the circumstances (1825: 19–20). Finally, the only just ends of war are compensation for the injury received and security against any fresh injury, and the law of nations should outlaw any violence not conducive to those ends (1825: 21, 26).

John Stuart Mill shared Bentham's and his father's anti-war disposition, but although he continued to think highly of James Mill's "Law of Nations," he was sympathetically skeptical of institutional solutions to the problem of war (Varouxakis 2013: 158–64). He seems never to have discussed the general causes of war or how to avoid it. In an intriguing fragment found among Mill's papers, however, his wife Harriet Taylor observes that the pre-modern world did not abhor war as much as we do today and therefore made little progress toward getting rid of it. That is because peace did not seem as preeminently important then as it does now. In few nations did all classes of the community enjoy the full benefits of civilized life, which include personal safety, liberty of commerce, undisturbed possession of wealth, and the freedom to expand one's energies in all directions. Moreover, the progress of civilization in general and of medicine in particular diminishes the physical suffering with which people are familiar, and as "plague, pestilence, and famine cease to be conspicuous among us, war stands out with ever increasing distinctness as a cause of human suffering, and the main agent in violent and premature death" (Taylor 1988: 616–17).

Although John Stuart Mill said little about the ethics of war in general, he was actively involved in the political debates of his day and in his discussions of current events occasionally made points that pertain to it. In "A Few Words on Non-Intervention," for instance, he argued that nations should not take sides in civil wars or uprisings against an established government except to counterbalance the intervention of other outsiders (1984a: 111–24). When the people are struggling against their own government for free institutions, there is obviously no question of supporting the government against them. On the other hand, however, if an oppressed people are to win enduring liberty, Mill maintained, then they must do so themselves. The situation changes, though, if they are struggling against foreign rule or a domestic tyranny supported by outsiders. Then the reasons for non-intervention no longer apply.

Mill followed the American Civil War closely. It engaged his "strongest feelings" because, he wrote, "I felt from the beginning [it] was destined to be a turning point, for good or evil, of the course of human affairs for an indefinite duration" (Mill 1981: 266). He was scathingly critical of the South and hoped that the war would last long enough, as in fact it did, to become unequivocally anti-slavery in character. In the context of rebuking those who wished that the North had not resorted to arms or who were pushing for it to come prematurely to terms with the South, he remarked:

War, in a good cause, is not the greatest evil which a nation can suffer. War is an ugly thing, but not the ugliest of things: the decayed and degraded state of moral and patriotic feeling which thinks nothing *worth* a war, is worse ... A man who has nothing which he is willing to fight for, nothing which he cares more about than he does about his personal safety, is a miserable creature ... As long as justice and injustice have not terminated *their* ever renewing fight for ascendancy in the affairs of mankind, human beings must be willing, when need is, to do battle for the one against the other.

(Mill 1984b: 141–2)

Mill applauded the North for having fought tenaciously and sacrificed so much "chiefly for the freedom of others," and he wanted Britain to have a defensive army like that of the United States, whose soldiers were not professionals but returned home to their civilian lives once the conflict was over (Varouxakis 2013: 166).

Mill discussed rebellion and insurrection in various other contexts as well. When was such political violence justified? It was defensible, he thought, only if it had a just cause and a reasonable prospect of success (Whitham 2014: 419–21; Williams 1989: 106, 110–1). By just cause, Mill generally meant that the violence served some fundamental utilitarian goal, such as upholding the freedom and basic well-being of the masses. In an 1867 letter, however, he appears cautious about revolutionary violence, expressing his "deep conviction" that it is justified only if (a) the oppression, tyranny, and consequent suffering are so intense that "to put an immediate stop to them is worth almost any amount of present evil and future danger" or (b) there are no peaceful and legal means of redress or those means have proved inefficacious despite having been pursued to "the utmost for a long series of years" (1972b: 1248).

Henry Sidgwick, the last of the classical utilitarians, wrote about war in his *Elements of Politics* and in some popular essays. In the former work, Sidgwick sought to outline the system of international rules, "for which it is desirable to obtain—and not unreasonable to hope—general acceptance" (Sidgwick 1908: 238). Of these, the most central is the "principle of mutual non-interference." Already widely accepted in international law, this principle makes it "the primary duty of a State to abstain from injuring any other State or its members (1) directly, or (2) by interference with rights of property, or (3) by non-performance of contract" (1908: 245).

If there has been a serious, unprovoked violation of its rights, a state has a secondary right to seek reparation. If reparation is refused or if "the outrage is gross and deliberate," the wronged state can legitimately use force—even if it leads to war—to obtain redress or secure itself against further violations (1908: 245). States should seek to arbitrate their differences, but sometimes this will be either impossible or undesirable: The violation of right may require immediate action, or the wronged state may view it as too serious to chance arbitration (1908: 264). The principle of mutual non-interference implies that no third party is obliged to participate in the conflict. However, if other states agree about who is in the wrong, then it can be both their duty and their interest to threaten intervention if they can form a league for this purpose that is strong enough to render improbable resistance by the aggressor. (Such leagues, Sidgwick speculates, might pave the way for a permanent federation strong enough to prevent wars.) Otherwise, neighboring states should remain neutral (1908: 267).

Sidgwick firmly rejects "national egoism" or the doctrine that states have no moral duties limiting the pursuit of their interests: "For a State, as for an individual, the ultimate end and standard of right conduct is the happiness of all who are affected by its actions." Although usually states, like individuals, best promote the general happiness by pursuing their own good,

> in the exceptional cases in which the interest of the part conflicts with the interest of the whole, the interest of the part—be it individual or State—must necessarily give way. On this point of principle no compromise is possible, no hesitation admissible, no appeal to experience relevant: the principle does not profess to [describe] what states and individuals have done, but to prescribe what they ought to do.
>
> (Sidgwick 1908: 299)

Still, Sidgwick writes, we should not exaggerate the divergence between the discrete interests of states and the general interest of the community of nations. It is usually in a state's interest to conform to the rules, at least if it can expect other states to do so as well.

As mentioned, Sidgwick favored arbitration as a way to forestall war but was alert to its limits. Because wars usually involve a conflict of principles, finding an arbiter whose wisdom and impartiality both sides can rely on is difficult. And with important rights at stake, a state will be reluctant to risk arbitration if it believes that force can settle the matter in its favor. Moreover, arbitration and legalistic proceedings are an "external method" to avoid war because they work no change "on the intellects and consciences of the disputants," who continue to advocate in their own interests (1998a: 53–5). Accordingly, Sidgwick stresses the importance of trying to reduce the causes of war "by cultivating a spirit of justice." To begin with, we should put ourselves in our opponent's place. If still convinced that we are in the right, we need to ask whether "there has been a divergence between our actions and our principles." If there has, this argues "for mildness and for a spirit of compromise." Finally, if fundamental differences of principle seem to divide the two sides, then we have the "difficult duty" of trying to see whether there is "an element of truth in the opponent's view which we have hitherto missed." Practically speaking, the opposed views of justice do not need to be completely harmonized, only reconciled enough that the difference between them appears less important than the evils of war. Cultivating a spirit of justice in these ways and seeking "no more than is our due in any dispute," tends, in turn, to promote the external method by making us more willing to submit our claims to arbitration (1998a: 59–60).

The utilitarian war principle

War has an obvious impact on human well-being, one that is almost always deleterious. For whatever good a given war might conceivably produce or whatever evils it may forestall, it will inescapably involve death and destruction, mayhem and misery. Indeed, it is exceedingly unlikely that any war, viewed as a whole, has ever been a welfare-optimal event or series of events. There will almost certainly have been some alternative state of affairs that the nations in question could have brought about instead that would have been better on utilitarian grounds. Indeed, frequently there will have been an outcome available to the belligerents that would have been better for each of them individually. That is why wars can sometimes look like collective folly. Even in periods of peace, the need to be prepared for war affects well-being, diverting human and material resources along channels that, viewed by themselves, are less productive of welfare than obvious alternatives to them.

However, even if war typically spells a collective loss of welfare, making the world worse than it might have been, this fact is far from settling the moral question of war. That is because an individual state affects but does not control the environment in which it must act. The question it faces is not how any other state should act nor how it would be best for all states to act but, rather, how *it* should act in the particular situation in which it finds itself. More specifically, a state must sometimes decide whether it would be right, in the given circumstances, for it to wage war against another state or states.

When, then, should a state go to war? The classical utilitarians did not answer this question with the directness and specificity we need. To be sure, we find them referring to national defense, to the protection of liberty, and to the vindication of certain rights—rights that they thought the international order should recognize and uphold—as just bases for a state to wage war, but their underlying utilitarian standard is rarely brought to the fore or explicitly connected to what they took to be legitimate grounds for war. Drawing on Chapter 2, however, the answer to our question is fairly straightforward.

Consequentialism entails that it is morally right for a state to wage war if and only if nothing else it could do would have better results. Call this the Consequentialist War Principle (CWP). Utilitarianism, too, entails CWP, but because utilitarians believe that individual welfare or well-being is the only thing that is valuable for its own sake, they would refine CWP by replacing "better results" with "greater expected well-being." Rewording things somewhat, we thus arrive at what I shall call the Utilitarian War Principle (UWP):

> (UWP) It is morally right for a state to wage war if and only if no other course of action available to it has greater expected well-being; otherwise, waging war is wrong.

This chapter and Chapters 4 and 5 discuss UWP, but much of what I say about it will also hold true of CWP, which is the more generic principle. Thus, readers who believe that things other than or in addition to well-being are intrinsically valuable or affect the goodness of an outcome may find it useful to think in terms of CWP even when it is UWP that is being discussed.

Let us look more closely at UWP. To begin with, it specifies when it would be morally right for a "state" to wage war. Because, strictly speaking, states differ from nations, *state* is the proper term to use here.[1] UWP focuses on states, not on sub-state, non-state, or supra-state political actors or collectivities or on the choices that individuals may face when their country is contemplating or has undertaken a war. One might modify or extend UWP to cover collective entities that are not states—I touch on this at a couple of points in this book—but UWP itself explicitly addresses only the central case of war between or among states, and that remains my focus. That's because it is important to settle this question before discussing other sorts of armed conflict.

UWP neither affirms nor denies that entities other than states, including lone individuals (Steinhoff 2007: 3–4), can be said with linguistic propriety to wage war. "War" can be defined in different ways. With regard to war between states, probably the only potential ambiguity to which one needs to be alert is that there are various kinds of wars that states can fight, from those that involve only restricted combat to those that engage all of a country's resources. UWP takes this fact into account. Among the alternative courses of action to be considered under UWP is that of fighting a war of a different type, scope, or intensity. Relatedly, UWP uses the phrase "wage war" rather than "go to war" because whether to fight a war is not a one-time-only decision.[2] Once a war begins, circumstances change, and a war that was initially justified according to UWP may cease to be so, and vice versa. UWP is forward looking: That a war was morally justified at time t does not entail that it is morally justified at time $t + x$. It is sometimes said that having justifiably embarked on a war, a state should see it through to the end. As a firm rule, however, this is inconsistent with UWP. That both sides in a given conflict could be waging war in accordance with UWP is vanishingly unlikely. It is less unlikely, though still improbable, that whereas at time t UWP justified state X's war effort, but not state Y's, at time $t + x$ the reverse is true.

If it is morally right for a state to wage war, then, of course, it is morally permitted to do so. Is it also morally required to wage war? The answer is that a state is morally required to wage war, as opposed to being merely morally permitted to do so, if and only if waging war has greater expected well-being than anything else it could do. This implies that if the well-being expected from some other course of action (A) is equivalent to that of waging war (W), and no course of action B, C, D, … etc. has equivalent or greater expected utility, then although a state must choose either A or W, it is not required to select one rather than the other. It acts rightly if it opts for either. This may sound like a purely theoretical point. But given the difficulties of estimating expected well-being, the possibility of ties may not be so remote.

UWP lays down the fundamental criterion for determining whether waging a given war is right or wrong.[3] Specifically, it requires, for a contemplated war to be right, not only that it does some good or forestalls some evil or even that its benefits outweigh its costs, but also, more stringently, that nothing else it could do (for example, to negotiate or simply to ignore the provocation) would have better results or, more precisely, greater expected well-being. UWP does not say what international rules states should adhere to or what rights, if any, states should be recognized as having, nor does it explicitly state how national leaders are to decide whether to lead their nations into war, that is, what guidelines or decision procedure they should follow so as to make it as likely as possible that they fight wars if and only if doing so accords with UWP.

I will say more about these matters in later chapters, but it is worth bearing in mind that war's ill effects are a given. Epistemic uncertainties may make it difficult to estimate the magnitude of harm ahead of time, but that people will be maimed or killed, that lives will be disrupted, and that things will be destroyed are guaranteed. By contrast, the presumed benefits of any prospective war typically lie further in the future, making them inevitably less certain and more speculative. Those benefits—for example, the deterrence of aggression or the upholding of freedom and self-determination—may indeed outweigh the costs, but to a large extent the costs are immediate and inevitable and occur regardless who wins whereas the benefits are more distant and conjectural and hang on victory falling to one side rather than the other, which, of course, is something that can rarely be assured. Because of this, when after the fullest reflection it remains uncertain whether an envisioned war would satisfy UWP, it is probably wisest to err on the side of caution.

Finally, it is worth emphasizing that UWP is universalistic in scope, taking into account the interests of everyone equally, including future persons, not just the interests of the nation (or the denizens of the nation) that is contemplating war. In principle, UWP takes into account the well-being of all sentient creatures, not just human beings. Although it is possible to imagine cases in which the moral assessment of a given war hinges on its impact on animal welfare, to simplify the discussion I concern myself here only with human well-being.

UWP is simple, but its widespread acceptance would have profound, practical ethical implications. It does not take much familiarity with human history to see three things. First, in deciding whether to wage war, states typically neglect or discount the consequences for other peoples. Justifications of war rarely take a universalistic form or, when they do, the universalism is spurious and what is thought to be good for one side (or for its rulers or for a dominant class) is presumed to be thereby good for humanity as a whole. Second and relatedly, arguments for war have frequently been conducted in terms that, if they do not ignore consequences altogether, focus on consequences that have little or nothing to do with how well or poorly the lives of individual people go (for example, when wars are fought to defend national honor or fulfill the destiny of a people). By contrast, this is all that ultimately matters for utilitarianism. True, there are rival understandings of well-being, and even when there is an agreed-upon conception, there are likely to be empirical uncertainties and disagreements about how best to promote well-being, so understood. But when it comes to war, subtle questions about the meaning or measurement of well-being are rarely involved because the goodness or badness of its effects on people is obvious and uncontroversial.

Third, it is uncommon for either side to have thought through, in any detailed or serious way, the probable gains and losses of fighting. True, the two sides are likely to believe that the stakes are high, that the benefits of fighting are great, that the consequences of not fighting are too terrible to contemplate, and that there is no feasible alternative. But conviction is not justification, and these beliefs are typically overconfident and only loosely grounded in fact. Even when they have some empirical basis, they are all too often riddled with mistaken assumptions and flawed assessments of likelihoods. In particular, seldom is sufficient thought given to alternatives that fall outside the political or ideological consensus of the time, such as conceding land or influence or relying on non-violent resistance. Widespread acceptance of UWP would change this for the better.

The case for UWP

One might embrace UWP because one believes that a utilitarian approach to ethics is the most plausible normative stance; hence, it is the approach to be taken when reflecting on the ethics of war. UWP, however, does not state a general criterion of right and wrong; rather, it is a fairly specific normative principle covering a limited ethical domain. Although utilitarianism entails UWP, the reverse entailment does not hold. With perfect consistency, one can accept UWP while rejecting utilitarianism as a general account of right and wrong. Indeed, one could even believe UWP to be true without believing that when wars are morally justified, this is because they maximize expected well-being. UWP states a bi-conditional, not an explanatory relationship ("if and only if" is not equivalent to "because"). Thus, it is possible that a theorist might grant that UWP is true, even universally true, but hold that what accounts for its truth is some normative factor or combination of factors other than welfare-maximization (perhaps with these factors varying from domain to domain or even from case to case). More weakly still, one might believe only that UWP is an extremely reliable ethical generalization, not a universally or necessarily true proposition.

Let us look more closely at why non-utilitarians might accept UWP as providing a satisfactory or basically correct criterion of when it is right for a state to wage war, beginning with those consequentialists who dissent from utilitarianism because of its value theory. Although almost always granting that well-being is intrinsically valuable, these consequentialitsts believe that some other things (for example, knowledge, equality, beauty, or personal affection) are valuable for their own sake, independent of their effect on human well-being. Even so, they may reasonably think that when it comes to waging war, at stake are welfare consequences so profound as to dwarf, for all practical purposes, any intrinsically valuable non-welfare consequences. They may further believe, quite plausibly, that trying for the sake of theoretical completeness to take into account those other consequences would make matters needlessly complicated or even prove counterproductive. In this way, non-utilitarian consequentialists might come to accept UWP as essentially correct—as practically speaking the most pertinent and useful basis for assessing the waging of war.

What about non-consequentialists? Why should they embrace UWP? The main reason is that UWP states an intuitively plausible normative principle. Common-sense morality balks, I believe, at the proposition that fighting a war can be right even though the overall results of fighting would be worse than not fighting. It is therefore implicitly committed to CWP. And if well-being is understood broadly enough to encompass goods such as liberty and self-determination that are essential to human flourishing—as Mill and almost all contemporary utilitarians believe— then upon reflection most people, I submit, will find UWP intuitively correct as well.

Some non-consequentialists appear to want consequences to play no role at all in determining the rightness or wrongness of waging war (e.g., Roff 2009: 81). The vast majority of contemporary non-consequentialists, however, believe that consequences, although not the whole story morally, are relevant to the deter-mination of right and wrong and, further, that in some circumstances the results of our actions may be all that really matters. They are especially likely to place primary importance on the outcomes of our choices when those choices have the potential to affect the well-being of many, many people for better or worse and in deep and important ways, as is undoubtedly the case with decisions about war and peace. So, consistent with their various theoretical commitments, these non-consequentialists could join commonsense morality in endorsing UWP as an intuitively acceptable, middle-level normative principle, a principle the cogency of which is evident upon reflection and that also coheres well with the judgments we are inclined to make about specific cases. Or, short of this, they may find that UWP offers a useful public standard for the assessment of war, around which it may be possible to build a political consensus.

Finally, even if some non-consequentialists find themselves unable to endorse UWP, they should find it helpful to have its implications spelled out because, when it comes to deciding whether to wage war, the principle is likely to capture at least part of what they think is normatively significant. Because, as I have said, most non-consequentialists place value on human well-being, even if they think that its promotion must sometimes yield to other moral considerations, it should be important to them to know what UWP implies about a given decision to wage war. Only then can they decide whether other moral considerations are significant enough to warrant the loss of welfare that would come from deviating from UWP in that particular situation.

In this context, it is worth noting that many of the reasons non-consequentialists have for rejecting a utilitarian or consequentialist account of right and wrong do not apply to UWP. For example, critics of utilitarianism contend that it is insensi-tive to questions of distribution, that it demands too much of us as individuals, or that it can too easily conflict with ordinary moral requirements such as keeping one's promises or telling the truth. They urge that utilitarianism is too impersonal and coldly calculating, and they maintain that it ignores one's individual attachments and personal commitments and the specific moral obligations that grow out of our various everyday relations with others. I believe that utilitarians can answer these complaints. However, the point here is that they lack bite or miss the mark altogether when it comes to UWP. When war and peace are at issue, we want our decision-makers to focus on the consequences of the alternatives open to them and to be committed to acting so as to make people's lives go as well as possible. We want them to be impartial, dispassionate, and empirically minded—to be rational deliberators who look objectively at the big picture and the long run, basing their decisions on the most accurate and detailed understanding they can obtain of the circumstances in which they are operating and the likely results of the alternatives open to them (Goodin 1995).

Some objections to UWP rebutted

Most of the standard criticisms of utilitarianism as a comprehensive moral theory are, I believe, inapplicable to its criterion of justified war, UWP, which is a relatively specific normative principle with a limited reach. Still, we can anticipate some likely objections to that principle.

To begin with, critics of UWP are likely to object that utilitarian reasoning is susceptible to abuse—in particular, that it can be used to justify all sorts of immoral wars. Even when initiating manifestly aggressive and purely self-aggrandizing wars, states often claim to be acting for the greater good and defend their actions, at least in part, on grounds that sound utilitarian. To the critics, this is evidence of the bankruptcy of the utilitarian approach. It must be conceded that devious, deceitful, or deluded leaders have often rationalized the immoral wars they wished to fight by specious appeals to the greater good. However, they have not refrained from also exploiting various non-utilitarian rationales—appealing, for example, to religious duty, to the glory or honor of the nation, or to some historical injustice it has allegedly suffered. When it comes to war, utilitarianism is no more vulnerable to rationalization and misuse than are other moral approaches, including conventional just war theory.[4] Even if it were, this would not show that it fails to provide a satisfactory normative criterion for assessing wars, only that the criterion has to be handled with care. In particular, one must distinguish candid, serious, and empirically grounded thought about outcomes from groundless assertions about the greater good and from sophistic arguments or state propaganda that takes a superficially consequentialist form but merely rationalizes a course of action determined on other grounds. No normative principle is shown to be incorrect because those who are morally reckless, self-deceived, or unprincipled abuse it.

The proper response to superficial and fallacious utilitarian arguments for war is not to abandon consequentialist thinking to the ignorant and unscrupulous, but rather to strive to do it better—that is, more accurately and more carefully and with greater awareness of the various illusions and mishaps to which human reasoning is prone. Although political leaders can fumble or manipulate utilitarian calculation and although, when it comes to matters of war in particular, the assertions on both sides about what will or will not bring about the most good are prone to be poorly grounded, tendentious, or even entirely spurious, to take UWP seriously is to push against this—that is, to seek to examine with as much specificity and meticulousness as possible the probable results of waging war in a given situation, taking into account the interests of all. By insisting that the right answer depends on the likely outcomes of the alternatives in the particular circumstances we face, and on nothing else, UWP provides the only possible antidote to baseless assertions about the greater good.

The above rejoinder, however, does not address what many will see as the major problem with UWP, namely, that when applied to real situations, it is hopelessly inconclusive because of epistemic obstacles confronting any attempt to use it (Werner 2013: 41). Chapter 2 discussed this sort of challenge to utilitarianism in general, but it is necessary to examine it further in the context of UWP. The epistemic obstacles in question are of two types, one a result of UWP's value theory, the other of its consequentialism. First, it will be urged that the concept of well-being is elusive, that the things that promote it are extremely variable or even unknowable, and that UWP ends up requiring us to compare goods that are, in fact, incommensurable (Coates 1997: 173–5). Second, it will be urged that, even if we could plausibly assign values to different outcomes, the consequences of the various possible courses of action open to any state contemplating war are too uncertain and unpredictable for UWP to yield a determinate answer either way. Let us consider these objections in turn.

In responding to the first set of claims, it bears repeating from Chapter 2 that we already know quite a lot about human well-being—about what it is for people's lives to flourish or fail to flourish, about the sources of their suffering and satisfaction, and about the various things that conduce to, or thwart, their faring well. Far from being entirely ignorant about these matters, we broadly agree about the things that are good for people and the things that damage their interests, blight their prospects, or make their lives go poorly. Although more work is need to clarify and refine the notion of well-being, of which there are competing philosophical conceptions, and although we have a lot left to learn about the biological, psychological, and social factors that affect individual welfare, when it comes to questions of war, as previously suggested, we are not dealing with subtle questions of well-being. Maiming or killing people, orphaning children, destroying farms and factories, dislocating civilians, damaging a country's cultural heritage, and ripping up its economic infrastructure—these are patently destructive of well-being. On the other hand, there is no question that physical and psychological security, personal liberty, political self-determination, and respect for territorial integrity promote well-being and that war may sometimes protect these goods.

Still, weighing and comparing the relevant goods and evils can be challenging, and a number of philosophers believe that many values (for example, liberty and equality) are incommensurable, meaning (roughly) that it is not possible to measure and compare them against each other. This is a vexed topic in contemporary discussions of value theory and decision-making, especially for those who believe in a diverse range of intrinsically valuable goods. By contrast, UWP appeals to an apparently monistic standard, namely, well-being. Yet, on closer inspection this monism may be more terminological than substantive because at least some conceptions of well-being oblige us to make comparisons of its different aspects on an essentially intuitive basis. But, again, it is easy to exaggerate the problems facing UWP because even those philosophers who stress that various values (or various aspects of well-being) cannot be reduced to a common measure also believe that in practice we often can and do make reasonable comparisons and trade-offs among them.

Utilitarians long ago gave up belief in anything like Bentham's hedonic calculus.[5] They tend, like Mill, to take a broad view of the things that are important for human flourishing, including among them, for instance, respect for individual autonomy and the upholding of basic rights. Undoubtedly, UWP invites extremely hard questions, such as: In terms of their long-run contribution to human well-being, are the goods that this war seeks to secure and that it has such-and-such a likelihood of bringing about, worth the projected loss of these many lives and this much material damage? Posed this way, the question may seem daunting indeed, but whenever a nation weighs recourse to war it is precisely tough questions of this sort that one should be asking and that the relevant decision-makers should be debating, as carefully and with as much precision as they can muster.

This brings us to the second obstacle confronting any effort to apply UWP, namely, that the consequences of our choices are only imperfectly foreseeable. Even if we could correctly assess and compare the goodness or badness of various outcomes (our first problem), our knowledge of the future is inevitably tenuous and incomplete, especially insofar as it involves anticipating how others will respond to what we do. When it comes to questions of war and peace, the future is too unpredictable, the critic of UWP alleges, for us to make reliable judgments about the likely results of the alternatives open to us. This allegation is not entirely groundless. Even decision-makers sincerely trying to adhere to UWP can misjudge the probable effects of the courses of action they are considering, either overlooking some possible outcomes altogether or miscalculating their likelihood. They can be also unaware of, or fail to attend to, some alternative courses of actions. In addition, faulty background assumptions and various kinds of bias can distort their assessments as can wishful thinking, anchoring, framing effects, and the other sorts of cognitive error to which all human decision-making is prone. Emotion, self-interest, and social pressure can also cloud their judgment.

Nevertheless, the critic of UWP overstates the hopelessness of our epistemic situation. Much of the time we manage to navigate through the world with some success. We anticipate future events more or less correctly. Things go according to plan; our expectations are fulfilled. Moreover, fuller discussion, empirical testing, the ventilating of assumptions, and the consideration of divergent perspectives can improve our anticipations of the future, our knowledge of the probable results of different courses of actions. An appreciation of our own fallibility can also help as can an awareness of the various ways, logical and psychological, that reasoning can go astray. When it comes to war in particular, it may be possible to learn from the past by studying the flawed thinking that has characterized so many decisions to wage war and comparing it to what an impartial, well-informed observer who had undertaken to apply UWP would have decided, looking at the facts and probabilities and taking into account the interests of all. At the very least, history can teach us to be more modest and circumspect and to acknowledge our own epistemic limits.

Uncertainty about the consequences of our actions should make us cautious about going to war; it should not lead us to believe that the morality of resorting to arms can be determined independently of its consequences. There are, in fact, many wars, the waging of which unarguably violated UWP, and others about which we can assert with reasonable confidence, I believe, that fighting them accorded with UWP. About some wars, it may not be obvious what careful utilitarian reflection would show. However, when it comes to big, complicated, real-world questions of war and peace, we have no reason for assuming that the correct normative principle, whatever it may be, will always give us simple and effortless answers.

Given this, and given that no state (to my knowledge) has consciously adhered to UWP and that few thinkers have used it to examine either current or past wars,[6] it seems premature to discard it as unworkable. And even if the epistemic problems I have canvassed are as serious as the critic of UWP believes they are, it would not follow that UWP should be rejected. It might simply be the case, as I have intimated, that a normative principle, namely, UWP, which upon serious reflection we judge to be plausible, reasonable, well-justified, or just plain true, is often difficult to apply and that sometimes conscientious people may reasonably differ over specific cases. That would be unfortunate, but it might be the way things are. We cannot rule out the possibility that getting the right answers to some important moral questions may be problematic. Nor should it be surprising that it can often be difficult to assess morally large-scale decisions that affect the lives of thousands or even millions of people in countless ways.

In this context, let us consider World War II.

World War II as a test case

As discussed in Chapter 2, when non-consequentialists criticize utilitarianism, a standard technique is that of counterexample. The critic tries to imagine some scenario where utilitarianism implies a course of conduct that conflicts with our moral intuitions and then on this basis concludes that the theory should be repudiated. When it comes to war, however, it is difficult to come up with realistic examples where utilitarianism has implications that would strike one as counterintuitive or seriously problematic. David Rodin, however, has argued that World War II poses this sort of challenge to utilitarianism (Rodin 2002: 10–11; 2007: 147). Because the Allies' war against German and Japanese aggression is almost universally seen as about as clear an example of a morally justified war as one can imagine, utilitarians must be able to show that the Allies were right to fight. This, Rodin believes, they cannot do.

Let us look, then, at World War II. Around 55 million people, Rodin says, died because of that war, an additional 40 million were made homeless, and there was enormous, nearly incalculable damage to the world's cultural and material wealth. From a utilitarian or consequentialist perspective, Rodin suggests, the price the world paid for stopping the Nazis may not have been worth it. In response, the first thing is to acknowledge—who could deny it?—that the human costs of World War II were truly staggering, horrendous almost beyond belief, and that this fact should give anyone pause. We should not glibly and automatically say, "yes, but of course, it was all worth it."[7] Although I think that the Allied war effort was indeed morally justified on utilitarian grounds, this is not a judgment to be made lightly. And it is a strength of utilitarianism that it continually points to the costs or likely costs of any war for real flesh-and-blood human beings and asks whether the good to be achieved warrants paying that price.

In the case of World War II, a utilitarian justification of the war would begin by pointing out that the figure of 55 million that Rodin uses cannot possibly refer to deaths that resulted from the Allies' decision to take up arms. Millions would have died from Axis brutality and aggression even if Britain and the United States had stayed out of the war and the Soviet Union had immediately capitulated.[8] Moreover, for utilitarians the issue is not the costs of the war as a whole, but the decision that each country faced whether to fight or not. For instance, was the entry of the United States into the war at the end of 1941 the best course of action available to it, that is, the course of action with the greatest expected utility, taking a long-run view and the well-being of all into account? Answering that question is less daunting than an irrelevant weighing of the gains and losses of the war as a whole, and it certainly seems reasonable to believe that the answer is yes.

Although U.S. entry into the war resulted in more American deaths than would have occurred otherwise, it probably resulted in no more—and indeed probably fewer—deaths overall than if it had stayed out of the conflict and left the other belligerents to battle it out to the end. The United States undeniably tipped the balance decisively against the Axis powers and ensured their demise. That this outcome was an enormous good, no one would deny, given the long-term cost to civilization itself of Nazi dominion in Europe and unopposed Japanese hegemony in Asia—the cost to world culture, to the rule of law, to humanitarian values, and, of course, to liberty (deemed by Mill "one of the principal ingredients of human happiness, and quite the chief ingredient of individual and social progress" [Mill 1977: 261]). True, at the time Russia was a pretty nasty place, and who can tell how the Nazi or Japanese regimes might have evolved and what life might have been like under their rule twenty or thirty years down the road? Even so, it is hard to deny that resisting the Axis forces advanced the expected well-being of humanity. Flipping the issue around, we can ask whether an objective and impartial person could plausibly believe that refraining from violent resistance to Japanese and German aggression would have been the optimal course of action. The answer is obvious: To believe so would be to unmoor oneself from historical reality.

So far we have been looking back at World War II from decades later, and Rodin is right to say that moral theory is primarily concerned with forward-looking assessment of how one ought to act. "It is on this count," he contends, "that consequentialism is most disappointing as a moral theory of warfare" (2002: 11). That is because he believes that the final consequences of World War II could not have been reliably predicted in 1939 when Britain made the decision to go to war. He wisely points out that wars are hugely complex events, whose eventual outcome is shaped by a whole variety of factors, and that they often have an internal dynamic that subverts the original objectives and intentions of those who initiate them. But all European political leaders of the time knew what they were getting into. They had lived through World War I, and they knew that if there were another world war, the struggle would be fearsome and terrifying and that it would spell devastation on a previously unknown scale. Furthermore, even if the odds were against Britain, this does not entail that it was wrong to wage war. If the stakes are high enough, an action with a low probability of success may have greater expected utility than any alternative to it. Finally, even if the utilitarian case for Britain's going to war in defense of Poland was debatable in 1939, it was as evident then as it is now that utilitarianism condemns German and Japanese aggression and that U.S. entry into the war spelled their ultimate defeat, however exactly this would play out.

Suppose that I am right about this and that utilitarianism can "answer the question [of World War II's justification] confidently in the affirmative." To this Rodin responds, "would this capture what we feel to be morally most important about the Second World War? I believe that few would think so" (2002: 12). This remark is open to interpretation. I take it to mean that we know immediately and intuitively that the war was justified and that utilitarianism, with its demand that we look at the projected costs and benefits, fails to capture this. By analogy, if your spouse is drowning, you do not stop and calculate, weighing the risks and reflecting on possible alternative futures (perhaps I'd be happier with someone else?), you simply leap in and try to save her. In response to this point, utilitarians have several things to say.

To begin with, as discussed in Chapter 2, utilitarians are concerned not only with people's actions but also with their character and motivational structure; they want people to have a strong intuitive commitment to certain values and moral principles, values and principles that are more specific than the general goal of bringing about as much well-being as possible. This is because, utilitarians believe, in acting from these more specific motivations, people will in fact produce more good on balance and over the long run. Thus, for example, Mill averred that utilitarianism "enjoins and requires the cultivation of the love of virtue up to the greatest strength possible" (1969c: 237) and in our own time R.M. Hare (1979) maintained that utilitarians want people to be firmly and categorically opposed to slavery and to resist it in all circumstances, even if it is possible to imagine far-fetched situations in which a slave system would maximize well-being. In the same vein, it is clearly good that people be stoutly opposed to everything the Nazis stood for. Utilitarians will want them to look at the Nazis with revulsion and think "yes, they should be opposed at all costs."

These are important points about utilitarianism, properly understood. Still, the matter is a little different with regard to political leaders, who have the authority and power to lead their nations into war. Naturally, utilitarians want them to have sound moral instincts and to adhere to certain moral guidelines, but when it comes to decisions about war and peace they also want them to stop and think and to examine the likely consequences of the alternative courses of action open to them. With so much at stake, they have to be able to step back from the intuitive convictions that utilitarians want all people to have (in this case, that one must always resist fascism) and to think through their decisions in a concrete and detailed consequentialist way.

Although World War II undoubtedly raised profound and sometimes terrifying moral choices for many countries, it poses no basis for rejecting UWP. That principle, with its focus on the likely real-world consequences of the decision to go to war, makes those decisions neither easier nor harder than they actually are. Ironically, although Rodin criticizes utilitarianism for being insufficiently unequivocal in its endorsement of World War II, it turns out that his own anti-consequentialist, rights-oriented framework fares no better. Skeptical of the right of national defense, his book concludes that "there is no way to understand the fighting of defensive wars as morally justified." True, when it comes to a regime as repugnant as Nazi Germany, he writes, we may nevertheless feel that we simply "must" fight. Still, "if we do so … our argument cannot be conceived in terms of right and justice" (2002: 198–9). This feckless conclusion, I think, only strengthens the appeal of a utilitarian approach.

Notes

1 In this book, however, I often forsake terminological purity for stylistic convenience and, like most writers, frequently employ *state*, *nation*, and *country* interchangeably.
2 I do not mean to suggest that there is always an unambiguous, initial decision to wage war. A state might slide into war as a result of many small choices, and it can sometimes be difficult to say exactly when a war began.
3 H.M. Roff believes that because of future uncertainty, utilitarianism can tell us only when it is reasonable to go to war, not when it is right to do so. Utilitarianism can pronounce on the latter, she thinks, only retrospectively (2009: 80–1). As I have formulated UWP, however, this is incorrect.
4 For example, in a 1991 meeting with Vatican officials the leaders of Iraq's Christian churches defended their country's invasion of Kuwait on just war grounds (Coates 1997: 152).
5 Bentham himself was well aware of its limits; see Quinn (2014).
6 Gruzalski (2006) is a noteworthy exception.
7 This is especially true for Americans, who tend to have a sanitized and overly romantic view of U.S. involvement in the war; see Adams (1994).
8 Lackey (1989: 23) writes that the Allies were responsible only for the 5.5 million Axis soldiers and 1 million civilians in Axis countries whom they killed. But from a consequentialist perspective, this exaggerates things in the opposite direction. The Allies were responsible not just for their direct killings but for all the deaths that were a foreseeable consequence of their intervention.

4

UTILITARIANISM, PACIFISM, AND JUST WAR THEORY

The Utilitarian War Principle (UWP) states that it is morally right for a state to wage war if and only if no other course of action has greater expected well-being. As previously explained, utilitarianism entails but is not entailed by UWP.[1] The point of explicitly identifying UWP and differentiating it from utilitarianism is to emphasize that one can accept that normative principle while favoring some other general ethical theory or no ethical theory at all.[2] In line with this, Chapter 3 spelled out the meaning and merits of UWP, advanced reasons why non-utilitarians might find it an attractive normative principle, and answered some objections to it.

In particular, it defended UWP against the criticism that it is unworkable and should therefore be rejected. But even if that criticism can be rebutted, it points to a genuine problem: In practice, how should utilitarians or other adherents of UWP decide questions of war and peace so that those decisions conform best to that principle over the long run? Chapter 2 quoted John Stuart Mill on the importance of following "intermediate generalizations" or "corollaries from the principle of utility" instead of "endeavour[ing] to test each individual action by the first principle." Indeed, "whatever we adopt as the fundamental principle of morality," he writes, "we require subordinate principles to apply it by" (Mill 1969c: 224–5). UWP is not, of course, "the fundamental principle of morality." Nevertheless, applied to the present context, Mill's remarks suggest that even if UWP provides the theoretically correct criterion for distinguishing justified from unjustified wars, because of the difficulty of applying that criterion accurately in practice, policy-makers may need to follow certain secondary guidelines or lower-level rules or principles. Doing so may reduce the epistemic and other difficulties that can impede employing UWP successfully.

What secondary principles, if any, might suitably play this role? Two possibilities suggest themselves: adopting the pacifist principle or following the *ad bellum* principles of just war theory. This chapter explores these two possibilities, rejecting the former but arguing that utilitarians and other friends of UWP should embrace the latter principles as normative guides. It then rebuts some final objections to the utilitarian approach to war.

The pacifist principle

Pacifism means different things to different people. For some, it involves a commitment to non-violence in all one's relationships, that is, to living a life that honors the value of peace. For others, too, pacifism is not primarily about war, but rather reflects a belief that all life is sacred and to be respected or that it is always wrong to kill another human being or, perhaps, even to kill any living creature whatsoever. At the very least, though, a pacifist is one who opposes war. Some pacifists see opposition to war as a personal or lifestyle choice; for others, it is an obligation imposed by their particular religion or vocation, whereas for yet others, it is a universal moral duty, incumbent on everyone. This latter position, which Chapter 1 labeled "anti-war pacifism," is what most people understand by pacifism: namely, the categorical rejection of war on moral grounds.

In trying to square his support of the Allied war effort in World War II with his pacifist opposition to World War I, for which he went to jail, Bertrand Russell distinguished traditional anti-war pacifism, which repudiates all war, from "relative pacifism." This holds "that *very few* wars are worth fighting, and that the evils of war are *almost* always greater than they seem to excited populations at the moment war breaks out" (Russell 1943–4: 8). More recent writers (Bazargan 2014; Fiala 2010) have used the label "contingent pacifism" to refer to views like this, which oppose war in general but allow for some exceptions. Far less extreme than traditional anti-war pacifism, this selective sort of pacifism amounts to little more than a strong moral presumption against war. This is something that many people may find congenial.

In any case, by the "pacifist principle," it is anti-war pacifism—the blanket moral condemnation of war—that I shall have in mind. Any humane person will want people to believe, and to be disposed to act on the belief, that war is a dreadful thing and should be strenuously avoided. The pacifist principle, however, goes further than this, affirming unconditionally that a state should never wage war, ever. It rejects all wars as immoral and forbids us to fight them. Absolutist in character, the principle brooks no exceptions. For those who embrace it, the principle most likely rests on some prior, more fundamental deontological principle or argument—for example, that one has an overriding duty not to kill other human beings; that it is always, and under all circumstances, wrong to take any human life or to participate in the taking of any human life; that killing in war inevitably and in all cases violates the right to life of those who are slain, not only civilians but combatants, too; or that, whatever one's reasons, it is always wrong to act in ways that cause innocent people to die, something that can hardly be avoided in war.

The pacifist anti-war principle obviously collides with utilitarianism, which conspicuously abstains from condemning war across the board. If waging a given war would have better results than not fighting it, then a state is morally justified in waging that war. Why, then, might utilitarians want people to follow the pacifist principle? They might desire this if they believed that the antecedent in the "if–then" conditional two sentences back is never satisfied—if they believed, that is, that waging war is never, in fact, the optimal course of action. If so, this could lead utilitarians to endorse the pacifist principle. After all, if something—torturing sentient animals for fun, say—always produces less expected welfare than do the obvious alternatives to it, then utilitarians have no hesitation in telling us never to do it.

Is it true that waging war is never the best option open to a state, that is, that some alternative course of action will always have greater expected well-being? Certainly, it seems reasonably to believe (1) that states have fought many wars that failed to satisfy UWP and were therefore wrongful and should not have been fought. Perhaps this is true of most wars that states have waged. Could one plausibly go further and maintain (2) that almost all past wars flunk the UWP test or, even, (3) that absolutely all of them do? Proposition (2) strikes me as doubtful, but perhaps it is true, whereas I am confident that proposition (3) is false and that on some occasions states have been justified, according to UWP, in resorting to arms. In Chapter 3, I argued that U.S. entry into World War II was one such occasion. A proponent of (3) would have to debunk this and other historical examples that critics are likely to bring forward. In any case, propositions (1), (2), and (3) each suggest, on inductive grounds, that it is likely—or possibly very, very likely—that any wars that states might consider fighting in the future will be immoral. If so, then this fact might lead utilitarians to a kind of sophisticated pacifism that holds that although wars can in principle be morally justified and, indeed, sometimes actually are morally justified, this is so rarely the case that in practice we will get the best results if we never even entertain the possibility of going to war but, rather, internalize in ourselves, teach our children, and proclaim to others the pacifist principle that war is categorically wrong and that no nation should ever again fight one.

Certainly, the truth of proposition (1), (2), or (3), if any of them be true, should guide us in determining whether a given state, in the particular circumstances it faces, would act rightly in waging war. Recourse to war is fraught with the gravest risks to human well-being, and the knowledge, if knowledge it be, that nations have seldom, if ever, been justified in waging it would be salutary. Yet, the sophisticated pacifist goes beyond this and proposes on consequentialist grounds that pacifism be our sole guiding principle regarding war. Utilitarianism, the reasoning goes, is so likely to rule out as immoral any future war, the waging of which might be contemplated, that we should dispense with UWP and not appeal to it at all. We should do this, our imagined pacifist argues, because if we apply UWP to the war decision before us, we might err and decide (incorrectly) to go to war, whereas we know ahead of time (based on induction from past history) that waging this or any other war would almost certainly be wrong. And even if this pacifist stance leads us on rare occasions to err morally by failing to fight wars that, according to UWP, we should have fought, we still do better overall and in the long run, the argument continues, by adhering to the pacifist principle and refusing ever to appeal to UWP or to regard war as a live option. In sum, over the course of time, we are more likely to act in accord with UWP, fighting only the wars it authorizes, if we never base decisions about war and peace on the direct application of UWP but rather cleave firmly and unconditionally to the pacifist principle.

A strategic or indirect consequentialist approach like this may be sound in some cases. For example, although it is logically possible that slavery could maximize net welfare, in the real world it never does. Consequently, the results are better if we teach people that slavery is categorically wrong and should always be resisted and if we internalize and act on that principle ourselves than they would be if we encouraged people (ourselves included) to weigh the consequences of each and every instance of slavery before deciding whether to oppose it (Hare 1979). Analogous arguments can also be advanced, quite persuasively I believe, with regard to state-sponsored torture or the punishment of innocent persons. But when it comes to questions of war, this sort of reasoning is unconvincing.

It might seem obvious that a world in which everyone believed that wars should never be fought would be a better world because no wars would be fought. But whether that is true depends on what the imagined world without war would be like. If such a world had more injustice, oppression, or aggression—in short, more misery and less well-being—than a world with the occasional war, then it might not be a better world. A world in which people did not care enough about combating these evils ever to incommode themselves or risk their own safety by taking up arms against them might be a worse world. Furthermore, for one to follow the sophisticated pacifist and repudiate all wars may or may not be the best way to bring it about that human beings fight no wars. It depends on whether most other people can be brought to categorically repudiate war. If most people have trouble accepting the pacifist principle or have trouble sticking to it when push comes to shove, then advocating it might not be the optimal strategy. Sticking with UWP might have better results.

Suppose, what seems entirely plausible, that in the foreseeable future the vast majority of people are not likely to be brought to believe that we should never, ever wage war regardless of the circumstances (although they will, of course, continue to believe, as they do now, that war is terrible and ought to be avoided if at all possible). Imagine, then, that a nation finds itself in a situation similar to those that in the past have led nations to resort to arms. There will certainly be people arguing for going to war on various grounds, moral and otherwise, sound and spurious. Suppose further that the war in question would be morally unjustified. How is that war to be effectively argued against without looking at the facts, that is, without bringing the utilitarian perspective to bear directly on the issue? Simply to reaffirm one's categorical opposition to war, as our sophisticated pacifist does, and to say "we don't have to look at the details to know that this war would be wrong," will be unconvincing when the war party is making arguments, giving reasons, and pointing to facts. By requiring us to focus on the human costs and benefits of any possible war, to examine likely outcomes, and to weigh alternative courses of action, utilitarianism invites decision-makers to be specific and empirical. If a prospective war is indeed wrong (as we are now supposing), then arguments that focus on consequences and alternatives are likely to be more effective in opposing it than is refusing to debate the particulars of the situation with the proponents of war. In modern times, most countries face the decision whether to wage war, or at least full-fledged war, only at infrequent intervals when the circumstances seem exceptional, when what is at stake appears very important, and when emotions run high. It is precisely here that the unequivocal rejection of all war that the sophisti-cated pacifist wants us to teach is likely to be ineffective and to be set aside as only a generalization open to exceptions—which, of course, is exactly what it is for our sophisticated pacifist.

Still, the sophisticated pacifist may worry that reliance on UWP invites us to adopt a way of thinking that is too congenial to war. With its calculative instrumentalism and an outcome-oriented the-end-justifies-the-means attitude, a utilitarian approach to war, it is alleged, makes it too easy to rationalize war. In this vein, Stuart Hampshire, the distinguished philosopher, once blamed the Vietnam War on the "coarse, quantitative, calculative Benthamism" of America's civilian leadership (Hampshire 1970: 4; cf. 1978: 4–5). But an acceptance of UWP does not require a hawk-like mentality—indeed, as I have been discussing, it has rather pacifistic implications—and the reasoning that Hampshire rightly spurns "as a counterfeit model of rationality" is also a parody of sensible, informed, and judicious consequentialist thinking. Indeed, as Hampshire himself makes clear, America's foreign policy and defense experts viewed the whole issue entirely in terms of American interests: They were realists, not utilitarians. Rather than lead-ing us to the crude, benighted reasoning that Hampshire criticizes, UWP requires us to focus on concrete harms and benefits to real people. It does not bias ethical analysis toward war.

Here there is an instructive analogy with capital punishment. Critics of the death penalty frequently fear that utilitarianism, because of its concern to promote net social good, is too inclined to condone execution (because of its presumed direct and indirect deterrent effects). Others, however, have the opposite con-cern. They worry that a utilitarian approach will lead us to refrain from executing people who (they believe) deserve it (because depriving them of their lives will bring no social benefit beyond what imprisonment would accomplish). Both sides reject a utilitarian or consequentialist approach to punishment because it might not favor their intuitive conviction that we should (or should not) execute murder-ers. Likewise, whereas critics such as Hampshire believe that a utilitarian approach conduces to war, other theorists seem implicitly to believe that it will incline us too much toward pacifism by making it too difficult to justify going to war. They, too, would like questions of war and peace to be decided without reference to, or at least with less concern for, the expected consequences of the alternatives before us. But trying to insulate one's antecedent, pro-war or anti-war convictions from the test of UWP seems morally and intellectually irresponsible.

Just war theory

There is no compelling reason, then, for utilitarians to champion the pacifist principle as a moral guideline. Nearly everyone agrees that war is terrible and should be avoided if at all possible, and UWP already places a high justificatory burden on any state contemplating war. But what about the principles associated with just war theory? Might they provide useful secondary principles?

Chapter 1 provided an overview of just war theory, the expositors of which sometimes note that it is really a family name designating a number of closely related theories because different thinkers have developed and elaborated the basic ideas in different ways. (In this respect, it is rather like utilitarianism.) Nevertheless, among contemporary just war theorists there is, despite some variation in presentation, broad agreement on the basic principles that should, according to the theory, govern the moral legitimacy of recourse to war—the principles of *jus ad bellum*.[3] Accordingly to mainstream just war theory, then, a war is just if and only if it meets the following six conditions: (1) legitimate authority, (2) just cause, (3) right intention, (4) last resort, (5) proportionality, and (6) reasonable prospect of success. (Some just war theorists add additional criteria, for example, that the war be publicly declared, that it be carried out in the right spirit, or that it aim at a just peace. Most of these moral concerns can be captured by the six criteria that I discuss and about which there is consensus.)

When just war theory states that a war is just if and only if it meets these conditions, it is using the word "just" in a broader sense than people sometimes do. By "just" the theory means "morally justified," "morally permissible," or "morally legitimate." If a war is morally justified because it meets the six criteria, then, according to just war theory, it is permissible for a state to fight it (although it must do so according to the rules of *jus in bello*, discussed in later chapters). Meeting these criteria, however, does not entail that a nation must wage war, that is, that it is morally required to fight, only that it is permitted to do so. Implicitly, just war theory allows states to decline to prosecute wars that it would be morally legitimate for them to undertake.

If the six *jus ad bellum* conditions are met, then a state is morally justified in waging war; if they are not, then the war is unjust and should not be fought. If one side is fighting a just war, then the other side is fighting an unjust war. However, the fact that one side is fighting an unjust war does not entail that the other side is fighting a just war. It is possible that neither belligerent is waging a just war, that is, that both sides are acting wrongly. For example, if two states were battling over territory belonging to another state, which neither of them had a right to possess, both sides would be in the wrong. (A few just war theorists deviate from the mainstream. They believe that if a nation's resort to arms meets most of the *ad bellum* criteria, it may be just on balance even if not completely just and, relatedly, that both belligerents may have some degree of justice on their side.)

Let us turn, then, to the six conditions that standard just war theory says must be satisfied for a war to be morally justified:

1   *Legitimate Authority:* Only a competent, duly constituted or legally designated political entity, with authority to speak and act on behalf of its population, can authorize war.

This condition rules out vendettas and private wars. As just war theory sees it, wars aim at some publicly identified goal sought by an organized political collectivity. They are, properly speaking, something that happens between states or state-like collectivities, not simply between groups of individuals. The legitimate authority criterion implies that a warlord locked in a power struggle with other military groups after a state has collapsed would not be fighting a just war. He may have an army, but he lacks legitimate authority.

The legitimate authority criterion also implies that wars fought by a duly consti-tuted state must have been authorized or brought about by the appropriate public figures in a legally or politically pre-designated way. In the United States, for example, if the president waged war contrary to the will of Congress, he would be acting unconstitutionally. The war would be unjust because he lacked legitimate authority for waging it. Is the legitimacy in question moral or legal? Just war theo-rists lean toward the latter position, so that even murderous tyrants such as Hitler or Stalin are seen as having legitimate authority to wage war (Frowe 2011: 59; Lee 2012: 82–3).

The early just war theorists assumed that only sovereign states can have legiti-mate authority to wage war. Contemporary just war theorists, however, are more flexible and are prepared to expand the concept of legitimate authority to include, in some circumstances, supra-state actors such as the United Nations and sub-state actors such as secessionist or national liberation movements. The latter might have legitimate authority to wage war if they can plausibly be said to represent a nation, a people, or another collective entity that has political goals or aspirations. Here the concept of legitimacy seems to have moral content. Thus, the Continental Congress can be seen as having had legitimate authority in 1776 for taking up arms against Great Britain in order to win independence for the thirteen colonies because it could reasonably claim to represent the American people. By contrast, many guerrilla organizations or terrorist groups (think of the Red Army Faction in West Germany or the Symbionese Liberation Army in the United States) patently lack any legitimate authority whatsoever for waging war.

2   *Just Cause:* Because war is so terrible, the reason, goal, or purpose for which a state undertakes it must be morally compelling; some very important value or principle must be at stake. It is not enough that a nation proclaims or even believes that it has right on its side. It must have a reason for going to war, the justice of which would be evident to any impartial person.

A war cannot be just unless the cause for which a state fights is just. However, this is only a necessary, not a sufficient condition: A war with a just cause will be unjust if the other principles of *jus ad bellum* are not met.

What, specifically, constitutes just cause? Traditional examples of just cause include protecting the innocent, repelling invasion, restoring rights wrongfully denied or rectifying other injustices, and punishing wrongdoing. Although just war theorists usually speak of "just cause" in the singular, some have argued that a state might have several just causes, each of which is insufficient to justify war by itself but which, when added together, collectively provide morally adequate grounds for war (Fotion 2007: 72–82; cf. McMahan and McKim 1993: 502–6.)

These days the only universally agreed example of just cause is defense against armed aggression (discussed in Chapter 5). This includes not only a nation's fighting back against armed attack—for example, Poland's resisting German invasion in 1939—but also other nations coming to the aid of the victim nation. It also encompasses recovering wrongfully seized territory (the 1982 Falkland Islands War) or dislodging an aggressor after it has successfully occupied another country (the 1991 Gulf War to liberate Kuwait from Iraq). More controversially, some just war theorists hold that in some circumstances the right of national defense licenses preemptive attack or even preventive war.

Today, many just war thinkers believe that humanitarian intervention can be a just cause for war—more precisely, that other nations are justified in waging war to stop a state from committing genocide or grossly abusing its own population (as happened in Rwanda in 1994). Although usually based on a modern appeal to human rights, this endorsement of humanitarian intervention is in line with the traditional, pre-modern view that just cause can encompass protecting the innocent and punishing wrongdoing.

3 *Right Intention:* That a just cause for war exists is insufficient; it must be the real reason the state goes to war, its underlying intention or motivating purpose. In other words, just cause cannot be a mere pretext. Right intention also includes the idea that when resorting to war, a nation must have as its ultimate aim the restoration of peace or *jus post bellum.*

The point of this criterion is that a state's goal in waging war must be limited to and circumscribed by its just cause. A state is justified in waging war and wreaking the destruction and damage that this inevitably involves only if it is acting so as to remedy the wrong that gives it a just cause and only to the extent that waging war is necessary for achieving that just cause.

Identifying the intentions of a collective actor such as the state is notoriously difficult, however. Various actors or bureaus in the state machinery can have different and possibly incompatible intentions and motives. Which of these matter? Often, indeed, the very idea of collective intent is only a useful fiction (as when judges try to surmise the intent of Congress in passing a particular law despite the fact that its members had different understandings of the legislation's meaning and likely results and a variety of reasons for voting for it). Furthermore, in deciding to wage war a state can have more than one intention—it can be trying to bring about more than one thing. The just intention criterion requires that, in waging war, a state must intend to correct the wrong that gives it just cause, not that it have no other reasons for fighting. The criterion can be interpreted, then, as insisting only that a state act in a way that is consistent with the hypothesis that it is a unified actor motivated by just cause and just cause alone. In other words, if what a state says and does is incompatible with one's believing that it is acting for moral reasons or on the basis of just cause, then it is waging an unjust war. The fact that it might have a just cause does not matter if it is clear from its actions that this is not its reason for fighting.

4   *Last Resort:* War is a great evil, and nations must always take sincere and meaningful steps to avoid it—for example, through negotiation, diplomacy, or boycott. Even if they have a just cause, states should not go to war unless all other options have been exhausted.

The rationale for this criterion is obvious. States should always, in the old catch-phrase, "give peace a chance." They should not go to war unless they absolutely have to, that is, until they have tried all reasonable alternatives to it. This criterion is especially important because in international disputes both sides typically believe that they are in the right. For example, suppose that after expanding its territorial waters, a nation sinks the fishing vessels of other nations that enter those waters. Those nations may believe that they have just cause for war, and the first nation may also believe that it has right on its side. Although nations have certainly gone to war over issues such as this in the past, clearly neither side is justified in doing so, even if the other *ad bellum* conditions are met, until diplomacy, negotiation, international law, and mediation have not only failed to resolve the outstanding issues, but also show little or no prospect of being able to do so.

Just war theorists concur, however, that "last resort" should not be taken too lit-erally because there will almost always be some further step short of war that a state could conceivably take—even after its territory has been invaded. Furthermore, some alternatives to war may have undesirable consequences, perhaps worse than war, and sometimes waiting longer might make prosecution of the war, when it inevitably comes, even more destructive than it would otherwise have been. So in applying the last resort criterion, one must make a comparative judgment about the expected benefits and costs of continuing to seek peaceful resolution to the dispute.

5   *Proportionality:* Even if a state's cause is just, for the war to be just the good which is at stake must outweigh the evils the war will cause to all sides, com-batants and non-combatants alike.

This criterion speaks to the possibility that even if a state has good moral grounds for going to war, it might be wrong to do so because the war would cause harm that is excessive or out of proportion to the injustice that the state seeks to rectify or the good it hopes to achieve. For example, suppose (as seems historically plausible) that although the NATO states had just cause for resisting the USSR's invasion of Hungary in 1956, doing so would have precipitated a worldwide nuclear war. If so, then those states were right not to have gone to war with the Soviet Union even if they had just cause for doing so.

In determining whether it would be right to fight, a nation must weigh and compare the costs and benefits of doing so. These include not only such things as loss of life, destruction of infrastructure, the reclaiming of lost territory, or freedom of movement at sea, but also less tangible goods and evils. Proportionality requires that, given the justice of the cause, the benefits of war are sufficiently weighty to justify its costs. (A minority of just war theorists holds that proportionality requires only that the war not produce a lot more harm than good [e.g., Lackey 1989: 40–1].) Most just war theorists take the straightforward view that one counts all the goods and evils that can be expected to result from a given war and weighs them equally (e.g., Johnson 1999: 27–8; Orend 2006: 59). However, some recent just war theorists put less weight on the deaths of combatants than they do on those of non-combatants (Bazargan 2014: 7), exclude from the proportionality calculation goods that are not contained in the just cause but are only side-effects of pursuing it (Hurka 2005: 40, 43, 45–6; 2007: 199), or insist that not all harms are to be included among the evils weighed by the proportionality principle (Lee 2012: 85–93).

6   *Reasonable Prospect of Success:* A state should not wage war, even if its cause is just and the other criteria are met, unless it has a reasonable chance of success.

Given the horror of war, it cannot be right to fight when there is little or no likelihood of success. For example, a small state might have just cause for resisting a large and extremely powerful nation from taking over an island that it owns. According to this criterion, however, the small state is not justified in going to war if the death, destruction, and suffering that would result from doing so would be futile or pointless. To some patriots, this may sound cowardly, but the leaders of a nation have a responsibility not to waste its resources or the lives of their fellow citizens.

Success, however, must be defined relative to a state's war aims, and these may be more modest than the goal of total victory or the other side's unconditional surrender. For example, a country might fight back against a much more powerful adversary, which has the wherewithal ultimately to defeat it, in order to try to force a negotiated settlement or to give the country's allies time to marshal their forces. Judged against these war aims, it may have a reasonable prospect of success. More controversial is whether the reasonable prospect of success criterion is met if the small nation's war aim is only to make the aggressor pay a price for its aggression or to maintain its national pride.

The principles of *jus ad bellum* as intermediate principles

In refining or expanding upon these principles and in illuminating them with both historical and imaginary examples, contemporary just war theorists have had valuable and insightful things to say about war, although they differ somewhat among themselves in how they interpret and develop their shared principles and in what they take their implications to be for various cases. Obviously, the Utilitarian War Principle and the principles of *jus ad bellum* are not identical in meaning, nor are they logically equivalent. Depending upon exactly how one interprets the *ad bellum* principles, they might conceivably forbid some wars licensed by UWP or permit some wars that UWP would condemn. Nevertheless, it is difficult to envision real-world scenarios in which a war condemned by one would be approved by the other. For this reason, utilitarians and other friends of UWP should take an approbatory attitude toward the received principles of *jus ad bellum*, accepting them as providing a helpful way to analyze questions of war.

The principles of last resort and reasonable prospect of success, despite some inescapable vagueness, draw attention to factors that are patently relevant from a utilitarian perspective. Given the destructiveness of war, waging it is unlikely to satisfy UWP if there are viable alternatives to it or if there is no realistic chance of succeeding. Utilitarians will also find the proportionality criterion congenial. Although broadly consequentialist in character, it is not, however, identical to UWP. The proportionality criterion insists that the goods resulting from a given war outweigh its evils or that the latter not be excessive or out of proportion to the former, but not that waging war be the optimal course of action. On the face of it, the criterion calls for no comparative analysis. It requires that the war be proportional but not that its expected net benefit be greater than the expected net benefit of alternative courses of action. Nevertheless, from a utilitarian point of view, this is acceptable. The point of embracing the criterion is not to replicate UWP but to provide a rule or test that may be somewhat easier to use. Utilitarians will naturally favor interpreting the principle so that it counts all expected goods and evils rather than picking and choosing among them based on one's intuitions about which harms and benefits should be considered, as some contemporary theorists are inclined to do. But only in some cases will this matter.

Legitimate authority, right intention, and just cause are non-consequentialist principles, but utilitarians have reason to endorse them, too. The legitimate authority requirement, even when interpreted flexibly enough to license some civil wars and national liberation struggles, helps to restrict the incidence of war. Although one can imagine hypothetical situations in which one rightly wages war without the moral, political, or legal authority to do so, in the real world sticking to the principle will produce better outcomes on balance. On the face of it, right intention, too, is a non-utilitarian consideration. Utilitarians believe that whether an action is right or wrong is distinct from whether the actor's motives or intentions are good or bad. Sometimes people do the right thing for a selfish or dishonorable reason, and sometimes people act wrongly despite having a good aim or purpose. Nevertheless, someone who is ill motivated or has unsavory intentions is likely to produce bad consequences, and it is improbable that a state that is not motivated by just cause—that is not trying to do the right thing—will actually be fighting a war it should be fighting.

The just cause criterion requires that a state have a morally compelling reason for waging war. Utilitarians can certainly embrace that principle. Just cause can, however, also be interpreted more narrowly to require that some principle of justice or right underlies the case for war or at least that the case for war is compatible with the principles of justice. But utilitarians can accept and, indeed, insist on this, too. Following Mill, they believe that the principles of justice identify "certain social utilities which are vastly more important, and therefore more absolute and imperative, than any others are as a class" (Mill 1969c: 259). Thus, as utilitarians see it, it is almost inconceivable that going to war in violation of those rules could possibly be a welfare-maximizing course of action—though there could well be cases where the ordinary precepts of justice come into conflict.

The just cause principle, as generally understood, permits states to wage war only to defend some important right or to remedy or forestall some serious wrong, for example, by warding off armed attack. Among other things, it rules out fighting wars to intimidate rival states, to acquire natural resources, to expand a state's territory beyond its settled borders, to further a particular religion, or to impose some favored ideology on another people. These are restrictions that it makes perfect sense for utilitarians to advocate and adhere to, given the extreme improbability that wars fought on such unjust grounds would satisfy UWP. In adhering to the just cause principle, then, we run little danger of failing to fight wars that UWP says we should fight, and by restricting ahead of time, in this way, those situations in which we may permissibly entertain the possibility of waging war, we reduce the risk of going to war based on an erroneous belief that doing so maximizes expected well-being.

My suggestion, then, is that utilitarians and other advocates of UWP adopt and encourage others to adopt the principles of *jus ad bellum* as intermediate or secondary principles. Although ultimately subordinate to UWP, they would be seen as providing the workaday framework in which to examine the morality of resorting to war. Not only do the *jus ad bellum* principles draw our attention to considerations that are relevant and important from a utilitarian perspective, but also they are principles that are widely known, utilized, and taught (for instance, at the U.S. military academies) and that many people find intuitively plausible. They provide a focused structure for discussing the morality of war, use of which may often be easier, less contentious, and more reliable than direct and immediate appeal to UWP.

I am not arguing, however, that UWP be abandoned in favor of the principles of *jus ad bellum*. First, those principles are not self-interpreting, and their application to specific cases requires some care. Utilitarianism provides a vantage point from which this can be done. Second, at present the principles lack theoretical foundation. Although originally grounded in a theological or natural-law framework, the principles of *jus ad bellum* are, it seems, endorsed by just war theorists today out of respect for tradition or on the basis of moral intuition, commonsense morality, or a commitment to human rights. None of these rationales is entirely satisfactory. Utilitarianism, however, can potentially tie those principles together and provide them with needed theoretical underpinning. The rules of *jus ad bellum* are important and should be taken seriously because and only because adherence to them promotes well-being by increasing the likelihood that wars are fought when and only when UWP says they should be fought.

Friends of UWP would wish to see it entirely usurped by the *ad bellum* rules only if they believed that doing so would yield better results in the long run, as judged by UWP, than would allowing UWP to retain ultimate normative authority. This would be the case only if we imagine both (a) that acknowledging the secondary normative status of the *ad bellum* principles would lead nations to rationalize wars that UWP, properly applied, does not authorize or to rationalize not fighting wars that UWP, properly applied, says should be fought, and (b) that such erroneous rationalizations would not occur or would occur less often if the issue had been decided purely on *jus ad bellum* grounds without any reference to UWP. This seems far-fetched.

Viewing the *ad bellum* principles as intermediate or secondary principles ultimately subservient to UWP allows one to tolerate counterinstances or exceptions to them as well as a degree of indeterminateness in their formulation that would be unacceptable if one viewed them, as just war theory is committed to doing, as necessary and sufficient conditions for waging justified war. A utilitarian approach thus sidesteps fine-tooth, interpretative questions that just war theorists attempt to answer on the basis of their moral intuitions. It also relieves the temptation, to which some just war theorists succumb, to remove possible redundancies by reducing the six principles to a smaller set. This is because from a utilitarian perspective the principles serve only a practical purpose. UWP already provides the theoretically correct answer to the question of when a state is morally permitted to wage war. To best aid decision-makers to act in ways that are consistent with UWP, we want to provide them with neither too many nor too few guidelines. Utilitarians will seek, of course, to interpret and refine the *ad bellum* principles so that their application yields results that are as consistent as possible with UWP, but there are limits to this because principles that are too detailed or too complex cease to be of much practical help. And UWP is always there for decision-makers to fall back on in situations where the *ad bellum* principles fail to give them clear direction or where the circumstances are exceptional or anomalous.

If utilitarians see merit in employing the just war principles as secondary principles, then how exactly should they understand these rules? One possibility is to consider them as basically pragmatic guidelines, generalizations, or "rules of thumb" that assist in the application of the utilitarian criterion but that lack any normative weight in their own right (Smart 1973: 42). Analyzing a prospective war with their aid draws attention to various aspects of the issue that need to be considered, making it less likely that in deciding either to wage war or to refrain from it we will contravene UWP. In practice, following these guidelines will usually suffice to give us the correct moral answer and to do so in a way that may run less risk of error than would attempting to utilize UWP directly and without the aid of any practical prescripts. Although rules of thumb assist our decision-making, they are rightly put aside without compunction or regret when one believes that one is in circumstances to which they do not apply or in which reliance on them would lead one astray. This is not to say the rules are not to be taken seriously. In the case of war, they provide a valuable framework for public discussion and analysis, and one must have good reasons for setting them aside in any particular case.

A second possibility, however, is to treat these secondary rules as genuinely moral in character, as having normative force in their own right. When a person has internalized a rule as part of his or her moral code, the person does not look at the rule instrumentally; it is not something the person can pick up or put down as the occasion demands. Rather, the person will tend to feel guilty when his or her conduct fails to live up to the rule and to disapprove of those who act contrary to the rule. Utilitarians have good reasons for wanting people to internalize in this way certain important rules. As mentioned in Chapter 2, this way of thinking about rules does not commit one to a rule-utilitarian criterion of right. While retaining their familiar, act-oriented criterion of right, sophisticated utilitarians can agree that in some situations having people strongly inclined to act in certain rule-designated ways, to reproach themselves for failing to do so, and to criticize others for not living up to the rules can have enormous social utility.

As I shall discuss in later chapters, I believe that combatants should view the rules of *jus in bello* in just this way. They should, for instance, not even entertain the idea of directly and intentionally killing civilians even if, hypothetically, there were reason for thinking this to be the welfare-maximizing course of action. Civilian immunity is not a mere rule of thumb. Rather, a commitment to it should be part of the intuitive moral code of all combatants. I see no advantage, however, to encouraging either policy-makers or observers who are weighing the rightness or wrongness of resorting to arms to embrace the *jus ad bellum* criteria as fully fledged moral rules rather than simply as aids to applying UWP. Encouraging people to internalize a firm moral commitment to certain rules and to feel guilty about failing to adhere to them makes the most sense from a utilitarian point of view when the rules are relatively unequivocal, when deviating from them almost always has poor results, when following them greatly simplifies everyday decision-making, and when people's adhering to them improves social coordination and helps to establish a stable system of rights and expectations. These considerations do not apply, at least not with much force, to a state's decision whether to wage war. That decision is not a routine one where we want to facilitate rapid decision-making, nor are we dealing with a situation in which rules are necessary to coordinate the expectations and conduct of large groups of people. The *ad bellum* criteria are important, but there is no clear welfare benefit to regarding them as genuine moral principles, which one should reproach oneself and others for violating, rather than as useful guidelines or pragmatic rules of thumb, especially given their somewhat indeterminate character and the possibility of exceptions to them.

With the principle of just cause, however, things may be different. That wars should not be waged in the absence of just cause, that is, without a moral justification, will be more than a mere rule of thumb for utilitarians. Indeed, it would make little sense for a utilitarian or indeed for any moral person to view the requirement that, for a war to be right, there must be a compelling moral reason for it as merely a practical guideline, which might conceivably be set aside. That simple requirement, however, has little substantive normative content. But suppose we understand the just cause criterion to mean, more specifically, that the reason for war must involve or at least not contradict the principles of justice. Will utilitarians view that more specific criterion as a genuine moral principle or only as a rule of thumb? Because of the importance they place on justice (understood as the most important of the moral rules that people should adhere to), that the case for war must be consonant with those rules will be, for utilitarians, more than a mere pragmatic generalization. I say more about this in the next section.

Three supposed counterexamples

For the reasons I have given, utilitarians and other adherents of UWP should view the rules of *jus ad bellum* as secondary criteria or intermediate principles—more specifically, as practical guidelines for determining whether a state would act rightly or wrongly in resorting to arms. This blunts the objection that UWP is unworkable or too difficult to apply in practice. Even though the *ad bellum* rules have no independent deontic status, it is beneficial to encourage people to analyze the case for going to war in terms of them for at least two reasons. First, being more specific than UWP itself, they may be easier for decision-makers and others to understand and apply, and, second, being already fairly well known and rather commonsensical, appealing to them may resonate more widely than would UWP and yet lead to no judgments or decisions that would conflict with UWP.

Still, introducing secondary principles as convenient guides to decision-making will not satisfy those who believe that UWP is unsatisfactory because it has implications that sometimes diverge from our moral intuitions. Chapter 3 rebutted the contention that World War II provides such a case, and it seems improbable that critics can find any current or historical war where (a) there is a consensus among informed people about its rightness or wrongness, and (b) UWP implies a judgment that contradicts this consensus and, as a result, is so morally problematic that it calls UWP into question. Perhaps, though, there are telling hypothetical examples where UWP has implications that would strike one as counterintuitive or seriously problematic. Let us examine three supposed counterexamples. Doing so will, I believe, sustain UWP and clarify some points about the utilitarian approach to war.

The oil reserves

One putative counterexample revisits an issue that I have already touched on. It imagines that it would maximize net expected benefit for a powerful state, the economy of which depends on petroleum, to seize the underutilized crude oil reserves of a small nation. Although UWP would seem to authorize this, it would be unjust. Hence, argues the critic, UWP should be rejected.[4] This scenario is obviously fanciful. We must imagine that the small nation flat-out refuses to sell its oil at any price, that the more powerful state has no other way of obtaining it, that it cannot shake off its dependency on petroleum, and that no one foresaw this situation developing in time to avoid it.

But however far-fetched, let us grant this scenario for argument's sake. As stated earlier, like other moral persons, utilitarians will insist that wars should be fought only for just cause. This point does not settle the issue, though. Interpreted in a broad sense, the just cause principle requires that there be strong moral grounds for going to war, and here the imagined case for war is indeed a moral one. Ex hypothesi, it is being fought to maximize expected well-being, taking into account the interests of all. In a narrower sense, however, the war lacks just cause because, by violating the rights of the small nation, it runs contrary to the principles of justice.

At a general matter, utilitarians want people to internalize a firm commitment to justice. Following Mill, they emphasize the importance of people embracing and upholding certain basic rights and principles of justice for their own sake. Mill thought that the dictates of justice coincide with utility and, further, that even non-utilitarians acknowledge this (Mill 1969c: 241). The reason the two coincide is that the principles of justice single out "certain classes of moral rules, which concern the essentials of human well-being more nearly, and are therefore of more absolute obligation, than any other rules for the guidance of life" (1969c: 255). Thus, there are strong consequentialist grounds for encouraging people to inter-nalize a firm, non-instrumental commitment to justice and to feel guilt or remorse about behaving unjustly.

Likewise, when turning to war, there is a solid utilitarian case for instilling in people a commitment not just to the principle that there must be a sound moral reason for any war but also to the more specific principle that states must not wage war in violation of the principles of justice and right. In some situations, of course, those principles may conflict, with each antagonist appealing to a different one. When there are plausible but conflicting claims of justice, Mill thought, one has no recourse but to appeal to the more fundamental standard of utilitarianism. Still, keeping the scenario as it is—so that the larger nation has no colorable claim of right or justice on its side—then its seizing the oil fields would manifestly lack just cause in the narrow sense because it violates the territorial integrity and political sovereignty of the other state, thus transgressing its fundamental rights and violat-ing an established and important norm of international law. Yet these are rights that it makes sense for utilitarians to uphold, nay, to insist upon and to treat as of the greatest normative weight because doing so does so much to protect human well-being in the long run. Permitting states to ignore the basic, internationally accepted rights of other states whenever they believe that doing so would maxi-mize utility would be a disastrous policy.

The hypothesized circumstances could, of course, be so exceptional that even taking into account the general utility of upholding the internationally accepted rights of states, UWP would authorize seizing the oil reserves. Chapter 5 says more about the rights of states and about the possibility of justified infringements of them, but utilitarians and others who have internalized a firm commitment to respecting the basic rights of states, as utilitarianism says they should, will be reluctant to consider, let alone to countenance, violating the territorial integrity and political sovereignty of the smaller state. Because they do not, normally, even entertain the possibility of overriding basic rights in order to try to reap some gain in utility, they may well refrain from violating them even when UWP would (hypothetically) require this. From a utilitarian perspective, however, this is untroubling; utilitarians care about how people will act in the real world, not in purely suppositious circumstances, and in the real world we get better results overall and in the long run if people are resolute in upholding rights despite the possibility that this will lead them to act wrongly in some make-believe cases. Of course, if the imagined circumstances are extreme or desperate enough—suppose that the smaller state's sudden refusal to sell its oil will cause the larger state's economy to collapse and that this is its very reason for not selling—then even non-consequentialists may permit the smaller state's rights to be infringed or overridden.

Hopeless resistance

A second alleged counterexample imagines that a powerful and aggressive state attacks a smaller and weaker one. If resistance would be futile, then utilitarianism implies, it seems, that the smaller state would be wrong to resist.[5] This strikes some people as counterintuitive. How can it be wrong, they will ask, for a state to fight back? The first thing to point out is that the state would be doing so at the cost of the lives and well-being of some of its citizens, and, at the very least, these are to be sacrificed only for a very good purpose. On the other hand, however, some good might come from the small nation's resisting. Even apparently hopeless resistance may accomplish something, perhaps forcing the aggressor state to modify its original plans or dissuading it from undertaking similar campaigns in the future.

This is a point that both Bentham and John Stuart Mill made. Discussing a case where the aggression is a prelude to total destruction but successful resistance seems impossible, Bentham writes that nevertheless "prudence and reason may join with passion in prescribing war" because resistance may, "by gaining time, give room for some unexpected incident to arise" and may also "weaken the mass of inducements which prompt him [the aggressor] to similar enterprises" (1843a: 545). Similarly, in discussing why it is "right that a people inferior in strength should fight to the death against the attempt of a foreign despot to reduce it to slavery," Mill argues that such "iniquitous attempts"

> are very much discouraged by the prospects of meeting with a desperate though unsuccessful resistance. The weak may not be able finally to withstand the strong if these persist in their tyranny, but they can make the tyranny cost the tyrant something, and that is better than letting him indulge it gratis.
>
> (1972a: 854)

Elsewhere he adds:

> There would be a great deal more tyrannical aggression by the strong against the weak, if those who know they were not strong enough to succeed in the struggle, gave way at once ... Spirit and obstinacy themselves count for much, and how much can never be known till they are tried. The Greeks would never have resisted Xerxes or the Dutch, Phillip II if they had merely calculated numbers.
>
> (1972a: 947)

With the greatest values at stake and with disaster looming, desperate resistance may be better than doing nothing. It might accomplish something and, if not, it may still help to deter such aggression in the future. Even with a low probability of success, resistance may be the course of action with the greatest expected well-being. In many cases, however, yielding to superior forces does not spell catastrophe, and Bentham praises the Dutch for having prudently conceded to the British in 1652 (1843a: 545).

Even when the stakes are extremely high, sober consequentialist calculation may well dictate capitulation. Utilitarians and other humane people disapprove of pointless loss. Only in the rarest of circumstances will they urge the suicidal taking up of arms or laud fighting to the last man. Nevertheless, in many cases utilitarians will refrain from rebuking the victim nation for trying desperately to stave off defeat. One reason for this is that we tend to esteem those who sacrifice themselves in causes that seem hopeless because the virtues they display are such valuable ones to inculcate in people (cf. Ayer 1985: 275–6). But this admiration presupposes that the cause they sacrificed themselves for was a good one and that they freely chose to do so. Thus, we can join Bentham in extolling the Spartans at Thermopylae, but feel quite otherwise about the Japanese fighting on to total annihilation at Iwo Jima.

Suppose that the critic of UWP pushes the example further, postulating that a more powerful state is bent on exterminating the people of a weaker nation, that resistance is absolutely futile, and that it is known that absolutely no good will come from it, even taking into account the points made by Bentham and Mill. In these circumstances, the critic will ask, should not those in the smaller nation still try to kill as many of the aggressors as possible before being slaughtered themselves, contrary to what utilitarianism seems to imply? For utilitarians, to be sure, pointless killing is suboptimal. Again, however, they would hardly censure the uniformed combatants of the smaller nation for fighting on. To rebuke them for not submitting would be incompatible with promoting the virtues, including resolve, courage, and steadfastness, that we want soldiers fighting for a justified cause to have, even if in far-fetched circumstances, like those imagined here, those virtues lead them to act in a way that fails to maximize utility. When it comes to the smaller state's civilians, utilitarianism will see little point in criticizing ordinary citizens for trying desperately but hopelessly to ward off their fate. What good would come from doing so? On the other hand, however, there can be dignity in submitting to an unjust but inescapable fate peacefully and with your head held high—going to your execution calmly, for instance, rather than struggling with your guards in a desperate attempt to inflict some final injury on them.

Waging war versus fighting malaria

A third supposed counterexample takes issue with a basic implication of UWP, namely, that it is wrong for a state to fight if there is a better course of action open to it. Suppose that it has greater expected well-being for a state to wage a particular war than to refrain from doing so and to carry on as usual. Thus, it is right for the state to fight. But now suppose that there is a third thing it could do instead, for instance, to launch an all-out drive to eradicate malaria in the third world, which would produce even more well-being than would waging war. If so, then UWP now seems to imply that the state should not wage war because its combatting malaria would do more good.[6] This strikes some people as counterintuitive: If waging war is the right course of action when compared simply to not fighting, then how can that judgment change because of something that bears no intrinsic connection to the war or the issues it is about?

To begin with, the imagined scenario requires many improbable assumptions: that the state in question cannot both fight the war and mobilize against malaria; that it never previously realized the good that would come from its rallying to eradicate this disease; and that the welfare cost of deferring the malaria campaign until after the end of the war would be too high. But granting these implausible premises, suppose that the war in question involves the state's right to defend itself or a victim nation against armed attack or that treaty obligations or considerations of justice require it to take up arms. If so, then utilitarians might plausibly believe that in these circumstances waging war takes priority over aiding other nations to overcome malaria—that is, that it is better for states to do what justice requires or for them to be allowed to exercise their most basic rights than it is for them to aid less advantaged neighbors or act in other ways that are normally considered supererogatory. This is because of the long-term welfare benefits that flow from establishing and supporting a stable system of rights and rules governing the conduct of states, a point that I discuss further in Chapter 5.

Suppose, though, that the imagined case does not involve these factors. If so, then UWP would imply that the state in question is wrong to wage war because campaigning against malaria instead would have greater expected well-being. Although perhaps a surprising conclusion, it is not obviously counterintuitive. Ordinary Americans sometimes say, "We shouldn't be fighting over there when there is so much to be done at home." Although the malaria example concerns helping other nations rather than promoting domestic well-being, the quoted remark suggests that everyday morality is untroubled by the idea that waging a given war might be wrong because acting in other ways would accomplish more good.

It is important to note, furthermore, that UWP does not, despite what the counterexample seems to suggest, entail that the state in question should launch a massive campaign against malaria. The principle's remit is limited. In the imagined scenario, it affirms only that the state would be wrong to wage war because doing so would not be the optimal course of action. It does not, however, require the state to pursue the course that would be optimal, nor does it affirm that it or any other state acts wrongly if it fails to maximize well-being. This is pertinent because the force of the hypothesized counterexample rests partly, I think, on the insinuation that UWP requires states always to be acting for the general good and, more specifically, that it implies that wealthy states have a duty to put aside everything else in order to eradicate serious diseases in the third world. These are both controversial propositions. About them, however, UWP has nothing to say. As I have discussed, UWP does not entail that utilitarianism is the correct general theory of morality. If utilitarianism underwrites these two propositions and if one finds them objectionable, that would not impugn UWP. In fact, it is doubtful that utilitarianism does affirm these two propositions, or at least that was the opinion of Mill, Sidgwick, and the theory's other early defenders. They believed, rather, that it is for the best that the primary concern of each state should be the well-being of its own citizens. In any case, the pertinent point is that UWP entails nothing about the general duties of states. It specifies only when it is right or wrong for them to wage war.

To be sure, UWP implies that when deciding whether to wage war, states must consider more than their own interests, a proposition with which all non-realists concur. UWP goes further than this, of course, by forbidding states from going to war if this is not the best course of action open to them. However, when resorting to arms, few if any states concede that they are doing anything other than this. UWP treats this pretense seriously, insisting that states should wage war if and only if this really is for the best, taking everyone's interests into account.

Notes

1 Chapter 3 also identified the Consequentialist War Principle (CWP), a broader normative thesis available to non-utilitarian consequentialists.
2 This point having been made, however, it is a stylistically awkward and a bit artificial always to frame the discussion in terms of UWP and its adherents rather than speaking of utilitarianism and utilitarians, and I shall not always bother to do so.
3 For different presentations of the *ad bellum* principles of just war theory, see Bellamy (2006), Besser-Jones (2005), Biggar (2007), Christopher (2004), Coates (1997), Coleman (2013), Cook (2004), Coppieters and Fotion (2002), Dower (2009), Elshtain (2003), Fabre (2012), Fisher (2011), Fotion (2007), Frowe (2011), Frowe and Lang (2014), Guthrie and Quinlan (2007), Hartle (2004), Johnson (2005), Lackey (1989), Lee (2012), Moseley (2009), Nathanson (2013), Orend (2005), Regan (2013), Rhodes (2009), Steinhoff (2007), Whetham (2011), Whitman (2006–7), and Zupan (2004).
4 I thank Chris Eberle for pointing out this objection.
5 I thank Uwe Steinhoff for raising this point. Note that the just war criterion of reasonable prospect of success seems to have the same implication.
6 Jeff McMahan raised this objection in a discussion of the utilitarian approach to war at the Stockdale Center for Ethical Leadership's April 2010 McCain Conference on "The Ethics of War Since 9/11," held at the U.S. Naval Academy, Annapolis, Maryland.

5

NATIONAL DEFENSE AND ITS LIMITS

Chapters 3 and 4 explored the morality of resorting to arms, specifically, the question of when, if ever, it is morally permissible for a state to wage war. This chapter continues that discussion. As we have seen, utilitarianism provides a clear criterion, the Utilitarian War Principle (UWP), for answering that central question: It is morally right for a state to wage war if and only if no other course of action has greater expected well-being. As I have argued, one can reasonably embrace this normative principle while reserving judgment on, or even spurning altogether, utilitarianism as a general account of right and wrong.

Although UWP seems simple, applying it can be difficult because the world is complicated and the future difficult to predict. To some extent we can mitigate this problem by adopting as a practical guide the familiar rules of just war theory. According to these, waging war is wrong if it is not a last resort, if it is undertaken without just cause, legitimate authority, the right intention, or a reasonable prospect of success, or if it will result in evil disproportional to the good being sought. Applying these familiar and more specific principles to a given conflict is often useful because they can be easier to wield than UWP itself and because any war that fails to meet them is unlikely to satisfy UWP.

Most people are apt to find these guidelines sensible, even if their application to specific situations is not always cut and dry. Perhaps the most important of them is just cause, the elementary requirement that states must have a strong and compelling moral reason for waging war. These days, national defense is the one and only universally recognized just cause—the only moral and legal justification for going to war that is accepted by virtually all states and all peoples. Almost everyone, pacifists aside,[1] agrees that states have a right to defend themselves, that is, to use necessary and proportionate force to repel armed attack on their political independence or territorial integrity. This right entails that in defending themselves states are acting as they are entitled to act, that they are at least prima facie justified in doing so, and that they do not have to demonstrate that no alternative course of action open to them would bring about more well-being. To most people, philosophers and non-philosophers alike, this seems obvious.

But what is the meaning of this right, what are its limits, and how does it fit into the larger utilitarian perspective on war? After explaining why utilitarianism underwrites a right of national defense and what exactly this entails, I defend the utilitarian account against its critics and show how it applies to current controversies over preventive war and armed humanitarian intervention, all the while probing the general problem of adherence to rules in exceptional circumstances. Now, establishing that utilitarianism endorses a right of national defense might seem a superfluous and unnecessary undertaking: another example of utilitarians trying to show that with some deft maneuvering their theory can, after all, accommodate our existing intuitions or considered moral judgments—in this case, the conviction that states have a right to defend themselves. But this impression is incorrect, for three reasons.

First, although utilitarianism, as I shall argue, does in fact uphold the right of national defense, its objective in doing so is not to match people's existing intuitions. Rather, it endorses that right because in a world comprised of more or less sovereign states, doing so promotes peace and security and, thus, human well-being. However, if I am wrong about this or if in the future the political universe were different enough from what it is now, then the right of national defense would lose its consequentialist underpinning and utilitarians would cease to endorse it.

Second, the consensus that states have a right to defend themselves conceals the fact that the exact content and contours of this right are contested matters. Against what sort of threats may a state defend itself? Does the right of national defense permit preventive war? Is it ever permissible to wage wars that are not an exercise of national defense as is the case, in particular, with armed humanitarian intervention? How, if at all, does the right apply to non-state entities, that is, to civil wars, wars of national liberation, or other irregular conflicts? Utilitarianism provides a coherent way of analyzing and dealing with these issues.

Third, despite the widespread belief that nations have a right to defend themselves, upon reflection it is not obvious what grounds this right (Fabre and Lazar 2014). The most common way of justifying it is in terms of the individual right of self-defense, with the right of national defense being seen either as analogous to that right or as representing its collective exercise (Pojman, 2000: 191; Vaughn 2010: 423; Walzer 2006b: 58). However intuitive that approach might seem, it has been subject to thorough and penetrating critique (Lazar 2014; Rodin 2002). This makes stating the utilitarian or consequentialist case for a right of national defense important, especially because it does not rely on extrapolation from our uncertain and variable intuitions about individual self-defense.

The right of national defense

As Chapter 2 explained, utilitarians insist on the importance of society's recognizing and protecting certain rights, and they seek to determine the exact set of rights, the institutionalization of which will produce the most desirable results. For Mill and subsequent utilitarians, one has a right to x because of the utility of society's protecting claims of that sort. Although they view rights in this instrumentalist way, utilitarians nevertheless desire to internalize in themselves and to inculcate and reinforce in others a firm, non-instrumental commitment to the most important of these rights and corresponding norms. Only in this way, they believe, can we obtain the increased social well-being that an entrenched system of rights makes possible.

Although Bentham and the utilitarian jurisprudent John Austin favored a legal positivism that made them skeptical of the idea of international law, one can easily expand on the reasoning of the previous paragraph and maintain that, on utilitarian grounds, we should endeavor to get states to adhere to certain rules of conduct toward one another and, more specifically, to acknowledge that each has legal and moral rights that should be respected. As we saw in Chapter 3, the great utilitarian thinker Henry Sidgwick advocated exactly this. In his view, utilitarians seek those rules of international conduct and concomitant rights that, given the world as it is and nations and people as they are, will bring about the most good, taking into account, among other things, the likelihood of nations being brought to accept and comply with those rules. Once in effect, those rules morally restrain a state's pursuit of national interest.

In Sidgwick's time and our own, one of the most widely accepted rules of international affairs is the right of national self-defense, which is deeply embedded in the international legal order. Supporting international law entails upholding that right. If supporting international law is morally important, as no doubt it is whatever flaws it may have, then this fact provides grounds for upholding the right of a state to defend itself simply because international law affirms that right. However, this argument only goes so far. For although it is unquestionably true that "states have a moral as well as a legal right" to defend themselves "as a matter of international law" (Mapel 2007: 2, 8–10)—assuming, of course, that their use of force is necessary and proportionate (Waters and Green 2010: 297)—this fact does not fully vindicate that right because one can always ask whether international law should uphold it in the first place and, if so, why, or whether it would be better if it acknowledged no such right. From a utilitarian perspective, however, the answer to that question is straightforward.

Article 1(1) of the United Nations Charter declares that its purpose is "to maintain international peace and security" and "to take effective collective measures for the prevention and removal of threats to the peace, and for the suppression of acts of aggression or other breaches of the peace." Pursuant to these objectives, the Charter forbids member states from using or threatening to use force "against the territorial integrity or political independence of any state" unless authorized to do so by the Security Council (Article 2[4]). However, "if an armed attack occurs" against a member state ("*agression armée*" in the equally authoritative French text), Article 51 permits "individual or collective self-defense," which it refers to as "an inherent right" ("*droit naturel*"). Acknowledging this right tallies with commonsense moral thinking: States are entitled to resist aggression; they do not have to prove that their doing so satisfies something like UWP. The right of national defense is what philosophers call a "claim right" as opposed to a "liberty right" or "privilege"; that is, it is not merely that a state has no duty not to defend itself if attacked but also that others are obligated to allow or enable the state to do so.

Although today it may seem obvious that states should not use force against other states except in self-defense, the Charter broke sharply with earlier political morality. Through the end of the nineteenth century, the conventional view had been that each state has a customary right, inherent in sovereignty, to wage war whenever it pleased (Ruys 2010: 11), and even those who took a more moralistic perspective held that if any important right of a state had been violated and reparation was subsequently refused, then it could seek redress by force, including, if necessary, by war (e.g., Sidgwick 1908: 263). In dramatically restricting the right of states to resort to force, the UN Charter obviously seeks to diminish as much as possible the role of war and violence in international affairs. This effort has not been as effective as those who drafted and ratified the Charter hoped that it would be, but few would deny that it represents a step in the right direction and that institutionalizing the new norm has made the world a somewhat safer and more secure place.

To be more precise, the UN Charter can be seen as affirming two logically distinct, but intertwined, norms: (1) Non-defensive wars are illegal (except for military action authorized by the Security Council). (2) Defensive wars, that is, wars in response to armed attack, are permissible (assuming those attacks are illegitimate, that is, neither authorized by the United Nations nor themselves a defensive response to an initial aggression). Focusing on (2), is there any plausible rationale, utilitarian or otherwise, for abandoning it? I can see none. One can, of course, debate what constitutes an "armed attack," but dropping (2) would effectively gut the first norm. Aggressors would be in violation of international law, but their victims would have no legal right to resist. That is a logically possible position, but not very enticing. Upholding the legal right of national defense promotes peace and security, which in turn make possible various goods that are essential for human flourishing.

If international law recognized no right of national defense, it might still permit other states to come to the victim nation's assistance, but that is not an inviting proposal, either. If the victim nation has no right to resist, it is difficult to see the rationale for permitting other countries to intervene on its behalf. One might perhaps hold that, instead of resisting, the victim of aggression should appeal to the World Court or the United Nations for assistance. But, of course, the World Court has no enforcement power, and by the time the United Nations acts, if indeed it chooses to act, the victim nation will almost certainly have already suffered loss or harm that might have been avoided or reduced had it been allowed to defend itself. Resistance will often have better results than will hoping for eventual rectification of the status quo ante by other parties. True, in some cases, resisting a much more powerful aggressor may make matters worse for the victim nation.

Capitulation might be its most prudent option. This is no argument against a right of national defense. International law permits a state to fight back when attacked; it does not require it to do so.

In the absence of an operational and effective world peace-keeping force, for international law not to recognize a right of national defense would come close to decriminalizing aggressive war, making it a crime without a penalty. True, states will almost certainly resist grave attack whatever the law says, so a potential aggressor has some reason to be deterred in any case. But this natural or pre-legal deterrence can only be enhanced by the community of nations recognizing, as it does now, that the victim state is morally and legally entitled to fight back, that is, that it has right on its side. Furthermore, if international law were to fail to recognize a right of national defense against illegal and unwarranted attack, a right that is now universally acknowledged, this would only bring international law into disrepute. If, for example, international law could not have affirmed something as simple as Kuwait's right to have resisted Iraq's 1990 invasion, then it would hardly seem worthy of respect.

Given the tangled nature of disputes among nations, which often involve a long and sometimes obscure history of grievances on both sides, there is a lot to be said for retaining the simple and salient rule that the aggressor is the state that attacks first and the defender is the state responding to that attack. Instead of considering the larger context, the so-called "priority principle" focuses only on the question of who initiated the use of force (Lee 2012: 74). Elizabeth Anscombe once objected to this. "Why," she asked, "*must* it be wrong to strike the first blow in a struggle? The only question is, who is in the right." (1981b: 52). One might expect a proponent of UWP to agree with this, but a sophisticated utilitarian will appreciate the enormous benefits of upholding this simple rule, a rule that we can reasonably expect states to understand and adhere to.

A utilitarian inclined toward pacifism might argue, to the contrary, that in the long run better results for humankind will come from states' eschewing a right to use force under any circumstances, defensive or otherwise. However, even if a world in which all states refused ever to resort to war would be a better world—and this, as discussed in Chapter 4, is open to doubt—that fact would not entail that a state should renounce its right of national defense in today's world, in which not all states have absolutely and irrevocably committed themselves to non-violence. It is possible, of course, that by refusing on principle to defend itself with force, a state might set an example to others or in some other way produce the most good in the long run. But this is an extremely speculative hypothesis for a state to act on, and it certainly provides no basis for repudiating national defense as a moral and legal right.

More generally, one might worry that in upholding a right of national defense one is taking the current state system for granted and acquiescing in a blinkered Westphalian status quo. Perhaps some alternative to it might have superior results—true world government, for instance, or perhaps a world with no states or government at all. If so, then utilitarians would advocate moving in that direction.

Nevertheless, this would not prevent them from upholding the right of national defense in the current world just as a communist might condemn stealing in today's society despite believing that a world without private property would be better. From a utilitarian perspective, rights are not timeless; they can evolve and change. But if a right is vindicated, it is vindicated only by the expected consequences of its promulgation in the world as it actually is.

More on the utilitarian approach

The two basic non-consequentialist strategies for justifying a right of national defense are the reductive strategy and the analogical strategy (Rodin 2014: 123). Both are problematic, but by taking an instrumental view of the right of national defense, utilitarians escape the problems associated with each. The reductive strategy endeavors to show that the right of national defense is simply the coordinated exercise of the right of self-defense of thousands or millions of individuals. Because of the striking differences between the two rights and, in particular, the severe limits on when individuals can kill in self-defense, this strategy seems unpromising. The analogical strategy, on the other hand, contends that the state has a right to defend itself that is analogous to the right that an individual enjoys because the state has value in itself, has a moral personality, or represents certain collective values (Eckert 2009). That proposition will strike many, as it does utilitarians, as dubious.

In defending the right of national defense, Michael Walzer employs elements of both strategies. In his view, states have a right to defend themselves because in so doing they are guarding the "common life" of their citizens.

> Over a long period of time, shared experiences and cooperative activity of many different kinds shape a common life … a process of association and mutuality, the ongoing character of which the state claims to protect against external encroachment. This protection extends not only to the lives and liberties of individuals but also to their shared life and liberty, the independent community they have made, for which individuals are sometimes sacrificed.
>
> (Walzer 2006b: 54)

By participating in that common life, citizens tacitly transfer their defensive rights to the state, which protects their right not only to live, but also to live in a manner of their own choosing. This, then, is the moral basis of sovereignty; it is what grounds the right of national defense. On this topic as on so many others, Walzer's thinking has been extremely influential, but he has his critics, too. They have queried his implicit contractualism and raised tough questions about the concept of a common life and whether its preservation can plausibly be seen as the moral basis of existing states or as grounding their right to use defensive force (e.g., Rodin 2002: 141–62; 2014: 69–79).

Utilitarians look at the matter differently, as I have explained. For them, the right of national defense rests on the beneficial consequences of recognizing and upholding such a right, not on whether individual states represent some form of common life that is worth preserving. On the other hand, utilitarianism easily and straightforwardly captures what is sound in Walzer's position. Civilization presupposes organized political life, and human flourishing requires a reasonably just and secure social order. In today's world, preserving and respecting that organized political life by granting the state a right to use force to resist armed aggression protects the ability of human beings to live securely, safe from external predation, and thereby helps to foster and to preserve goods that are worth promoting on almost any theory of value. In the case of both liberal democratic and non-liberal but "decent" societies (Rawls 1999b: 4), those goods include the ability of individuals to exercise some degree of self-determination and control over their future.

From a utilitarian perspective, then, there are compelling grounds for affirming that states have a moral right to defend themselves against aggressive attack. Even apparently small infringements of territorial integrity or political independence may be quite serious if they prefigure more grave violations or if freedom, self-determination, or other values that utilitarians and others care about are at stake. In addition, deterrence and future precedent are important factors; in resisting aggression, a state is helping to uphold an established and valuable international norm. As with other rights, though—think of free speech—there can be situations in which, all things considered, one would be wrong to exercise it (for example, by saying needlessly hurtful things, when one could simply hold one's tongue). Thus, in response to some armed assaults, even necessary and proportional counterattack could conceivably be unjustified. However, the possibility of exceptional circumstances does not entail that the right in question should not be upheld or that the rights-holder should be interfered with. The full repercussions of exercising a given right in a particular situation are likely to be somewhat uncertain. For this reason and because we cannot secure the benefits of upholding a particular right and at the same time make its exercise contingent on its maximizing utility in each case, there is a strong presumption that in exercising a right that is grounded in utility, such as the right of national defense, a rights-holder acts permissibly.

But what about states that are oppressive or represent forms of "common life" that are not worth preserving? Do they have a right to defend themselves? Later in this chapter, I argue that regimes have no right to resist armed intervention aimed at preventing or halting genocide or other serious humanitarian abuses. Like disreputable people, however, shabby regimes do not automatically forfeit all their rights; they are still entitled to resist certain sorts of aggression. Generally speaking, one's rights are not dependent on one's moral character. This is why enthusiastic volunteers from Oxfam may not burgle the homes of selfish persons on the grounds that they ought to be giving more to charity than they do and why we are not free to assault bad people or damage their property even if it is true that they deserve to suffer. True, wrongdoers may forfeit certain rights that others have—that is why they can be justly punished—but as a general matter it is not only the good who have rights. From a utilitarian perspective, this is both because of the benefits of inculcating a general respect for persons and because of the infeasibility of proceeding in any other way, given the difficulty of knowing which people are so bad that it would be beneficial to ignore their rights. And, again, the rights of persons or other entities are not, in general, contingent on the use they make of their rights. My right to free speech, for example, is not conditional on my having something valuable to say, although, to be sure, I may justly be prevented from falsely crying "fire" in a crowded theater. These points apply equally well to states. In most cases, what matters is a state's *de jure* sovereignty not the goodness of its rule. Upholding the right of national defense against armed attack, not selectively but across the board, strengthens the general ban on states' initiating non-defensive warfare.

Answering Luban and Rodin

David Luban (1980: 165) rejects what he calls the "rule utilitarian" case for the ban on non-defensive war and for the concomitant right of national defense,[2] by which he means the argument, which I have been advancing, that endeavoring to uphold these two UN rules produces better results, in terms of human well-being, than would upholding any other rules or no rules at all, and that this is what justifies them. Luban contends, to the contrary, that by putting the priority on peace and security, the utilitarian approach "does not really answer the question of when a war is or can be just; rather, it simply refuses to consider it." Luban thinks that to focus on the results of upholding the UN norms "is simply to beg the question of *jus ad bellum*" (1980: 165). But one might well think that it is Luban who begs the question by assuming that the right of national defense must have some "deeper," non-consequentialist rationale.

Luban suggests in passing that the utilitarian approach ignores "the moral stature of a state" as well as "the empirical likelihood of escalation in a given case," but does not expand on these points (1980: 165). I discussed the first of these issues at the end of the last section and return to it later. The second issue seems to be a variant of the familiar point that even when a rule is justified on grounds of utility, there will be exceptional cases in which adherence to it produces suboptimal results. However, the utilitarian case for an absolute ban on murder, say, or for upholding an almost unconditional right of free expression does not presuppose that there could never be a case in which taking someone's life or preventing someone from speaking would make the world a better place.

Pushing Luban's second criticism further, David Rodin has challenged the whole consequentialist rationale for the right of national defense. Specifically, he rejects the contention that granting nations a right to defend themselves deters aggression, arguing that it is only "a crude speculation based on vague assumptions about human behavior" and that whether a norm permitting national defense would better promote peace and security than a norm prohibiting it is an "untested" proposition, which has "no determinate answer" (2002: 12, 117). This strikes me as tendentious and hyperbolic. True, we are dealing with empirical matters, and no conclusion we draw will be beyond question but, as argued earlier, it is difficult to believe that denying nations a right to defend themselves will produce better overall, long-term results. To the contrary, it seems perfectly reasonable to believe that aggression needs to be discouraged and that acknowledging a right of national defense helps to deter it.

Rodin contends, to the contrary, that upholding a state's right to resist attack might disrupt international peace and security, rather than promote it, and thus be unwarranted on utilitarian grounds. His example is the decision of the Western powers (which he thinks was correct) not to intervene on Czechoslovakia's behalf in 1968 because of the danger of precipitating a general war with the Soviet Union (2002: 117–18). But this conflates two things: The right of national defense and the question whether other states should come to a defender's aid. Even if the West was right not to have intervened, this does not entail that Czechoslovakia lacked a right to defend itself. Utilitarians can consistently make a case for the right of national defense on grounds of deterrence and the importance of allowing people to govern themselves and to continue to enjoy a shared political life free from external interference or predation, while at the same time thinking it right, in some cases anyway, for other states not to come to the assistance of the victim nation (or even for the victim nation not to resist).

It bears repeating that the utilitarian argument for the right of national defense or, indeed, any other right does not rest on the premise that exercising that right will maximize expected well-being in each and every case. If, however, it were the case that a state's exercise of its right of national defense, although necessary for and proportionate to its defensive objective, would bring about less good than not exercising it—if, in other words, its waging defensive war would violate UWP—and if this were known, then according to utilitarianism the state ought not to defend itself. But, as discussed before, this does not imply that it should be criticized for doing so, still less that it lacks that right in the first place.

Rodin rejects as well a utilitarian account of the right of individual self-defense because it "fails to provide a moral justification for self-defensive killing in [each and every] particular instance." This is because in a particular case defending oneself with lethal force "may not enhance the deterrence utility of the rule" or might even incite future aggression (2002: 54–5). However, this criticism, which, if sound, would apply equally well to the right of national defense, misunderstands the way that utilitarians and other consequentialists look at rules. If they endorse a particular rule, it is because they believe that the expected benefit of upholding and enforcing that rule and of people's internalizing it and modifying their conduct accordingly will be greater than the expected benefit of upholding and enforcing any other rule or no rule at all. Once a particular rule is established, then people are at least presumptively justified in acting in accord with it. Their particular actions do not also have to "enhance the ... utility of the rule."

Rules rest on generalizations, and it is well understood among philosophers of law that given any rule ("No dogs in the restaurant," "Speed Limit 55") there will be cases that do not subserve, or that fall outside, the rationale of the rule (Alexander and Sherwin 2008: 15; Schauer 1991: 47–52). If a rule is a serious rule, however, this entails that it is routinely enforced even in atypical cases because of the importance of maintaining the rule and furthering general compliance with it. Moreover, from a utilitarian point of view, part of the benefit of having a rule or sustaining certain rights is that people then know that they may act in certain ways without having to calculate the consequences of doing so in each and every particular case.

Preventive wars

Because national defense has long been accepted as a legitimate *casus belli*, states have sometimes stretched the concept beyond reasonable bounds in order to rationalize attacking another state over economic or trade issues, preventing a rival from becoming too powerful, or pursuing some tendentious territorial claim. Because of this, Bertrand Russell, arguing from a consequentialist point of view, once rejected the right of national defense because he believed that it permitted nations to justify fighting almost any war they wished to fight. "So far as I know," he wrote, "there has never yet been a war which was not one of self-defence," and he pointed to World War I as a case in which all the antagonists viewed themselves as acting in self-defense (1915: 138).

Russell's contention is pertinent because utilitarians cannot say, as some other moral theorists can, that x is a right if in practice acknowledging x as a right has poor consequences. If identifying and upholding a right of national defense produced less net benefit over the long run than not doing so, then utilitarianism would entail that there is no such right. I have, however, already laid out the benefits of acknowledging that right, discussed the costs of refraining from doing so, and endeavored to rebut the claim that declining to recognize a right of national defense might have better results. Given this, then, the fact that the concept of defensive war can be abused does not tell against retaining the core legal and moral right of nations to defend themselves against armed aggression. If states have misused the right of national defense, appealing to it to rationalize non-defensive warfare, this does not imply that we should repudiate that right, but rather that we must delineate its contours more precisely and criticize states that play fast and loose with it.

To be sure, because defense against armed attack is now the only legal justification for war (aside from military actions authorized by the Security Council), international law and convention have expanded the legal category somewhat; it is seen as embracing preemptive strikes, assisting other states to fight back against armed aggression, and the recovery of illegally and unjustly seized territory, as in the case of Kuwait or the Falkland Islands. And individual states occasionally try to push the boundaries of defense even further to include, for example, overseas counterinsurgency activities or retaliatory responses to minor border incursions or to crimes committed against their citizens when they are abroad. Nevertheless, since Russell wrote the passage quoted above, the consensus international understanding of the right of national defense has become more precise and restrictive, in part as a result of lessons drawn from World War I.

First, that right is understood to apply only to armed attacks that are a significant assault on a state's territorial or political sovereignty; it does not encompass waging war to defend other interests—economic, strategic, or political—that a state may have or see itself as having. Second, that right is understood to license only military action that is a necessary and proportionate response to the original aggression. As with individual self-defense, a state cannot go beyond what is necessary to deflect the attack and prevent its renewal, nor can it aim at non-defensive goals. Third, the right of national defense does not license preventive war. It does not encompass a state's waging war to forestall a threat that has not yet materialized but that might unfold in the future—that is, to attack another state now to deprive it of the capacity of attacking in the future. This understanding of national defense represents a rejection of the older view that states may legitimately wage war to preserve the international status quo or maintain the balance of power by preventing a rival state from becoming too strong. Preventive war is now seen as aggressive, not defensive. On the other hand, the right of national defense permits a state to ward off an imminent attack, that is, to preempt an assault that is about to start or is in progress but has not yet struck home. In this case, a state is not initiating the war, but intercepting or heading off an attack that has already been set in motion.

Although drawing a line between them raises some intriguing philosophical questions (Nozick 1974: 126–30) and may sometimes be difficult to do in practice, the basic distinction between preemptive attack and preventive war is widely understood and accepted (Orend 2006: 74–83; Walzer 2006b: 80–5). As with individual self-defense, a state does not have to wait to respond until it has been struck; on the other hand, it cannot wage war simply to weaken an adversary's military potential. The reason for this is clear. Because states are prone to exaggerate their security needs (Mill 1825: 26; Sidgwick 1908: 290), the belief that they are justified in waging war to eliminate potential threats—that this is part of their inherent right of self-defense—increases international insecurity and the likelihood of war. As suspicion feeds upon suspicion, it creates a spiral of mistrust so that a state may feel compelled to attack now because of worries that its rival may be contemplating preventive war against it. This danger has long been recognized.

The case against preventive war

Within the community of nations, all this was seen as settled and uncontroversial doctrine until 2002 when the Bush administration developed a new national security policy as a prelude to launching war against Iraq (Crawford 2007; Frowe 2011: 74–5). Depending on how one interprets it, that document either redefines "preemptive" military action to include what had previously been considered "preventive" war or makes a case for preventive war when the stakes are high enough. Although the Bush doctrine may not have represented as much of a departure from past U.S. policy as is sometimes thought (Nathanson 2013: 146–7), under either interpretation it clearly challenges established international norms. The failure to find weapons of mass destruction in Iraq—the main *casus belli* among several shifting rationales for the war—has, of course, greatly reduced the appeal of the new doctrine. On the other hand, it has forced scholars to clarify the conditions that must be met for military action to be considered genuinely preemptive and to restate the case against preventive war.

Consequentialist in character, that case rests on two lines of argument. First, it emphasizes the profound epistemological obstacles confronting any state that is considering preventive war. In particular, its intelligence must be accurate, reliable, and correctly interpreted, and the danger must be grave and the situation urgent, with no non-military options available and little time for delay. However, because of bias, emotion, ignorance, short-sighted thinking, and various ideological or other blind spots, to which even intelligent people can succumb, the risk of error is high. Because of this and because of the grim consequences of miscalculation, the state contemplating war faces a burden of proof that it is, in practice, unlikely to be able to meet. The second argument points to the bad consequences of general acceptance of a principle licensing preventive war—a point, as intimated above, that has long been acknowledged—because it promotes international insecurity and increases the likelihood of war by creating a spiral of fear and mistrust. Even a state that harbors no aggressive intent may feel obliged to attack its rival because it fears that fear will lead the other state to attack it first.

In response to the first argument, Buchanan and Keohane (2004) have proposed setting up a multilateral accountability tribunal that would review any state's case for preventive war. This could bring some degree of objectivity to the decision, though the tribunal would have to be free from the politics and self-serving that now makes the UN Security Council unable reliably to fill this role. The tribunal would also, of course, have to be accepted as a legitimate epistemological authority by a critical mass of states. In any case, though, the point still holds that a state is extremely unlikely to have compelling grounds for believing that it is justified in waging preventive war. But it might possibly be the case, nevertheless, that such a war would in fact satisfy UWP and that the state in question knows it. It cannot be maintained that this could never happen. Some believe that Israel's bombing of Iraq's Osirak nuclear reactor in 1981, though only a quick one-time strike and not a preventive war, shows that there could be circumstances that are not so far-fetched in which preventive war might be justified (Fisher 2011: 172; Sinnott-Armstrong 2007: 215). But it is easier to imagine hypothetical cases than to find real ones in which preventive war against another state satisfied or would have satisfied UWP.

This brings us to the second argument, namely, that because of the likelihood of error and the instability and heightened risk of war that a rule permitting preventive war would lead to, it is best to retain the current norm forbidding it. It has been contended, to the contrary, that game-theoretic considerations disprove this argument (Dipert 2006: 47–9) and that there is an equally strong case for believing that a rule that permits preventive war would produce the best results because, as Cicero famously urged in his fifth philippic, it is better to crush evils at their birth than to wait for them to develop (Rodin 2007: 149). But these are implausible assertions with dangerous implications. In the real world, we know the bad consequences that have followed from states believing that preventive wars are permissible. As intimated above, there have been few, if any, justified preventive wars, nor do there appear to be any cases about which in retrospect we can confidently say that some state erroneously failed to undertake a preventive war, the fighting of which would have maximized expected well-being (Betts 2003). But, of course, even if this is correct, it does not preclude the possibility that in the future some state really might be justified in waging preventive war. In line with this, some critics reject the second argument because from the fact that there is a justified utilitarian rule against preventive war it does not follow that preventive war is necessarily wrong in each and every case.

As emphasized earlier, this is a point that utilitarians and other consequentialists have long recognized. Indeed, it is an inevitable feature of general rules. Circumstances can throw up exceptions to them. What, then, is a conscientious state to do if it believes itself to be in just such an exceptional circumstance? To begin with, of course, it has to bear in mind the epistemological precariousness of its situation given that the historical record indicates that states that have believed themselves to have been justified in waging preventive war have almost always, perhaps always, been mistaken, as judged by the criterion of UWP. This should induce hesitation. But suppose that the state believes, reasonably and with a high level of confidence—perhaps independent observers concur—that UWP either permits or requires preventive war. If so, it may feel morally compelled to wage preventive war in violation of the norm against it, even after taking into account the risk of error. Doing so, however, will have a negative precedential effect; it will tend, to some difficult-to-specify degree, to weaken that important norm. Taking this also into account, it may or may not maximize well-being for the state to wage war.

Dealing with exceptional cases

Suppose that it does and that the state in question would act rightly in waging preventive war in violation of the international norm against it. One possibility is that international law should be amended to permit preventive wars in just such circumstances. Or it could be that the state is morally justified in waging war even though the general rule cannot or should not be modified to authorize its acting as it does. In this case, one might simply condone the violation. Sidgwick seems to favor this. Just as "cases occasionally occur in which an individual is widely held excused for breaking a rule which it is yet thought desirable to maintain as law," he writes, so it is in the international realm. Indeed, "we must expect similar cases of approved or excused illegality to be more frequent in international relations" because of the relatively small number of states and the greater importance of any one state (as opposed to any one individual) relative to the whole (1908: 289). Following a line of thought suggested by Sartorius (1972), however, there is another approach utilitarians might take. This is to maintain that other states should criticize the war or at least withhold their full support for it, even though they believe that the decision to wage preventive war was correct, because of the importance of upholding and reinforcing the general rule against preventive war. Which stance one should take—turning a blind eye to the illegality or formally condemning it—has, I think, no general answer, but will depend on the particular case.

Let us pursue this further. On the view I am taking, the right of national defense does not encompass preventive war (as opposed to responding preemptively to an attack that is about to unfold or is already underway). Moreover, there are strong grounds for upholding the international norm against it, that is, for classifying it as illegal because it is non-defensive. However, as we have been discussing, there could be exceptional circumstances in which UWP approves a preventive war despite its violating an established norm that is justified on grounds of utility. In this case, it could be, as suggested in the previous paragraph, that international law and convention should recognize the war as a legitimate exception to the rule (like breaking the speed limit to take a woman in labor to the hospital) or that the rule itself should be explicitly revised to permit preventive war in such circumstances (like amending the traffic code to spell out in exactly which emergency situations one is permitted to break the normal speed limit). We could then say that the state in question had just cause for war.

Modifying the existent rule, however, or formally recognizing exceptions to it might be infeasible or undesirable. Upholding the established rule as it is and across the board might have better results. If this is so, then it would seem candid simply to say that in the case we are now imagining the state is morally justified in waging a war for which it lacks just cause (in the narrow sense of "just cause") because its doing so violates the rights of the state it is attacking. A passage in John Stuart Mill's *Utilitarianism*, though, suggests a different way of looking at the case. In discussing circumstances in which the need to prevent some grave harm trumps an accepted maxim of justice, Mill writes that "we usually say, not that justice must give way to some other moral principle, but that what is just in ordinary cases is, by reason of that other principle, not just in the particular case" (1969c: 259). This "useful accommodation of language," he writes, preserves the "indefeasibility attributed to justice" and rules out our having to concede that there "can be laudable injustice." Applied to the case at hand, this implies that the attacking state could point to the considerations that led it to breach the norm and contend that, in light of these, it was acting justly in the circumstances. Mill's approach will appeal to those who think that we should never grant the rightness of waging a war that violates the established rights of states (and in this sense is unjust or lacks just cause) or who believe that if war is justified, then the state waging it automatically has justice on its side. About these terminological matters, however, reasonable people can differ.

Armed humanitarian intervention

I have been arguing that there are compelling reasons for reaffirming and, indeed, strengthening the norm against preventive war and that any state would almost certainly be mistaken to believe that waging war to head off a non-imminent threat from another state or to eliminate its capacity to pose a threat in the future would satisfy UWP. This situation contrasts with that of armed humanitarian intervention, that is, with waging war to rescue the citizens of another state from genocide or other extreme abuses of human rights by their own state. Obviously, such intervention is not justified by the intervening state's right of national defense; indeed, the state that is attacked appears to have a right to defend itself against the intervener. Moreover, humanitarian intervention contravenes the legal norm that only defensive wars are permissible as well as the long-established "principle of mutual non-interference," which avers that states should refrain from interfering with the internal affairs of other states.

However, in contrast to preventive war, there are real cases in which armed humanitarian intervention appears to have been morally justified—for instance, India's intervention in East Pakistan, Vietnam's invasion of Kampuchea, and Tanzania's ouster of Uganda's Idi Amin—or in which armed humanitarian intervention would have been justified, had it been undertaken, as in Rwanda in 1994. Moreover, it is easy to imagine such cases in the future, cases in which humanitarian intervention would be morally justified, all things considered, even if it violates current international law, because intervention would save lives or prevent other serious abuses and depredations, resulting in less overall harm than non-intervention would have. Bulley (2010: 454–5) makes heavy weather of the fact that in order to protect some people, armed humanitarian intervention kills other people. He describes this as a "conundrum," an "ethical paradox," and a "moral dilemma." But any morally justified war involves killing in order to achieve some good great enough to justify that killing.

To be sure, there are those who are skeptical of humanitarian interventions, noting their entanglement with international politics and cautioning in a realist vein that such interventions tend to go awry, resulting in more harm than they were meant to prevent (e.g., Kuperman 2009; Miller 2010; Wilkins 2003). Although salutary, this skepticism should not be pushed too far. Confronted with genocide in Rwanda, for example, there are a number of things that other states could have done, including armed intervention, that would almost certainly have been better than what they did do, which was, in essence, nothing. To this, the critic can reply that even if armed humanitarian intervention would be theoretically justified if carried out properly, in the real world it is actually existing states that we are asking to intervene, and these states are flawed, error-prone actors with impure motivations. Moreover, humanitarian crises are rarely clean and simple, and various unpredictable factors outside the control of the intervening state can cause intervention to go amiss and make its aftermath regrettable. This latter point is one that utilitarians will acknowledge, indeed, emphasize: We need to act with the fullest possible knowledge of the situation we are facing, including the likelihoods of the possible outcomes of the courses of action open to us. In any given case, that knowledge might or might not lead to the conclusion that intervention would be worse than non-intervention.

The critic's first point is thornier, namely, that armed humanitarian intervention inevitably relies on states that are no angels themselves and that are all too likely to intervene in a maladroit or heavy-handed way. Spelling out the argument in more general terms, we are being asked to accept as our premises that (a) x is the welfare-maximizing course of action for agent A in situation S, (b) A could in fact do x, but (c) A, being the kind of person or entity it is, is bound to screw up—because A tends to be careless or ham-fisted, frequently acts selfishly, or exercises poor judgment in practical situations. Thus, the argument goes, it is better not to encourage A to do x. Yet this conclusion seems premature. After all, x is the right thing for A to do, and it is within A's power to do it. Rather than relieving states of the moral duty to rescue those threatened by genocide, we may, rather, want to encourage them to intervene in a careful, judicious, and proportionate way rather than in the self-serving, culturally insensitive, or benighted way that typically characterizes their foreign policy. On the other hand, a given state might be so inept or, worse, so imperialistic or its foreign policy so malign that we may not want to give it any excuse for invading another state.

These considerations complicate the moral assessment of humanitarian intervention, but they do not establish the pessimistic conclusion that it is always to be discouraged. By contrast with preventive war, from the engaging in which we want to restrain states even though their self-interest may incline them toward it, humanitarian intervention is essentially altruistic. Generally speaking, the practical problem is not to deter states that are keen to do so from intervening because it will have bad results, but rather to prod them to act even though doing so is without benefit to them. Most contemporary commentators concur with this, holding that armed humanitarian intervention is sometimes morally justified (e.g., Ang 2013; Heinze 2009; Pattison 2010) and, indeed, can be squared with the *ad bellum* principles of just war theory (Christopher 2004: 251–4; Fisher 2011: 234–6; Lucas 2003: 85–90). Various criteria have been proposed for assessing when armed humanitarian intervention is justified (Bulley 2010: 454–5; Meggle 2003; Tesón 2006) but they tend to be rather general and obvious (e.g., Pattison 2010: 23). With so many empirical factors in play, what is needed is careful, case-by-case analysis of the sort that UWP encourages, with close attention to the likely results of the available alternatives.[3]

Empirical uncertainties and the risk of untoward consequences will probably militate against armed humanitarian intervention in all but the most egregious cases. Altman and Wellman (2008), however, reject the idea that there must be a high justificatory threshold for armed humanitarian intervention, one that requires a "supreme humanitarian emergency" or widespread abuses of the most shocking kind. Rather, if the target state is illegitimate, then intervention is permissible when the risk it poses to human rights is proportional to the rights violations it can be expected to avert. Likewise, Jeff McMahan maintains that "a small-scale violation of human rights can constitute a just cause for a proportionally small-scale war" (2012: 287n). The point these authors are making seems correct, at least in theory, although there are other goods and evils that may need to be considered besides preventing or causing human rights violations. By the bar of UWP, it is clear that armed humanitarian intervention need not be restricted to genocide or situations involving the most extreme and extensive abuses.[4] But the more limited are the abuses in question, the more likely it is that the risks of intervention will weigh against it. And a norm permitting intervention to rectify or prevent relatively minor injustices—assuming that the nations of the world could be brought to embrace it—would risk states' coming to believe themselves justified in interfering with the domestic policies or institutions of other states whenever they thought that doing so would be for the best.

Article 42 of the UN Charter authorizes the Security Council to undertake military action "to maintain or restore international peace and security," and this includes intervention in ostensibly domestic matters if they disrupt or threaten to disrupt that peace and security, for example, by producing refugees or creating turmoil that has already led neighboring states to become involved (Regan 2013: 35). In general, though, armed humanitarian intervention appears to contravene the UN Charter. Some writers, however, have sought to square the two by arguing, for example, that "crimes against humanity" fall outside domestic jurisdiction (Christopher 2004: 248) or that Article 51 should be interpreted as granting substate groups a right to defend themselves, in which effort others can assist (Fletcher and Ohlin 2008: 138). In any case, many theorists favor revising international law to permit humanitarian intervention to prevent genocide or grave human rights abuses. In fact, with various international bodies seeking to formalize a "responsibility to protect" and with the willingness of the international community to countenance armed humanitarian intervention, at least in extreme circumstances, international law, which is a function of established or customary practice as well as formal treaties and accords, can plausibly be said to be gradually changing already.[5]

If international law permits or should be modified to permit armed humanitarian intervention in certain circumstances, either by the United Nations or by individual states acting unilaterally, this entails abandoning the notion that state sovereignty is legally inviolable. It shifts the balance between the rights of states and those of individuals, and modifies the rule that all non-defensive wars are illegal. Some attacks that are now illegal and against which it is permissible for a state to defend itself would become legal, depriving it of the right to resist in those cases. Legally acknowledging humanitarian grounds for war would not, however, affect a nation's right to defend itself against illegitimate attack. Instead, it would entail that the right to defend itself is something that a state can forfeit or have overridden by other legally recognized factors.

Utilitarians should almost certainly push for international law explicitly to permit armed humanitarian intervention to thwart genocide and other serious human rights violations, especially if the law specified clearly the conditions under which intervention is warranted and if there was some independent, non-political authority that could determine whether these conditions had been met. Even with procedural hurdles in place, however, such a change would not be risk free; the norm of non-interference is so important for international peace and security that one hesitates formally to recognize exceptions for fear they will be abused. But the consequences of failing to act in cases of extreme humanitarian abuses are so severe for the immediate victims and so damaging to the effort to sustain certain minimal standards of state conduct that there is a strong case for legal change. Although instrumentally very important, state sovereignty and, with it, the right of national defense are neither intrinsically nor absolutely valuable; rather, their boundaries have to be adjusted so as to maximize long-term human well-being in the real world.

Suppose, then, that although UWP justifies armed humanitarian intervention in a certain situation, such intervention would violate international law as it is now understood. UWP analysis will already have taken into account the possible negative precedential effects of such intervention, in particular, the possibility that it will weaken respect for the rule against non-defensive war in cases where that rule should be respected, and concluded that intervention is nevertheless justified. In the previous section, we wrestled with how to view a case of illegal but justified preventive war, but here the matter is more straightforward. That is because the clash is between "recognised international law" and "the development of international morality" rather than between the former and "the claim of national interest admitted as semi-legitimate" (Sidgwick 1908: 290). And we want international law to evolve in line with international morality so that interventions like the ones we have been considering are recognized as legitimate exceptions to the rule against non-defensive wars and the principle of mutual non-interference, if not through explicit treaty, then at least through established practice and precedent. For this reason, we need not hesitate to say that the intervening state is acting with just cause.

Non-state entities

Because our concern is with the right of national defense and its limits, I have focused on states, which are the bearers of this right. If a state is subject to illegitimate attack, then it has a right to defend itself and is at least prima facie justified in waging war. It has just cause for war and is entitled to use necessary and proportionate force to defend itself; it is not to be criticized for doing so even if it is unclear whether its waging war satisfies UWP.

But what about non-state entities, such as revolutionary, secessionist, anti-colonial, or national liberation movements? Can they claim something analogous to the right of national defense that legitimate states enjoy? I think not. There is no presumption, as there is with states exercising the right of national defense, that their resorting to arms is morally justified. Utilitarians support the right of national defense because of the importance of deterring aggression against states and thereby preserving the peace and security that is necessary for human flourishing. No analogous considerations argue for any sort of general right of non-state entities to take up arms. Could they, nevertheless, be justified in waging war? The consensus answer to that question is yes. It is reflected in certain international documents and, generally speaking, rests on argument by historical example, that is, by appeal to cases in which non-state actors seem intuitively to have had a strong moral case for going to war. As a conceptual matter, one does not have to have a right to ϕ for one to be justified in ϕ-ing.

To be sure, some just war theorists maintain that non-state actors can have "a right to fight" (Fabre 2012: 141–56; Gross 2015: 21–49). It turns out, however, that by this, these authors mean only (a) that non-state entities can satisfy the criterion of legitimate authority and (b) that sometimes those entities are morally justified in waging war—two propositions with which nobody today fundamentally disagrees. Implicitly, on their view A's being justified in waging war entails that A has a right to fight. This widespread way of speaking cannot be considered incorrect, but the concept of a right is being used in a weaker sense than when we are discussing the right of national defense. That right establishes a strong presumption that a state acts rightly in resorting to arms; it is the reason it is justified in waging war, not merely another way of saying that it is.

What I am skeptical of, then, is any attempt to specify clear and straightforward conditions, analogous to those governing the right of national defense, in which a non-state entity would automatically have just cause for waging war or some sort of right to resort to arms—prior to any consequentialist analysis. Again, this is not because I think that such entities are never justified in waging war. Rather, I doubt that such conditions can be identified with enough precision to be helpful. There are too many historical variables—too many different situations and too different types of actors with too many different types of goals—to identify some general rule stating when non-state entities are entitled to wage war, nor is it obvious what the benefits of such a rule would be. For one thing, it would hardly be a simple and salient rule like that licensing states to counter armed attack with military force, and the effort to turn it into a workable international norm or law would probably be futile and perhaps even counterproductive, leading in practice to more war than would be justified by UWP.

Although UWP explicitly deals only with states, it could plausibly be extended or modified to cover various non-state actors. Whether a non-state entity is justified in waging war would hang, then, on a detailed analysis of the particulars of the case in terms of the just war guidelines and, ultimately, something like UWP.[6] This puts a heavy justificatory burden on the non-state entity because there is no presumption, as there is in the case of national defense, that it is justified in waging war. But this is as it should be. When it comes to militarized conflicts involving non-state entities, there are in the world today too many spurious appeals to rights or supposed historical grievances, with too little attention paid to the consequences of war for flesh-and-blood human beings or to alternative non-violent courses of political action. Many struggles waged by non-state entities have not been morally justified, certainly not by the exacting standard of UWP. Even when those entities have been victorious, the long-run outcome has frequently been less good, I believe, than it might have been had some other, non-military course of action been pursued. However, victorious non-state entities often become states themselves and get to write their own histories; they develop a self-justifying narrative in which the new status quo whitewashes whatever violence brought it about. Because of this, the prevailing attitude toward the wars they fought tends to be too indulgent. It is important to insist, therefore, that it is wrong for a non-state entity to resort to violence unless no other course of action available to it would result, not merely in its triumph, but in greater net well-being, overall and in the long run.

Notes

1 See Ryan (2013) for pacifistic skepticism about the right of national defense.
2 In a later essay, however, Luban rejects preventive war on rule-utilitarian grounds similar to those given later in this chapter. See Luban (2004).
3 In line with this, Heinze (2005) argues persuasively not only that consequentialism provides the best justification of armed humanitarian intervention but also that it tallies well with commonsense moral thinking about it.
4 Nor in principle must it be restricted, as Altman and Wellman (2008) maintain, to interventions against illegitimate regimes.
5 For good overviews of these developments, see Bellamy (2015), Doyle (2014), Haines (2014), and Lucas (2014).
6 I reject the proposition (Dobos 2008) that the *jus ad bellum* requirements of last resort, proportionality, and reasonable prospect of success should be loosened for rebels—unless, of course, there were reason to believe that rebellions approved by the relaxed standards but not by the unrelaxed standards were in general likely to maximize expected well-being.

6

THE RULES OF WAR

Chapters 3, 4, and 5 upheld the Utilitarian War Principle (UWP) as the fundamental criterion for determining whether a state acts rightly in waging war, and they discussed the guidelines to be followed in employing that principle in practice, including acknowledging and respecting a right of national defense. Suppose, now, that war has broken out. If it is wrong for a state to fight that war, then obviously it should desist from doing so, and individual citizens should (some special circumstances aside, perhaps) oppose the war. As Sidgwick wrote, the duty of an individual whose nation is contemplating or has undertaken an aggressive or unjustified war is clear; it is "to use any moral and intellectual influence he may possess—facing unpopularity—to prevent the immoral act." But "how far he should go in such opposition" is "difficult to say" and "depends so much on circumstance that an abstract discussion of it is hardly profitable" (1998a: 52). It is even more difficult to say, in general, what either military officers or enlisted personnel should do if they come to believe that they are fighting, or being directed to fight, in an immoral war. Naturally, they will be reluctant to participate in that war, but they may see themselves as having a moral, legal, or professional responsibility to do so. Chapters 7 and 8 return to this issue.

Suppose, though, that a state is morally justified in waging war and that one is either a combatant engaged in fighting that war or one of the public officials charged with directing it. How, according to utilitarianism, is one permitted to wage the war? What constraints, if any, are there on one's conduct? From a utilitarian perspective, it might seem that if the war is morally right, that is, if no alternative course of action has greater expected well-being, then "the end justifies the means" and those involved in the fighting should be prepared to do absolutely anything as long as it helps to achieve victory (Rodin 2008: 54; Whitman 1993: 262). However, this is inaccurate and misleading for three reasons.

First, although it is true in a sense that utilitarians believe that the end justifies the means, it is, as Sidgwick reminds us, a universal end, "the happiness or well-being of humanity at large" which they seek to promote, "not the preservation of any particular state, still less its aggrandizement or the maintenance of its existing form of government" (1998b: 37). Taken literally, of course, the slogan that the end justifies the means can hardly be gainsaid. By definition, a means is a means to some goal or end; what else could justify a means other than the end at which it aims? Of course, what people mean when they reject this slogan is that one is not permitted to do anything whatsoever in pursuit of one's goals, and this is a truth that utilitarians have no trouble endorsing.

Second, utilitarians seek to maximize net expected benefit; they care not only about how much good a course of action can be anticipated to produce, but also about the costs of bringing that outcome about. Selecting the least harmful means of achieving a given objective is, of course, a matter of elementary rationality. More significantly, for utilitarians consideration of the available means affects whether it is right to pursue that objective in the first place, however valuable it may be in its own right. Thus, the fact that victory, viewed by itself, would be a better result than, say, surrender or a negotiated settlement, does not entail that it is right to fight in whatever way conduces to that victory. If the harm done by fighting in a certain way—say, to take an extreme case, by using nuclear weapons—is too great, then the utilitarian calculus will entail that the war cannot be fought that way even if this makes victory impossible. If the only route to victory is too costly, then war will not be the course of action with the greatest expected well-being.

The third reason that utilitarians do not believe that combatants and those who direct them are permitted to do absolutely anything to obtain victory, even if UWP indicates that they are in the right, is that their conduct should be restrained by what Michael Walzer (2006b: 127) dubs the "war convention" or what I shall call the "received rules of war." After providing an overview of those rules, this chapter explains and upholds the utilitarian view of them. Against rival understandings of the rules, in particular, those of Walzer and George Mavrodes, it not only shows how and why utilitarianism underwrites them but also argues that it provides the most satisfactory account of why they have the moral force they do.

The received rules of war

These rules, which constrain the conduct of hostilities, are of two sorts. One major component is the international law of armed conflict, all or part of which is now often referred to as international humanitarian law. It is based on the customary or accepted practice of states; on formal treaties and agreements among states, such as the 1949 Geneva Conventions; on the rulings of various national and international legal tribunals, such as those held at Nuremberg after World War II; on the writings of legal specialists; and, finally, in the words of the Hague Convention of 1907, on "the laws of humanity, and the dictates of public conscience" (Roberts and Guelff 2000: 70). These rules are often extensive and detailed, for instance, the provisions that govern the treatment of prisoners of war, the enemy sick and injured, and the population of an occupied territory. Other rules are simpler, such as those forbidding—to pick a few examples—taking hostages, declaring that no quarter will be given, abusing a flag of truce or Red Cross emblem, and soldiers' disguising themselves in civilian clothing.

Like international law generally, the law of armed conflict is real and binding on all states. As Sidgwick writes, "There *are* accepted rules of international duty, and the pursuit of national self-interest *is* restrained by them—imperfectly, no doubt, but still to an important extent" (1908: 240; see also Hart 1994: 213–37). Importantly, neither the legal nor the moral obligation to adhere to the law of armed conflict is contingent on a state's having agreed to do so. That a nation has signed a particular international accord or otherwise agreed to adhere to all or part of the international law of armed conflict may increase its obligation to do so, but its declining to ratify the laws of war does not free it from the duty to follow them. Worth noting here is that international agreements often begin life as treaties binding only on their signatories but over the years become absorbed, in whole or in part, into customary international law, binding on all states. Thus, it would be illegal (and immoral) for a state to abuse prisoners of war even if it had not ratified the Third Geneva Convention of 1949, which forbids torturing prisoners or treating them in cruel, humiliating, or degrading ways.

In addition to the positive law of armed conflict, almost all writers on the ethics of war believe that combat is (or ought to be) regulated by three broad normative principles. Traditionally identified as the rules of *jus in bello* or just conduct in war, they are the principle of necessity, the principle of proportionality, and the principle of discrimination and non-combatant immunity:[1]

Principle of Necessity: Force and violence are to be employed only if they serve some legitimate military goal.

According to this principle, it is wrong for the armed forces of a nation at war to employ force or violence that lacks a military purpose or that is unrelated to the objective of defeating the enemy's military. Looting civilian homes or raping women, for example, has no military rationale and is forbidden for this reason. The men who do it, even if they are in uniform and, indeed, even if they are carrying out orders, are not acting in a military capacity; what they do bears no relation to the just cause for which they are supposed to be fighting. The principle thus forbids rapine, carnage, or destruction that is needless from a military point of view. Combatants may not kill, destroy, or engage in any other kind of mayhem unless there is some military reason for it. At the end of the 1990–1 Gulf War, the United States eventually called off attacks on Iraqi soldiers who were fleeing back to Iraq from Kuwait after their army had been smashed. This was in line with the principle of necessity. At that point, the Iraqi soldiers were no longer a functioning army; continuing to slaughter them would have had no rational military purpose.

The word *necessity* is somewhat ambiguous. In this context, it means something like military benefit. The principle of necessity does not require that a belligerent have no other viable military option; it requires only that the violence it employs not be wanton—that is, that it be directed toward overcoming the enemy's military forces and thus have a military purpose.

Principle of Proportionality: The use of force or violence must be proportionate to the value of the military objective being sought.

This closely related principle should not be confused with the *ad bellum* criterion of proportionality, which requires that for a war to be just the harm it produces not outweigh the good it is intended to achieve. The *in bello* proportionality principle, in contrast, concerns specific military actions during a war. It goes beyond the principle of necessity and forbids violence that is excessive in relation to its military objective. Thus, even if bombing a dam served some military purpose, it might nevertheless be wrong if the devastation it wreaked outweighed the military value of destroying the dam. Likewise, it would be wrong to raze a village even if doing so were the only way to eliminate sniper fire coming from it. The principle has a comparative dimension because a military operation will violate it if there is an equally viable and effective but less destructive alternative.

Although most modern military leaders consider the cost to their own troops when deciding whether to undertake a particular military campaign and try not to squander the lives of the men and women under their command,[2] the proportionality principle requires them also to consider, to some extent, the cost to the other side. For example, it would be wrong, other things being equal, to mow down enemy soldiers when encirclement or other maneuver could have compelled their surrender. Or, to revert to our earlier example, even if killing fleeing Iraqi troops near the end of the Gulf War would have had some military utility, the principle of proportionality would have condemned it because slaughtering them would have been out of proportion to whatever modest benefit it might have brought. Finally, the principle of proportionality rules out using weapons, such as exploding bullets, serrated bayonets, or glass-filled projectiles, which cause excessive or unnecessary suffering or significantly reduce the likelihood of recovering from a wound.

The *in bello* proportionality principle does not necessarily require belligerents to keep force to an absolute minimum or to use the least amount of it compatible with attaining the aim in question.[3] Employing overwhelming, seemingly excessive force may sometimes result in less overall harm because it achieves the objective more quickly. Moreover, neither side's combatants have a duty to accept greater casualties in order to reduce casualties to the other side. Rather, the principle of proportionality requires only that the violence employed not be grossly out of proportion to the military goal that is being sought. That idea also plays a role in the following principle.

Principle of Discrimination and Non-combatant Immunity: Belligerents must discriminate between military and non-military targets. They are not to target non-combatants and must make reasonable efforts to avoid harming them.

Combatants are legitimate targets. Although a soldier may not support the war he has been drafted to fight, in putting on a uniform he becomes a legitimate target, and the other side does no wrong in trying to kill him. Government or party officials who, although technically not part of the armed forces, play a direct military role, for example, by picking targets for attack, overseeing combat operations, or handling logistics, may also be legitimate targets. Because they are deeply and actively involved in the hostilities, they are part of the war machine even if they do not wear uniforms or bear arms. In contrast, those who are not directly or immediately involved in the fighting but are, rather, ordinary civilians taking no part in the hostilities but simply going about daily life as best they can are non-combatants and have a right not to be harmed. Unlike the soldier or the civilian military official, they have done nothing to make themselves appropriate objects of attack.

The principle of discrimination and non-combatant immunity does not imply that genuine civilians may never be killed in war. It categorically prohibits deliberately targeting or attacking them, but it accepts that civilians may sometimes be injured or killed as a side-effect or collateral consequence of striking a legitimate military target. This is permissible if the collateral or unintended harm to them is proportionate or reasonable in light of the military objective and if a good faith effort was made to avoid harming them. Thus, although it would be wrong to bomb a civilian neighborhood in an effort to demoralize the enemy, it would not necessarily be wrong to bomb a munitions factory even though it is foreseen that the raid will kill civilians, assuming that the factory has sufficient military importance and that there is no alternative (such as sabotage by a commando unit) that could accomplish the same end without endangering civilians. The principle of discrimination and non-combatant immunity requires combatants to accept some increased risk to themselves in order to reduce the harm imposed on non-combatants. For example, in an effort to deal with enemy soldiers taking shelter in a residential apartment complex, the other side cannot blow up the whole estate, thus killing innocent women and children, just because this would be less risky for them than fighting door-to-door.

The three principles of *jus in bello* intertwine with the positive law of armed conflict. Although the latter tends to be more detailed and specific, some of its general statements reflect or incorporate the three principles, and those principles underwrite many of its particular provisions. In turn, those provisions help to make the principles' requirements determinate and specific. For this reason and because both the principles and the legal regulations are widely known and internationally accepted, even if not always adhered to in practice, I lump them together as the "received rules of war."

My doing so is in line with the early utilitarian or proto-utilitarian William Paley, who held that the conduct of war is regulated both by (1) the law of nature, which rules out "acts of hostility" that have "no proper tendency to accelerate the termination or accomplish the object of war," and (2) the laws of war, that is, "those positive laws which the custom of nations hath sanctified, and which, whilst they are mutually conformed to, mitigate the calamities of war" (2002: 466–7).

Adherence to the former is a direct moral requirement whereas the authority of the latter rests on the general utility of observing them. Although the two are distinct, the law of nature ratifies the positive law of war. For example, both prohibit

> the slaughter of captives, the subjection of them to indignities or torture, the violation of women, the profanation of temples, the demolition of public buildings, libraries, statues, and in general the destruction or defacing of works that conduce nothing to annoyance or defence.
>
> (Paley 2002: 465–6)

True, if we consult morality alone, then there would seem to be no reason to distinguish between employing poison or assassination (both of which were condemned in Paley's day), on the one hand, and "other methods of destruction, which are practised without scruple by nations at war," on the other. But given that "civilised nations" now shun the use of poison and assassination and that introducing them would, Paley believes, only add to the horror of war without procuring any advantage to the nations engaged in it, then we have strong moral grounds for upholding their prohibition (Paley 2002: 466–7).

The received rules of war specify both the moral and legal duties of belligerents. Almost all governments officially endorse them, and the military establishments of all Western and many other nations incorporate them into their manuals of conduct, teach their officers to enforce them and their personnel to obey them, and punish those who fail to adhere to them.

Utilitarianism and the rules of war

The principal thesis of this chapter and Chapter 7 is that utilitarianism not only strongly endorses the received rules of war but also provides the most plausible and coherent moral basis for them. Those rules find their justification in the fact that adherence to them diminishes the destructiveness of war and, to some extent, makes peaceful reconciliation more likely after a conflict ends. This is true even though some of those rules, in particular, parts of the positive law of armed conflict, may seem arbitrary when looked at from the perspective of ordinary morality.

To take an example similar to Paley's, the law of armed conflict categorically prohibits exploding bullets but not flamethrowers, although both are equally ugly ways to kill someone. It outlaws many kinds of booby traps, such as those attached to graves or to food and drink, but does not ban their use across the board. It regulates in great detail the treatment of prisoners of war. Most of these regulations promote their humane treatment, but others, for example, the requirement that prisoners be allowed to purchase tobacco or to wear insignia of rank, seem relatively trivial from the moral point of view. It has also been alleged that the law gives too much leeway to military necessity (Wasserstrom 1972: 12–13, 19; 1974: 54; but cf. Cohen 1974). For these reasons, it cannot be said, without serious qualification, that the law of war embodies or gives coherent shape to distinctions or principles that loom large in everyday morality. Rather, the law of armed conflict is worthy of moral respect because, overall, it does so much to reduce the harm of war. In most cases, adhering to it promotes human well-being. Even if some of its provisions appear to lack a clear humanitarian rationale, obeying them helps to promote allegiance to the system of rules as a whole, which is valuable. States have a duty to be law-abiding members of the international community and to follow the rules that they have previously agreed to or that are widely accepted by the nations of the world.

This is not to say that we should rest content with the received rules of war and, in particular, the law of armed conflict as it is now. Shaped by the perceived self-interest of existing states, it has evolved in a piecemeal and somewhat vagarious way. Utilitarians and other humanitarian-minded people will naturally seek to refine, clarify, or modify the received rules or even to introduce entirely new ones in an effort to make them as welfare-promoting as possible, taking into account the likelihood of potential belligerents and the people who fight for them being brought to accept and comply with those rules. Thus, James Mill proposed the following "comprehensive and highly important rule":

> That in the modes of carrying on war, every thing should be condemned by the law of nations, which, without being more conducive, or more in any considerable degree, to the attainment of the just end of the war, is much more mischievous to the nation against whom it is done.
>
> (1825: 21)

Presumably, Mill intended his rule to guide the international community in adopting more specific restrictions on warfare, for the comprehensiveness and generality of his rule make it a poor candidate for legal formalization. By contrast, the International Campaign to Ban Landmines is an example of a conscious effort to push the international law of war in a reasonably specific, welfare-enhancing direction. It culminated in the Ottawa Treaty of 1997, the 162 signatories of which are required to cease making anti-personnel mines, to destroy existing stockpiles of them, and to clear any territories they have mined.[4]

While endeavoring, where possible, to add to or otherwise improve upon the received rules of war—perhaps, for example, by interpreting them to restrict more closely attacks on dual-use facilities (Shue and Wippman 2002)—for the foreseeable future utilitarians will probably be more concerned with trying to see that the current rules are subscribed to as widely as possible, that potential combatants and their leaders are taught the rules and internalize a commitment to them, that all military organizations make adherence to them part of their organizational culture, and that further mechanisms are found for institutionalizing and enforcing them.

Most writers on the ethics of war accept that the positive law of armed conflict has, as a whole, a utilitarian or consequentialist justification. Its restrictions find their moral value in the humanitarian good that comes from belligerent parties abiding by them. However, when we turn to the other component of the received rules of war, namely, the rules of *jus in bello* promulgated by just war theory—necessity, proportionality, and discrimination—the situation is a little different. These principles seem to tally with our pre-theoretical intuitions about moral conduct in war, appearing intrinsically important or worthy of respect independent of the results of obeying them. This leads most contemporary just war theorists to believe that those principles, especially that of discrimination and civilian immunity, do not have a consequentialist rationale (e.g., Lee 2012: 165). This is incorrect, though. Utilitarianism underwrites all three normative principles and explains why adherence to them is so important.

Sidgwick on the rules of war

In probing the utilitarian approach to the rules of war, it is helpful to begin with Sidgwick. As he saw it, the goal for utilitarians is to identify the "rules of international duty, applicable to the conditions of war" (1908: 279), to which it would be desirable for states to adhere, and he was upbeat about the progress that had already been made in establishing "rule after rule of military practice, tending to limit the mischief of war to the *minimum* necessary for the attainment of its ends" (1998a: 58). But he was no utopian theorist designing ideal rules for perfect states. The rules have to be "capable of being effectively maintained by the *consensus* of civilised communities," and they have to leave "out of consideration the *justice* of the war on either side" (1908: 279). Let us look more closely at three aspects of Sidgwick's position.

First, the rules of war must apply equally to both sides, ignoring the question of which side is in the right. This might seem perplexing. Surely, one wants to say, it makes all the difference whether it is right for a state to fight. This is true. On the other hand, it is infeasible, Sidgwick argues, to promulgate one set of rules for just combatants and another for unjust combatants. Both states will almost certainly believe (or at least assert) that they are in the right, and even if there were general agreement that one side is in the wrong, there is no practical way to impose special restrictions on how it fights.

There is nothing quite like this in peacetime. True, we could say to a desperado something like "well, if you are going to rob banks, then at least you should avoid injuring anyone," but we do not travel very far down this road. We are much more concerned with getting people to desist from criminal conduct than we are with getting them to carry out that criminal activity in the morally best way on the assumption that they are going to do it anyway. With war it is different. Try as we will to discourage it and, more specifically, to bring morality to bear on the decision whether to wage it in the first place, wars will continue, rightly or wrongly, to break out, affecting the lives of thousands and sometimes millions of people. The goal of the rules of war is to reduce to the greatest extent possible the damage that those wars do. This project makes perfect sense from a utilitarian perspective.

The second important aspect of Sidgwick's position is that the rules must be ones that most states will accept and that they can reasonably be expected to observe. Sidgwick does not elaborate on this, but presumably he believes that states will not follow rules of war that restrict too greatly their fundamental interests, nor can those rules be so onerous that battlefield combatants will not stick to them when push comes to shove. There is no utility in promulgating rules that will be ignored when it really matters. To be effective, the rules should be supported by a consensus of states, but—and this is the third point—unanimity is not required. In particular, we are seeking a consensus of *civilized* states. In saying this, Sidgwick presumably thought there were objective criteria for distinguishing civilized from uncivilized states and that it was the moral opinions of the former that count. On the other hand, it is not implausible, I think, to maintain, at the risk of some circularity, that insofar as it abjures the received rules of war, a state is, to that extent and in that respect, uncivilized. In any case, the important point is that the rules of war retain their force even if some state or small number of states ignores them. A rogue regime cannot, by its aberrant conduct, veto international law or annul the received rules of war.

With these points in mind, Sidgwick identifies the following general principle:

> The aim of a moral combatant must be to disable his opponent, and force him to submission, but not to do him (1) any mischief which does not tend materially to this end, nor (2) any mischief of which the conduciveness to the end is slight in comparison with the amount of the mischief.
>
> (1908: 268)

These two limitations clearly correspond to the previously identified principles of necessity and proportionality, and their utilitarian rationale is evident. Sidgwick admits that the second principle in particular is vague and interpretations of it will differ. Moreover, its application will vary with changes in the arts of war and "in the circumstances and prevailing sentiments of civilised men." And in discussing the more specific implications of his general principle, he acknowledges various difficulties in applying it as well as points on which opinion is changing or has recently changed.

Michael Walzer (2006b: 129–33) has criticized Sidgwick's principle. He concedes that ruling out purposeless or excessive violence would eliminate a great deal of cruelty in war, but he contends that Sidgwick's principle would still permit any act of war that a belligerent deems conducive to winning. That is not entirely accurate: Sidgwick's principle forbids needless or disproportionate violence, not just violence that the perpetrator believes to be needless or disproportionate. Still, Walzer is correct that, guided by Sidgwick's principle, it would be difficult to condemn combatants for doing whatever they honestly believed was necessary and reasonable for victory. In any case, Walzer's more important contention is that Sidgwick's principle omits an important part of the war convention, namely, the principle of discrimination and non-combatant immunity. As I shall discuss later, there is some truth in this. However, to be fair to Sidgwick, he clearly believed that his general principle precluded attacking civilians. For example, he wrote that refraining from "inflicting personal injury on noncombatants" is an "important rule … which—we may confidently hope—will in future restrain civilised belligerents" (1908: 269). And he rejected the idea that an enemy can be coerced into submission by harsh treatment of its civilian population.

Brandt's approach

Richard Brandt was a leading twentieth-century utilitarian, and his widely cited 1972 essay, "Utilitarianism and the Rules of War," was the first sustained discussion of this topic since Sidgwick. It is still the best known. Despite its insights, though, the essay has serious shortcomings.

Brandt's approach is distinctive. He begins by asking which rules of war are morally justified. His answer is that they are the rules that would be selected by rational people choosing behind a veil of ignorance—that is, not knowing what wars their nations will be fighting in, what weaponry they will have, or what role they as individuals will occupy in that war. And what rules will these people choose? They will select rules of war that "maximize expectable long-range utility for nations at war" (Brandt 1972: 150). This is an idealized version, Brandt explains, of what representatives at international conferences on the regulation of war, such as the Hague or Geneva Conventions, attempt to do. That is, on the assumption that many of their nations will be at war at some point, the delegates try to decide, "in the light of calculated national self-interest and the principles of common humanity," what rules they are prepared to commit themselves to in advance without knowing "how the fortunes of war might strike them in particular" (1972: 151).

Those rules must not prevent a belligerent in a serious conflict from using whatever force is necessary to overcome the enemy (1972: 152). One might wonder why utility-maximizing rules must not significantly inhibit the ability of a belligerent to prevail in a conflict. Perhaps rules that sometimes did prevent a state from doing what was necessary to win would be utility-maximizing, and behind a veil of ignorance one would not know when, if ever, that would happen to one's own state. But, as Brandt explains, "neither side will consent to or follow rules of war which seriously impair the possibility of bringing the war to a victorious conclusion" (1972: 154). Thus, rational, impartial persons choosing behind a veil of ignorance will want rules of war that maximize utility in the real world, which entails that those rules have to be acceptable to states that are neither impartial nor in ignorance of their strategic situation and military capabilities.

States can easily, Brandt argues, agree to rules forbidding actions, such as abusing prisoners of war or harming civilians or their property in occupied territories, that contribute little or nothing to victory. Adherence to these rules imposes no military cost and benefits both sides. Moreover, direct calculation of utility cannot justify deviating from these rules; they are "absolute" (1972: 147). Thus, a military commander may not kill his prisoners because keeping them alive might threaten an important operation. Because states do not know exactly what the future will bring, it can also be in their collective self-interest to accept and follow more demanding rules of a humanitarian nature, rules that increase the cost of victory but do not affect the ultimate outcome of the war or jeopardize the ability of either party to prevail. Whatever military gains or losses come from following these rules are likely to be distributed evenly, Brandt argues, so that neither side gains a long-term advantage if the rules are observed (1972: 161).

In line with this, Brandt proposes the following principle for serious wars where the stakes are extremely high (as they were, he says, in World War II): "Substantial destruction of lives and property of enemy civilians is permissible only when there is good evidence that it will significantly enhance the prospect of victory" (1972: 156). Because following such a rule would reduce human suffering and yet not seriously impede the pursuit of victory, Brandt reasons, both parties to a war could accept it. In minor wars where less is at stake, there will be a higher and more demanding standard of what counts as "good evidence" and "significantly enhance." What a state may do when the stakes are high and what it may do when they are low both reflect the following general principle, which is, Brandt writes, applicable to all types of war:

> A military action (e.g., a bombing raid) is permissible only if the utility (broadly conceived, so that the maintenance of treaty obligations of international law could count as a utility) of victory to all concerned, multiplied by the increase in its probability if the action is executed, on the evidence (when the evidence is reasonably solid, considering the stakes), is greater than the possible disutility of the action to both sides multiplied by its probability.
>
> (1972: 157)

At first glance, this general principle seems simply to apply the utilitarian criterion of right to any contemplated military action. However, Brandt's principle involves no consideration of alternatives. It requires that military actions produce more expected good than harm, but not that they have greater expected good than alternative actions would have. This may have been an oversight on Brandt's part. Perhaps, though, he thought that it would be too difficult for belligerents to follow the full utilitarian principle, even though it provides the theoretically correct basis for appraising military operations, and so was proposing a simplified version of it.

In a utilitarian spirit, Brandt's principle refers to "the utility ... of victory to all concerned." However, Brandt believes that because both sides in a major struggle will have persuaded themselves that their cause is just, "it makes very little difference whether the more general principle uses the concept of the utility of victory by one side for everyone concerned, or the utility for that side only" (1972: 157n). This is a curious thing to say because there is a clear difference between the utility of victory for one side and its utility for everyone, even if belligerents are prone to confuse the two. Furthermore, although both sides are likely to believe that they are right to fight, they may not believe that their victory, although best for them, maximizes the well-being of all. Accordingly, they may find Brandt's general principle too restrictive to accept as a criterion of morally justified military operations.

This problem aside, Brandt's general principle, whether he saw it as equivalent to the utilitarian criterion of right or only as a truncated version of that criterion, is far too difficult to use in practice, requiring, as it does, calculating the expected net utility of each and every military action. It is analogous to telling automobile drivers that they should drive their vehicles in a way that promotes overall utility without giving them any more specific traffic rules to follow. In war, actors need secondary rules to guide them; they cannot possibly make the calculations required by Brandt's principle with any accuracy. Indeed, as R.M. Hare remarks:

> If armies were to say to soldiers when training them, "On the battlefield, always do what is most conducive to the general good of mankind," or even "of your countrymen," nearly all the soldiers would easily convince themselves (battles being what they are) that the course most conducive to these desirable ends was headlong flight.
>
> (1972: 175)

What is odd about Brandt's stance in this essay is that he is a rule utilitarian; he believes that right and wrong are determined, not by direct appeal to utility, but rather by the set of rules, the promulgation and acceptance of which would maximize utility (Brandt 1979, 1992). But the rule that he thinks it would maximize utility for belligerents to follow is either act utilitarianism or something quite close to it. By contrast, in maintaining that the secondary principles utilitarians should follow do not define "the right act," this book follows Sidgwick in adhering to an act-utilitarian criterion of right. On the other hand, in certain sorts of situations I advocate taking these rules as seriously as any rule utilitarian does and, indeed, as seriously as most non-consequentialists do, maintaining that some of them are so important for people to follow that they should internalize a commitment to them, consider their observance intrinsically important, and refrain from violating them in all but the most extreme circumstances.

One of these rules is the principle of discrimination and civilian immunity. Adherence to it does so much to reduce the harm of war that it should not be treated as a mere guideline or rule of thumb. Rather, it should be an inflexible part of the personal and professional moral code of combatants.

Walzer's critique of the utilitarian approach

From a utilitarian perspective, I maintain, it is desirable to affirm and, as far as possible, entrench the right of civilians not to be attacked and to oblige warring states to take whatever steps they reasonably can to avoid injuring them or their property. Brandt errs in not recognizing this, and Sidgwick, too, fails to give civilian immunity the importance it warrants from a utilitarian perspective. Like Paley and James Mill (1825: 22), they treat it, not as a stand-alone principle, but only as an aspect of the principle that gratuitous and unnecessary violence, violence not conducive and proportional to the military goal being sought, is to be avoided. In my view, however, utilitarians want states and quasi-state actors to recognize, uphold, and institutionalize the principle of civilian immunity without regard to considerations of military advantage; to have military establishments pledge their allegiance to this principle and to train their troops to follow it; and to have individual soldiers internalize a commitment to it.

Michael Walzer (2006b: 131–5), however, doubts that utilitarianism can ground the principle of non-combatant immunity, for at least three reasons. The first is that calculating the likely effects over time of different possible restrictions on combat is enormously difficult (see also McMahan 2010a: 504). This is perhaps true as a general proposition, but one can hardly take seriously skepticism (e.g., Lee 2012: 207) about the long-term beneficial effects of adherence to the rule that belligerents are (a) not to attack civilians and (b) to minimize incidental harm to them. The direct and indirect civilian casualties of war are often shockingly high,[5] and one of the simplest things the world can do to reduce those casualties is to continue insisting that belligerents always discriminate between combatants and non-combatants and minimize harm to the latter.

Walzer's second argument, which many others have also advanced (e.g., Kutz 2005: 167; Primoratz 2007: 25; Zupan 2004: 18), is that the long-term utilitarian case for respecting civilian immunity will inevitably run up against belligerents who argue that in their particular situation, victory requires putting aside the principle of civilian immunity, contending that their victory is so valuable that whatever is useful to achieving it should be permitted. In response, the first point to make is that belligerents who argue this way are almost certainly wrong, and indeed it is doubtful that Walzer and like-minded thinkers really believe otherwise. States may talk themselves into believing that victory hangs on deliberately targeting civilians or not taking due care to avoid harming them, but it is difficult to find cases in which this has actually been true. And even in the unlikely case in which refraining from directly attacking civilians did prevent one side from winning, there is a good chance that its victory would not have satisfied UWP in the first place or at least that it would not satisfy it if killing civilians is the price of winning. Furthermore, the principle of non-combatant immunity is so beneficial that it is worth upholding across the board even in the (hypothetical) case in which permitting its violation would maximize utility. As discussed before, we cannot obtain the benefits of having fixed rules and yet countenance one's violating them whenever one believes that doing so would be for the best. Utilitarians will therefore want the principle of discrimination and civilian immunity to be part of the "intuitive" moral code (Hare 1981) of combatants, that is, to be a principle that guides their day-to-day conduct and that it would deeply disturb their conscience to violate.

Against a utilitarian account of non-combatant immunity, Walzer (2006b: 133) argues, third, that "no limit [on the waging of war] is accepted simply because it is thought that it will be useful." Rather, it "must first be morally plausible to large numbers of men and women; it must correspond to our sense of what is right" (see also Lee 2012: 206; Norman 1995: 165; Primoratz 2007: 26–7). It is true, of course, that if the rules are to be effective, then belligerents must find them morally acceptable. But Walzer's contention rests on a false dichotomy. The rules can seem "morally plausible" to men and women in uniform just because of the humanitarian benefits of following them. True, when a rule, such as not targeting civilians, has become part of a combatant's moral code, he or she will see adherence to it as being intrinsically important, as one of the duties incumbent on those who bear arms. But that does not entail that the true justification of the rule lies somewhere other than in its consequential value. Moreover, many of the received rules of war do not correspond to a pre-existing "sense of what is right." When thinking about war, we do not, I believe, have an antecedent conviction that it is wrong to prevent medical supplies but not food or other crucial provisions from reaching enemy troops or wrong to use hollow point bullets or blinding lasers but not fragmenting grenades or incendiary weapons. These restrictions are morally plausible, to be sure, but only because, despite being somewhat arbitrary, they help reduce the harm of war.

To this line of argument, Walzer responds that utilitarianism lacks "creative power." Beyond insisting on necessity and proportionality, utilitarianism "simply confirms our customs and conventions, whatever they are"; it does not provide us with customs and conventions (2006b: 133). To be sure, utilitarians believe, correctly, that general adherence to those customs and conventions—the received rules of war—promotes net human well-being. However, the phrase "whatever they are" renders Walzer's statement false. Utilitarians have no difficulty criticizing existing rules if they are suboptimal or counterproductive, nor will they hesitate to propose utility-promoting refinements or additions to those rules. It is true, of course, that utilitarians are not free to remake from scratch the received rules of war, any more than they can reinvent the rules of commonsense morality. They must work with the accepted rules as they find them. In his *Methods of Ethics*, Sidgwick (1966: 453–7) maintains that utilitarianism and commonsense morality roughly coincide. Although the latter is not expressly utilitarian, it tends over time increasingly to move in a utilitarian direction. As a general proposition, this is debatable, but it seems reasonably accurate with regard to utilitarianism and the received rules of war. Adherence to them clearly promotes human well-being, and their evolution over the decades has been in a welfare-enhancing direction.

In repudiating a utilitarian approach to non-combatant immunity, Walzer contends that "the rules of war are grounded in a theory of rights" and, more specifically, that the principle of non-combatant immunity is premised on the idea that non-combatants have rights, which means that "they cannot be used for some military purpose, even if it is a legitimate purpose" (2006b: 137). This view is orthodoxy among contemporary just war theorists. But Walzer's contentions are erroneous.

To begin with, a rights-based approach fails to account for those aspects of the received rules of war which, although beneficial, are conventional in character and do not correspond to any antecedent rights of individuals, such as some of the Geneva Convention's detailed provisions governing the treatment of prisoners of war. The same point holds for the more abstract principles of necessity and pro-portionality. It is wrong for belligerents to use violence that is unrelated to some military objective or that is excessive or disproportionate in relation to it. But it is strained to claim that they have these duties *because* enemy soldiers have a prior right not to be killed if the military objective in question could be obtained in a less costly way or that civilians have a right that their amusement parks but not their highways and phone lines be preserved from attack, a right that supposedly pre-exists the rules of war.

Nor can we say even that the principle of discrimination and non-combatant immunity is grounded in a "theory of rights." First, as I shall discuss in Chapter 7, Walzer and some other rights theorists believe that in exceptional circumstances, it is permissible to target civilians.[6] Possibly they are correct to believe this but, if so, it is hard to see how rights theory explains why they are. Second, whether or not they agree with Walzer on this point, the vast majority of rights theorists believe that it is permissible to kill civilians if their deaths are both incidental and proportional to the goal being sought. But, again, it is hard to see how the fact that civilians have a right to life explains why it is permissible to kill them in these circumstances. One can contend, I suppose, that in this case the rights of the civil-ians were respected because, in being killed, they were not "*used* for some military purpose," but for the people whose lives were treated as expendable, that is small consolation. Things are made murkier by the fact that even if rights theory some-times permits killing civilians, it entails or seems to entail that those individuals have a right to defend themselves against the combatants who are justifiably threat-ening them; if they were to exercise that right, however, then the just combatants would now have a right to target them directly (Steinhoff 2007: 95–7).

Some rights theorists lean toward anti-war pacifism, believing that it is wrong not only to kill civilians deliberately but also to act in ways that foreseeably bring about their deaths because doing either violates their right to life. Other rights theorists, as I have just mentioned, believe that it is wrong to kill civilians inten-tionally but not necessarily wrong foreseeably to bring about their deaths. Finally, some rights theorists hold that in certain circumstances it is permissible to target civilians directly. Thus, when it comes to war and, specifically, to how we are to understand civilian immunity, so-called rights theory is inconclusive. Indeed, it seems fair to surmise that which of the above positions a rights theorist favors and how he or she develops that position are determined by what moral trade-offs the theorist is willing to accept. The belief that individuals have rights does not settle the issue one way or the other; it does no real work.

I am certainly not claiming that combatants and non-combatants do not have rights. Rather, that they have the rights they do is the conclusion of the argu-ment, not its premise. That is to say, combatants and non-combatants have certain specific rights because of the enormous utility that comes from recognizing and protecting those particular claims and entitlements. Consequentialist considera-tions justify the rules of war, which in turn determine the rights that people caught up in war have and that states and their combatants are bound to respect.

Mavrodes's conventionalism

I have been arguing that a rights-based approach cannot fully explain, underwrite, or morally justify the received rules of war, including that of civilian immunity. Utilitarianism can. Those rules are ones that we can reasonably expect belligerents to understand, accept, and endeavor to adhere to, and the following of which greatly promotes human well-being. Although some modification of those rules may be possible and desirable, for the foreseeable future, at least, there is no feasible, fundamentally different set of rules, the promulgation of which is likely to have greater expected utility.

The utilitarian approach resembles in certain respects the view, famously put forward by George Mavrodes (1975), that the rules of war are a mere convention and that our obligation to adhere to them is a convention-dependent moral obligation like the obligation to drive on the right-hand side of the road if that is the practice in our country. Civilian immunity from direct attack is a convention, Mavrodes argues, and as with the other conventions that make up the rules of war, for example, not taking hostages or not using bacteriological weapons, our obligation to adhere to it depends on others doing so as well. The standard objection to Mavrodes is that although it may make sense to view some of the received rules of war—regarding, say, the delivery of Red Cross packages to prisoners of war—as mere conventions, which we have a duty to obey only if others do so as well, our obligation not to kill civilians seems intuitively to go deeper than this. That obligation rests, it is claimed, not on a contingent custom, practice, or agreement, but on the fact that doing so is simply wrong. In other words, the wrongness of killing civilians is independent of, and prior to, the convention.

Some writers hold that it is intrinsically evil for combatants to kill civilians but not necessarily wrong for them to kill enemy combatants, at least if those combatants are wrong to be fighting, because the former are innocent and the latter are not (Anscombe 1981a, 1981b). Mavrodes and other writers have thoroughly debunked this idea. Some civilians may have worked hard to bring about an aggressive war, conscious of its unjust character, whereas some soldiers may be fighting only because they have been drafted into the army or do not know any better; they may even oppose the very war they are fighting. It is implausible, then, to equate one's status as a combatant or non-combatant with guilt or innocence. Indeed, some have argued that because civilians in a democracy bear responsibility for the wars their state wages, they cannot claim to have a right not to be harmed by the wars they have authorized (Green 1992; Held 2004: 67).

On the other hand, combatants are, and non-combatants are not, part of an armed and organized military force, geared toward fighting. The contrast between the two is salient and easy to grasp; moreover, it seems intuitively important because it coincides with the fact that the general point of military action is to defeat the army of the other side. Thus, the contrast makes for a workable norm, adherence to which has great utility, even though it does not coincide with the distinction between those who are guilty and those who are innocent. Indeed, contrary to Fullinwider (1975), it does not even coincide with the distinction between those who pose a threat and those who do not. The rules of war permit a belligerent to attack enemy soldiers who are off-duty or deep behind the frontlines and currently pose no threat; indeed, with some exceptions (for example, military medical personnel), they permit attacking all those who are in uniform even if the person is employed as, say, a cook, valet, or press officer and does not represent even a potential threat. Of course, all such personnel help the military machine to function and that machine does pose a danger. But then so do people in all sorts of civilian occupations, such as farmers and the manufacturers of combat boots, dog tags, and ready-to-eat meals. They, too, contribute to the war effort and, thus, to the military threat one faces.[7] They do not, however, participate in the fighting either directly or indirectly, nor are they members of a military organization that is engaged in fighting.

Utilitarians deny that the lives of combatants matter less than the lives of civilians or that an intrinsic wrongness attaches to killing the latter but not the former. They are thus in broad agreement with Mavrodes that the principle of discrimination and civilian immunity does not reflect a difference in the value of the lives of combatants and non-combatants or in their fundamental moral status as human beings but is, rather, a rule or convention, which is justified in terms of its expectable results. That convention greatly reduces the harm of war, compared to having no such convention. Utilitarians also agree with Mavrodes that in principle alternative conventions are possible (1975: 124–5). Some of these might, theoretically at least, have better results, but few if any of them are live options. For instance, a plausible-sounding, but infeasible, rule would be one that prohibited imposing any harm at all on civilians or their property. Such a rule would, if adhered to, greatly reduce the death and destruction that war brings, but states would not adopt it because, by making war almost impossible, it would be tantamount to pacifism. If, however, there were a rule that, unlike this one, could be the basis of a viable convention and the embracing of which would have better results than the current rule, then, according to utilitarianism, we would have an obligation to promote its adoption.

Utilitarians, however, differ from Mavrodes in how they understand one's obligation to respect civilian immunity. Mavrodes believes, as I have said, that obligation is convention dependent; for him, this means that the convention is the source of the obligation and that if the other side does not adhere to it, then one has no obligation to do so either. For utilitarians, the source of one's obligation to support and adhere to the convention is the duty to promote well-being. Respecting civilian immunity produces better results than would following no rule at all, and there is no practicable rule that would have better results. But whereas Mavrodes holds that one has no obligation to follow the rule if others do not, for utilitarians the matter is more complex. For them reciprocity is not the central issue; the question is whether advocating, supporting, and internalizing a commitment to the rule is a utility-maximizing policy. There are situations in war and elsewhere in which no good at all follows from sticking to a rule if others do not, and there are weapons and tactics that we cannot reasonably expect one side to refrain from employing when it would be militarily advantageous to do so if the other side does not. With civilian immunity, however, it is different.

Consider a state fighting an opponent that deliberately targets civilians or that is indifferent to the collateral damage it inflicts on them. Its conduct violates the convention, but although it may thus weaken the convention, it does not destroy it. So the state that is fighting the rogue opponent still has reason to adhere to the rule because doing so helps maintain and reinforce the current, welfare-enhancing convention, whereas violating it would serve only to undermine it further, making it more likely that other states, too, will ignore it in the future. Suppose, however, that there were no such convention. Even so, there would still be strong utilitarian grounds for adhering to the principle of discrimination and civilian immunity as part of an effort to establish such a convention.

But suppose that endeavor were hopeless and that nothing the state could do would help to bring the convention about. A utilitarian-minded state would, of course, still continue to follow the principles of necessity and proportionality, which in turn ordinarily rule out attacking civilians. However, it would seem that a state would have no reason to adhere to the principle of discrimination and civilian immunity if it believed that doing so was not the welfare-maximizing course of action in a given tactical situation. Rather, it should simply choose the means of attacking the enemy likely to cause the fewest deaths and injuries, counting combatant and civilian causalities as equivalent (Lackey 1989: 64–5; Lefkowitz 2008: 159–60). This is incorrect, however. Given the likelihood of believing oneself to be in exceptional circumstances when one is not, there are strong grounds for the utilitarian-minded state to cleave to the rule across the board, training its troops to see it as their duty always to respect civilian immunity. This is because minimizing harm to civilians is almost always the welfare-maximizing course of action, and the danger of harming civilians when, on utilitarian grounds, one should not is significantly greater than the risk of missing a chance to harm them in those very rare cases when this would in fact be the correct utilitarian thing to do. Lefkowitz (2008: 163–4) writes that utilitarians will "regret" and indeed "lament" the fact that they will inevitably be unable to identify, and will therefore miss, opportunities to maximize expected well-being by intentionally targeting non-combatants. This, however, misconstrues the psychology of those who, as utilitarianism requires, have internalized a strong moral and professional commitment to civilian immunity.

The deep morality of war

Although simple and, in a way, obvious, a utilitarian approach to the rules of war captures well why they matter so much. It is also easier to square, than are some other ways of thinking about those rules, with some of their distinctive and otherwise troubling features—in particular, the fact that the rules have to be such that states can reasonably be expected to endorse them; the fact that they apply to both sides equally whether they are right to fight or not; the fact that aspects of the rules seem somewhat arbitrary from a moral point of view (for example, the outlawing of poison gas but not flamethrowers or the fact that some combatants may be morally innocent); and the fact that the rules, while seeking to minimize the harm done to children and other innocent civilians, permit belligerents sometimes to bring about their deaths.

These features of the received rules of war have led some to distinguish them from what they refer to as the "deep morality of war." By this, they mean that the received rules do not accurately capture the true morality of combat; rather, they are a kind of pragmatic concession to the lamentable reality that general rules, if they are to be effective, cannot draw the fine distinctions that morality does. Thus, Jeff McMahan maintains that for various practical reasons, the rules of war cannot follow morality in holding (as he believes) that soldiers fighting on the unjust side act wrongly in killing combatants on the other side and that the just side may in some circumstances permissibly target civilians (McMahan 2006, 2009, 2010a: 497–9). For writers such as McMahan, the received rules of war lack deep moral grounding. Now, to be sure, there is probably room for improving upon the received rules of war, and utilitarians, as I have said, will endeavor to win recognition and acceptance of the best possible set of rules. But even if the rules were the best they could be, McMahan believes that they would still be morally inadequate because, basically, they could never ensure that individuals are treated only according to their moral due.

Utilitarians and other critics of this view deny that there could be a morality of war that was different from the best possible rules for regulating war. McMahan and like-minded thinkers fail to appreciate the limits to what can be imposed on combat in the name of morality. The moral and legal regulation of war is not aimed at distributing its harms based on fairness, desert, or rights or on the differential moral liability of individuals to attack. Rather, it aims at minimizing as far as possible the destructive effects of war. The received rules of war presuppose armed conflict. They endeavor to regulate it but not to make it impossible, and in doing so they sometimes permit or forbid actions that are not permitted or forbidden by the rules of law and morality that are appropriate in ordinary life. In particular, war cannot be fought without violating the rights that people have in normal times; to suppose that it could is a philosopher's chimera (Shue 2008: 111). Philosophers such as McMahan "over-moralize war," giving us, in effect, an "account of what individual responsibility in war would be like if war were a peacetime activity" (Walzer 2006a: 43; cf. Shue 2010: 519).

Some utilitarians have used the term "deep morality of war" to capture the difference between act-utilitarian appraisal of a given war and the public rules that utilitarians will support for use in deciding whether to wage that war (Sinnott-Armstrong 2007: 204). Earlier chapters of this book fit with this way of looking at things. Although UWP provides the correct or "deep" criterion for determining whether it is right for a state to wage war, utilitarianism recommends that in practice one follow certain secondary principles, specifically, the traditional *jus ad bellum* guidelines. The latter are intended to assist us in establishing whether waging war would satisfy UWP. But whether to wage war is an infrequent question and, when it arises, it involves the most serious consequences. Thus, it makes sense, even when following the *jus ad bellum* rules, never to have UWP too far out of view.

When it comes to the received rules of war, however, the situation is different for we are dealing not with one big moral question, but with the countless choices that combatants must make in the course of a war that is already in progress. The rules governing combat, I have been arguing, are not mere rules of thumb; they form part of the intuitive morality that utilitarians want combatants to internalize and embrace and to feel guilty about violating. There are not simply guidelines intended to help them to make correct act-utilitarian decisions when they are fighting. Although something like Brandt's general principle might state the theoretically correct utilitarian criterion of when a military operation is morally justified, telling combatants to conform to it would be pointless because doing so would require knowledge they do not have. Moreover, urging them to adhere directly to the utilitarian standard will have bad consequences because, in endeavoring to follow it in the heat of war, they will almost certainly err—both because of the inherent uncertainties of the situation and because bias, emotion, and self-interest will distort their judgments.

McMahan (2010a: 505) rejects the idea that, when it comes to war, a different kind of morality applies. Utilitarians agree. For them, there is just one ultimate moral standard, but it has radically different implications in war than it does in times of peace. When it comes to war, utilitarianism seeks to salvage as much good as possible in what is, to say the least, a non-ideal situation, by upholding and endeavoring to strengthen and perhaps to refine the received rules of war. Those rules and the moral convictions that it is appropriate for combatants to have will differ from the rules and moral convictions that are appropriate for peacetime, but both sets are grounded in the same ultimate moral imperative.

Notes

1 For different presentations of the principles of *jus in bello*, see Bellamy (2006: 124–5, 127), Coates (1997: 209–72), Coleman (2013: 151–62), Fabre (2012: 5), Fisher (2011: 76–9), Frowe and Lang (2014: xiv), Guthrie and Quinlan (2007: 35–43), Lackey (1989: 59–60), May (2007: 167–232), Orend (2006: 106–19), Regan (2013: 88–99), Rhodes (2009: 104–12), Steinhoff (2007: 3), and Whetham (2011: 80–1). Some of these presentations omit the principle of necessity even though the other principles can, as Crane and Reisner (2011: 69) and Dill and Shue (2012: 321–2) observe, be seen as flowing from it.

2 Before the fall of Singapore, Churchill expressed sentiments at odds with this:

> There must be at this stage no thought of saving the troops or sparing the population. The battle must be fought to the bitter end and at all costs … Commanders and senior officers should die with their troops. The honour of the British Empire and the British Army is at stake.
>
> (Quoted in Burleigh 2011: 263)

3 "The principle of proportionality is … in tension, but not necessarily in conflict, with the current US military doctrine, which favors overwhelming use of force in order to achieve decisive victory quickly and at minimum cost in terms of US casualties" (Roberts 2003: 184).

4 A number of important states, including Russia, China, and the United States, have yet to sign the treaty, so a ban on anti-personnel mines cannot be said, at least not yet, to be part of the customary law of war. For its part, the United States has pledged not to use anti-personnel mines outside the Korean Peninsula.

5 For some pertinent figures, see Downes (2008: 44–7).

6 Indeed, for Kamm (2012: 36, 38, 74), it seems, the circumstances do not have to be all that exceptional.

7 Anscombe (1981b) and Walzer (2006b: 146) contend that there is a morally significant distinction between contributing what soldiers need to fight and what they need to live so that, for instance, it is permissible to attack workers who make weapons for the army but not those who grow its food. Fabre (2009) has shown that this position is untenable. James Mill (1825: 21–2) acknowledges that civilians contribute to the war effort but wisely maintains that they should still be demarcated from combatants.

7

COMBATANTS AND NON-COMBATANTS

The received rules of war comprise the specific and often detailed rules that make up the positive law of armed conflict as well as the more general normative principles of necessity, proportionality, and non-combatant immunity. Those principles restrict the conduct of combatants independently of the law, but many of its provisions reflect those principles and, in turn, make their requirements more determinate. Chapter 6 contended not only that utilitarianism strongly supports the received rules of war, encouraging states and those who fight for them to adhere firmly to them, but also that only a consequentialist account satisfactorily explains why those rules have the moral force that they do. This chapter continues that argument, probing more fully the status, respectively, of combatants and non-combatants. In so doing, I reiterate some points made in Chapter 6, but that is unavoidable in expanding on these matters and refining and deepening our understanding of the utilitarian approach to the ethics of combat.

Are combatants morally equal?

The received rules of war and, in particular, the principle of discrimination and civilian immunity require one to distinguish between combatants and non-combatants, to directly target only the former, and to take reasonable steps to avoid harming the latter. But what justifies the attacking of combatants? The answer is easy if a state is fighting a morally legitimate war. In that case, its military forces are justified in assaulting those of the other side in an effort to win that war. In particular, if UWP shows that it is right for a state to fight, then the likely casualties on both sides have already been taken into account. One does not need to show both that a state acts rightly in waging war and then, separately, that it is permissible for it to use deadly force against enemy combatants.

War is a struggle between collectivities—between states or state-like entities. Soldiers, airmen, sailors, and marines are the human instruments of this struggle. Although it is individuals who do the killing, combatants on the opposed sides are not personal enemies. Combatants fighting in a justified war are warranted in attacking and possibly killing combatants on the other side not because of anything those men and women have done or not done to them personally but, rather, because they are the means of war employed by the other state and one is justified in warring against it. Some contemporary philosophers balk at this. Applying the norms of the civilian world, they think that one is justified in shooting at the warriors on the unjust side only if they are at fault, deserve to be attacked, or have through their actions in some way or other made themselves morally liable to attack. But this is the wrong way to look at it. That one is justified in attacking them hangs on nothing other than the fact that those individuals are part of the military machine now arrayed against a state that is justified in resisting it. The men and women who make up that machine may not know that their state is waging a morally unjustified war; they may have had little or no choice in becoming part of the military; and their duties may involve their doing nothing that threatens anyone on the other side. Nevertheless, in donning uniforms and playing however modest a role in that war effort, they have become part of a military machine that the other side is justified in trying to vanquish.

All this will, I think, seem obvious to most people. When fighting a morally justified war, a state is permitted to assault the other side's army and slay its soldiers (subject to the principles of necessity and proportionality and to the requirements of the other rules of war, such as, the duty to give quarter). Of course, not all warring armies are involved in justified wars. If they are not, then those armies should not be fighting. The received rules of war, however, do not condemn the ordinary personnel of those armies for endeavoring to kill troops on the opposed side. Those rules forbid their attacking non-combatants, of course, but allow them to target enemy soldiers even if the latter are prosecuting a morally justified war and their own side should not be fighting in the first place. How can this be?

Chapter 6 gave the simple but, I believe, correct answer to that question: The moral point of the rules is not to prevent or halt war, but to limit the harm it does once it has, for whatever reason, broken out. With this goal, the rules endeavor to regulate how war is fought; they seek to make it no more cruel and destructive than it absolutely has to be. If those rules are to have any success, they cannot simply forbid one side—or perhaps both sides if neither is waging a justified war—from fighting, telling its combatants that in killing anyone, whether a combatant or a non-combatant, they are committing murder. Such a rule would accomplish nothing because both sides are likely to believe that they are in the right; in any case, they have already committed themselves to fighting. After war has erupted and hostilities begun, better results come from setting aside the *ad bellum* question of whether the state they represent is right to fight and focusing instead on getting military personnel on both sides to control their own conduct and to follow certain rules, overall adherence to which significantly mitigates the damage of war.

In a sense, this is a pragmatic concession to reality, but there is no other choice. When war breaks out, we are in a non-ideal, suboptimal state of affairs. The received rules of war cannot remedy that. All they can strive to do is to lessen the death and destruction that follow. This implies imposing identical rules on both sides regardless of whether their armies are right to fight, rules that it is reasonable to believe that states and their fighters can be brought to accept and follow. There is, interestingly, a long-standing view that entails that this stance is not entirely pragmatic and result-oriented. It maintains, rather, that independent, largely non-consequentialist moral considerations make it appropriate for the rules of war to ignore whether the combatants whose conduct they seek to regulate are fighting in a justified war. This is because, or so it is argued, ordinary soldiers, airmen, sailors, and marines are not responsible for the rightness or wrongness of the cause they are fighting for. Even if the side for which they are bearing arms is in the wrong, they are either justified in fighting for it anyway or at least to be held morally blameless for doing so.

This is called the doctrine of the "moral equality of combatants." Embraced by a number of earlier writers and in our own time by Michael Walzer, it holds that soldiers on the justified and on the unjustified side of the conflict are moral equals in the sense that neither set of soldiers acts wrongly in fighting (Margalit and Walzer 2009; Walzer 2006b: 36–7). If the doctrine is correct, then the fact that the received rules of war do not distinguish between combatants based on the justice of their cause is not merely a practical necessity; it reflects a deeper moral truth. Combatants on both sides are, in the old-fashioned terminology of just war theory, "morally innocent"; they are not to be held responsible for the morality or immorality of the war their state is waging, and they do no wrong in attempting to kill combatants on the other side. Defenders of the doctrine marshal several arguments in its favor: For instance, that we cannot expect ordinary men and women to know whether the war they are fighting is justified or not, nor is this their responsibility; that if they willingly take up arms, then they consent to being attacked by those on the other side; and that if, to the contrary, they do not volunteer but are coerced or brainwashed into fighting, then they cannot be blamed for doing so.

The moral-equality-of-combatants thesis has a certain intuitive appeal. We rarely hold individual combatants responsible for the wars they fight or criticize or blame them for participating in them, focusing moral assessment instead on the political leaders who bring about those wars or lead their states into them. And, indeed, after a war has ended, depending perhaps on how it was fought, ex-combatants sometimes have a certain regard or fellow feeling for their former enemies based on their shared experience, seeing their erstwhile opponents as ordinary human beings just like them, no better or worse, who were swept up in a larger conflagration outside their control.[1] Jeff McMahan (2009), however, has mounted an extended and very influential attack on this thesis. We do not, it seems to me, need to explore the details of McMahan's arguments to see the force of his stance: If a given war is wrong, then it cannot be right for anyone to fight that war. This strikes many as an elementary truth.

Let us assume that it is (I say more about it in Chapter 8). Nevertheless, as I have suggested, in many, perhaps most, cases we do not wish to condemn, let alone punish, the ordinary men and women who participate in an unjust war. For a variety of reasons, we may be inclined to excuse their conduct or, at least, not to judge them too harshly. But this does not entail that in joining the fight they acted rightly. For example, about many Germans who fought in World War II, we may well want to say that because they either knew or should have known better, it was wrong of them to have participated in that war and to have killed Allied soldiers—even if the cost to them of having avoided service, and thus the morally unjustified killing of anyone, would have been high. Those who join the military, whether voluntarily or under some sort of constraint, are moral agents, responsible for the choices they make. War does not relieve them of their agency or moral account-ability. Now it may be, as I shall discuss in Chapter 8, that professional military personnel have competing responsibilities and that they should perhaps fight as their state directs, at least in a democracy, unless the war is seriously wrong, its wrongness is manifest, and their refusing to fight will do some good. Nevertheless, in many cases it will still be true, as McMahan believes, that in signing up to fight a war that one knows or should know is morally wrong or in allowing oneself to be enrolled in that fight, one is doing what it is objectively wrong for one to do.

Let us grant for the sake of discussion that McMahan is broadly correct and that it is not right for one to fight in a war that should not be fought. What are the implications of this? McMahan believes that those who fight in a morally unjus-tified war cannot fight that war in a just way even if they attempt to obey the received rules of war. This is (1) because they lack any legitimate targets to attack (because the combatants on the other side, the side that is morally justified in fight-ing, have a right not to be attacked [McMahan 2009: 15–16]) and (2) because the death and destruction they wreak will always be disproportional to the military objectives they hope to achieve (because they can have no legitimate military objectives in the first place [McMahan 2009: 24, 30; see also Hurka 2005: 45; Rodin 2008: 53]). But this is to misconstrue the principle of *in bello* proportional-ity as well as the principle of discrimination. If combatants fight within the rules, then they fight justly, that is, in an appropriate or legitimate way. And they fight within the rules if the harm they cause is proportional to the military, as opposed to the overall moral, value of their goal. Likewise, combatants fight in the correct way if they discriminate between combatants and non-combatants. They are not also required to distinguish between combatants based on whether the state they are fighting for is or is not right to be waging war.

McMahan understands this, of course. His point is that there is, in an important sense, no right way to wage a war that one should not be fighting in the first place. But what is the force of this? There are, obviously, morally better and worse ways to wage that war, and it is clearly preferable that those who are fighting an immoral war adhere to the received rules of wars. When we assess the conduct of war, McMahan wants us always to keep in mind that at least some of the combatants are in the wrong. Because the received rules of war abstract from that—because they are unconcerned with the rightness or wrongness of the war—they do not, in McMahan's view, reflect the true morality of the situation.

Imagine, then, William and Wilhelm shooting at each other at El Alamein in 1942, as permitted by the rules of war. In this respect, neither is to be criticized. But we should always bear in mind, McMahan would say, that it is wrong of Wilhelm to be fighting because German aggression brought about the war. Because of this, it is wrong of Wilhelm to shoot at William but not of William to shoot at Wilhelm. McMahan finds the rules of war deficient because they fail to capture this putative fact. But those rules do not purport to reflect the complete truth of William and Wilhelm's situation for the simple reason that they explicitly ignore the larger *ad bellum* issue. They do not say that from this broader perspective Wilhelm acts rightly in shooting at William. Rather, the rules forbid certain types of conduct and say, in effect, that if Wilhelm stays within the rules, then he is not a war criminal and is not to be punished for his conduct on the battlefield. Those rules neither approve nor disapprove of his being involved in the fighting.

McMahan believes that it is wrong of Wilhelm to shoot at William because he has done nothing to make himself morally liable to attack. It is undeniable, of course, that if nation A wrongly wages war against nation B, then nation A acts wrongly in attacking the individuals who are fighting on B's behalf. Employing the language of rights, McMahan and like-minded theorists maintain that just as nation B has a right that A not attack it so William has a right that Wilhelm and his comrades not shoot at him. But this means neither more nor less than that nation A is not justified in waging war against nation B. In no stronger sense does William have a right not to be shot at. He cannot plausibly contend that, despite having put on a uniform and joined the fray, he has a valid claim or entitlement that the troops he is shooting at not return fire. The world has never recognized such a right,[2] nor is there any reason to proclaim it now. Doing so would not make war less likely or less bloody, nor would it alter any combatant's conduct. Indeed, it would have no operational import at all. William's children can assert that right, the right not to be attacked, as can his elderly parents and the wife he left at home, and that Wilhelm and his comrades should respect their rights as non-combatants is beyond question. But for William to claim such a right himself would only make a mockery of the right that his loved ones really do have.

Imagine that Wilhelm fought with a unit that never violated the received rules of war. After the war, he comes to believe that Germany was in the wrong. If Walzer and the conventional view are correct, then Wilhelm should not feel guilty about having participated in the war. Rather, he will rightly think either that it was permissible for him to have done so or at least that he is to be excused for having fought because, let us suppose, he did not know any better and was only doing what the adults he respected told him was the right and patriotic thing to do. He will naturally feel some regret and rue the fact that he took up arms in a cause that was in fact immoral, wishing perhaps that it had been otherwise and that he could look back on those years in a different and more positive light. If McMahan and the revisionist view are correct, on the other hand, then Wilhelm should recognize squarely that he acted wrongly in fighting even if because of features of his particular situation, he is not to be judged too severely for having done so. Wilhelm should feel no pride in his military service, and indeed it might be appropriate for him to view it with a sense of guilt, shame, or remorse. However, even if he views his war participation as McMahan does, when Wilhelm reflects on his battlefield conduct, he should rightly believe that, in adhering to the rules of war, he conducted himself honorably. He should not feel the guilt, shame, or remorse that veterans who violated those rules should feel.

Contrary to the position I am defending, Christopher Kutz (2005: 167–8) suggests that if individuals knew that they would be liable to punishment for participating in immoral wars, just as they are for committing war crimes, then they might be deterred from fighting in those wars. This might sound like a good proposal, one that utilitarians should take seriously. However, only those who believe their side is probably in the wrong can potentially be deterred, and few combatants are likely to believe this. If they do, the prospect of post-war punishment if they surrender might well give them an incentive to fight harder. Further, the argument assumes that the just side will always win. But right does not make might, and it will often be the unjust side that prevails. Believing that it was in the right, as victors are almost always inclined to do, the unjust side will—following Kutz's line of thought—believe itself warranted in punishing those who, in its eyes, acted wrongly by fighting against it.

Combatant status

When war breaks out, it is crucial to be able easily to distinguish combatants from non-combatants. If an army at war cannot do so, then it is difficult for it to target only combatants, greatly increasing the risk to civilians. This is one reason that armies traditionally wear uniforms. (There are other reasons: Uniforms increase esprit de corps, and they make it easier for fighters to identify their comrades and to know their ranks and for leaders to control their subordinates and to direct military operations.) However, not everyone who fights, even if he or she wears a uniform, is a combatant, at least not according to the law of armed combat. It sets down certain conditions that must be met to qualify as a combatant. Failure to meet these conditions entails that one is not a legally recognized belligerent. Satisfying them—being accorded legal status as a combatant—brings with it certain protections and immunities. In particular, lawful combatants cannot be punished for their destructive deeds if they were following lawful orders and, if captured, they have certain rights as prisoners of war.

According to the Hague Convention of 1907 and the Geneva Convention of 1949, a lawful combatant is one who belongs to a military organization that meets the following four conditions:

1   It is "commanded by a person responsible for his subordinates"; that is, it must be a hierarchical group with a recognizable chain of command. The law of war does

not recognize as combatants isolated individuals bearing weapons or informal groups of them, however political their agenda may be. By contrast, a genuine combatant inflicts damage, not on his or her own initiative, but as part of a disciplined military organization, which controls the actions of its members. It regulates the conduct of its fighters and can punish them, for example, for violating the rules of war. It can also negotiate as a collective entity with other groups.

2   It obeys the received rules of war. Combatant status brings both privileges and responsibilities, in particular, the duty to adhere to the received rules of war. Violating those rules, however, does not automatically deprive one of combatant status as long as one's superiors subject members of the group to disciplinary action for such violations. However, if the group itself ignores the rules and never bothers to observe them, its members could forfeit their status as lawful combatants.

3   Its members wear a uniform or distinctive emblem that can be seen from a distance.

4   Its members bear arms openly.

The intent of these last two requirements is obvious. Together they work to make it easier to distinguish fighters from non-fighters and, thus, to protect the latter. However, these two rules were modified by Protocol I Additional to the Geneva Convention (1977), Article 44(3), which states:

> Recognizing ... that there are situations in armed conflicts where, owing to the nature of the hostilities an armed combatant cannot so distinguish himself, he shall retain his status as a combatant, provided that in such situations, he carries his arms openly: (a) during each military engagement, and (b) during such time as he is visible to the adversary while he is engaged in a military deployment preceding the launching of an attack in which he is to participate.

The revised rules decriminalize guerrilla warfare, legitimating certain irregular tactics and granting combatant status to guerrilla forces (provided they meet the other conditions). As we have noted, the rules of war are not static; they are subject both to gradual evolution as notions of what is acceptable practice change as well as to conscious and deliberate modification through treaties and international accords. Thus, as international attitudes toward guerilla warfare have changed, so has the law of armed conflict.[3]

The revised rules make it easier for non-conventional military forces to fight within the law, but they make life tougher and more dangerous for non-combatants. If guerilla forces operate among the civilian population, emerging only to fight and then fading away again, then ordinary people are more likely to be caught in the crossfire between guerillas and the forces arrayed against them. For this reason, one might doubt the wisdom of the 1977 changes. Some writers suggest, however, that the changes were necessary not to "unfairly disadvantage" smaller, less well-equipped military forces (Frowe 2011: 103) by denying them a "fighting chance" (Gross 2010: 38, 60; 2015: 45–6, 61–3). This strikes me as the wrong way to look at it. War is not a game, and the point of the rules that regulate it is not to ensure fairness or to level the playing field so that weaker forces have a chance to defeat stronger forces. We can see this clearly by considering a military or quasi-military organization that argues that the only way it can hope to attain its goals is by intentionally killing non-combatants. The civilian immunity rule, the group claims, unfairly disadvantages it because, were the group to adhere to it, it would have no prospect of success. To this, the obvious rejoinder is that we are concerned to protect the lives and well-being of civilians, not to ensure terrorists an adequate chance of achieving their ends.

Nonetheless, if the rules of war are to be effective, then they must be rules that the international community finds acceptable and that it is reasonable to expect that belligerents can, over time, be brought to embrace and conform their conduct to. Utilitarians are not seeking to identify an ideal set of rules, the following of which would, if they were in fact followed, reduce the carnage of war to an absolute minimum. That would be a perfectly hypothetical exercise. Rather, utilitarians seek to identify and promote those rules, the promulgation of which will do the most good, given the world as it actually is—that is to say, taking into account the likelihood that people and states can be brought to accept and comply with those rules. And if there are rules that are already generally followed and the following of which has good consequences, then there is a strong utilitarian case for adhering to them, even if better rules are imaginable (Moore 1968: 164). Sometimes it will make sense for utilitarians to advocate refining, modifying, or supplementing those rules in an effort to reduce further the devastation of war. But advocating rules that have little or no likelihood of being followed is pointless, however welfare-promoting those rules might appear to be in the abstract. None of this implies that there must be perfect compliance with the rules. That is not a realistic goal any more than it would be with municipal criminal law.

So, while one might regret that the 1977 changes heighten the risks to civilians, the revised rules do bring the formal law of war into line with contemporary international political morality, which accepts guerilla tactics and irregular warfare as morally legitimate (or potentially legitimate) ways of fighting—largely because they are associated with the anti-colonial and national-liberation struggles of the twentieth century, many of which are widely viewed as having been morally justified. The revised rules thus strengthen international law by increasing its perceived legitimacy. The modifications have some other potentially beneficial consequences, too. By recognizing that guerilla forces can be lawful combatants, the 1977 rules bring them under the umbrella of international law, encouraging them to respect that law and to adapt their conduct to the received rules of war, including necessity and proportionality, just as other lawful combatants are expected to do. The modified law of war offers them legitimacy in exchange for adherence to the rules. It also draws a line between lawful guerilla operations and violence employed by those who neither wear uniforms nor bear their arms openly before or during engagements but instead try to pass themselves off as civilians.

Civilian immunity from direct attack

As discussed in Chapter 6, the distinction between combatants and non-combatants does not consistently track the difference between those who are guilty and those who are innocent, between those who brought the war about or favored its being brought about and those who did not, or even between those who pose a threat to the armed forces of the other side and those who do not. Nor does the distinction capture any other difference between the two groups that would make it—absent the received rules of war—always wrong to attack members of the one, but not of the other. Moreover, it cannot be said that the lives of combatants are intrinsically less valuable or less worthy of preservation than are the lives of non-combatants.

These days many philosophers who study the ethics of war seek to identify exactly when and why certain individuals are morally liable to attack and to what degree they are liable (Frowe and Lang 2014: xvi). However, even if these principles could be spelled out, they are unlikely to coincide with the conventional combatant/non-combatant distinction. Moreover, they would almost certainly be too complex to serve as feasible rules of war, that is, as rules that could actually guide combatants and war leaders, because following the principles would likely require detailed knowledge of what individuals on the other side knew and did, which no combatant could possibly have. To this, the likely rejoinder is that the principles would nevertheless capture the true morality of the situation. But from a utilitarian perspective, once war has erupted, the objective is to mitigate its horror and destruction and thereby salvage as much well-being as possible by regulating it as best we can. By contrast, the project of identifying who would properly be exposed to harm, and how much harm and what degree of risk they would properly be exposed to, if war were somehow to be fought in accordance with our everyday intuitions about desert, liability, or moral responsibility—intuitions that it is, by and large, utility-maximizing for us to be guided by in peacetime—is an entirely theoretical endeavor, one with little bearing on the real world.

Judged from the perspective of ordinary peacetime morality, the conventional combatant/non-combatant distinction is somewhat arbitrary, but it captures the widespread conviction, over the centuries and in many cultures, that there is a significant difference between attacking armed men and attacking women and children or others who have no significant involvement in the war. Moreover, the line between armed warriors and ordinary civilians is salient and easy to work with. Recognizing that line and insisting that only combatants may be attacked have the most profound benefits. To the extent the rule is followed, it reduces significantly the harm of war. This is why the distinction has the moral importance it does, and why combatants and others should be taught to respect it.

The principle of non-combatant immunity holds that combatants should never directly attack civilians who steer clear of any involvement in the fighting (thus, the ban would not apply to civilians who snipe at enemy soldiers entering their town). Contrary to what some writers insinuate (e.g., Nagel 1972: 126), utilitarians endorse this rule and stress its importance. To begin with, directly attacking civilians will be almost always be wrong either because doing so lacks any military rationale whatsoever or because whatever military advantage it might bring is insufficient to justify the harm suffered by the civilians. But even if there were a military case for attacking civilians in a particular set of circumstances, doing so would almost certainly fall short of the utilitarian goal of maximizing net, long-term well-being, taking everyone's interests into account. For this reason, then, civilian immunity should be viewed as a distinct rule, not as a mere entailment of the principles of necessity and proportionality. That means that it is to be respected and upheld for its own sake—even in the rare, but imaginable, case in which attacking civilians would not violate those principles.

When interpreting the principles of necessity and proportionality, the benchmark is military value or advantage. It would be unreasonable and infeasible to tell combatants that the standard of assessment should not be military benefit but the good of all because of the difficulty of interpreting this rule in practice and because it would prohibit combat operations by armies that lack *ad bellum* justification for fighting. So understood, necessity and proportionality would never be accepted as rules in the first place. With civilian immunity, the situation is different. It is not unreasonable for states to accept this restriction on their combat activities and, despite occasional violations of the rule, the nations of the world do, in fact, concur that belligerents should not target or directly attack civilians.

Utilitarians should thus insist on treating civilian immunity from direct attack as a distinct and independent rule that combatants should always follow. Moreover, this rule is a real rule. This entails that combatants are not to decide on a case-by-case basis whether to respect civilian immunity. It is not a mere guideline, to be put aside if the circumstances seem to dictate doing so. Rather, from a utilitarian perspective, it is desirable to affirm and, as far as possible, entrench the right of civilians not to be attacked. Utilitarians want states and quasi-state actors to recognize, uphold, and institutionalize this right; to have military establishments pledge their allegiance to it and to train their troops to follow it; and to have individual soldiers internalize a commitment to the rule as part of their professional code.

Still, one can imagine exceptional circumstances in which attacking civilians would not only contribute to victory but would also be the utility-maximizing course of action—perhaps because it would result in fewer deaths overall than would attacking combatants only. As a result, some who appreciate the utilitarian importance of respecting civilian immunity believe that there can be justified exceptions to it; thus, civilian immunity is not absolute (Fisher 2011: 100–1; Glover 1999: 84–5). Many non-consequentialists agree with this. In particular, Michael Walzer (2006b: 251–68) famously maintains that sometimes the rule of civilian immunity must yield to direct utilitarian calculation. Specifically, he believes that in certain special circumstances, which he calls a "supreme emergency," a state may be morally justified in directly attacking civilians if this is the only way to preserve a political community that would otherwise be destroyed (see also Rawls 1999b: 98–9).

There are several objections to Walzer's widely discussed stance. First is the difficulty of specifying the exact circumstances that constitute a supreme emergency and thus permit a belligerent to override civilian immunity. Second is the fact that states could easily imagine that they are in a supreme emergency when they are not. Third is the precedent effect. Even if a state acts rightly in violating civilian immunity, doing so sets a bad precedent, increasing the likelihood that in the future both it and others will break the rule when they should not. For example, even if, as Walzer believes, Britain faced a supreme emergency in the early years of World War II, it continued to bomb German cities with great ferocity long after any such emergency had passed.

For these and related reasons, Stephen Nathanson (2010: 146–59; 2012: 25–35) rejects Walzer's position, arguing from a utilitarian perspective that the civilian-immunity rule should not be revised, nor should exceptions to it be permitted. Rather, utilitarians should endorse it categorically and belligerents should stick to it unconditionally. Nathanson is correct. If there is ever a utilitarian rationale for treating a rule as, in practice, categorical and without exceptions, the civilian-immunity rule would seem to be such a rule. Given the rule's enormous humanitarian benefit, we get better overall results if military strategists and soldiers in battle never even entertain the idea of directly and intentionally killing civilians. This could, hypothetically, lead them to forgo certain opportunities to maximize well-being by killing non-combatants. Even so, we achieve more good in the long run by insisting that combatants always follow this rule than we would from adopting any other stance.

Let us examine this more closely. Suppose that some soldiers or those in charge of them believe that in their precise circumstances adhering to the civilian-immunity rule would jeopardize their ability to prevail over the enemy. It cannot be denied that they might be correct and, further, that it could also be the case that directly attacking civilians would, in this particular situation, be the utility-maximizing thing to do. However, although theoretically possible, this is extremely improbable. Even if we assume that intentionally killing civilians makes it possible to win a particular skirmish, battle, or campaign, it may contribute little to ultimate victory. And even if it does, striving for victory, especially when pursued this way, may not be the optimal course of conduct—especially given how rare it is for states to be fighting wars that are justified on utilitarian grounds. Moreover, violating the rule will weaken the commitment of these soldiers to civilian immunity and have a negative precedential effect, increasing the probability that in the future they or other combatants will rationalize slaying civilians when they should not. For these reasons, then, it is overwhelmingly likely that there will be alternative courses of action that are welfare-superior to a belligerent pursuing victory in defiance of this recognized rule of war.

Even if the soldiers in our example were in an exceptional situation where, all things considered, directly targeting civilians really would maximize expected overall, long-term well-being, taking into account the interests of all, they will almost certainly not be justified in believing that they are so situated, for that would require evidence they will doubtless lack. Furthermore, the temptation to violate civilian immunity generally occurs in circumstances that are far from conducive to making reliable moral judgments—soldiers in the heat of battle or military strategists emotionally absorbed by the effort to prevail over another state. Indeed, it is hard to imagine worse epistemic conditions for making a balanced, objective, long-term assessment of the costs and benefits of breaking a rule, general adherence to which is so very important.

Finally, the well-trained and conscientious soldier will not find it easy to violate the civilian-immunity rule for any reason, including the belief that doing so is the course of conduct with the greatest expected well-being. Indeed, he will be appalled at the very prospect of killing civilians intentionally and on purpose. To do so would go against his personal and professional moral code and traduce his conscience. In addition, he may have taught subordinates to respect civilian immunity or criticized enemy soldiers for violating it. Moreover, as a utilitarian he approves of this situation; that is, he approves of his having a character structure that makes it virtually impossible for him to attack non-combatants. And he knows that utilitarians will not blame or criticize him for adhering to a rule that they want combatants to be as firmly committed to respecting as possible. He understands, too, that if he were to slay civilians, he would court moral censure and possibly risk punishment as well and that utilitarians will approve of this.

Contrary to what I have been arguing, Kutz contends that if combatants know that civilian immunity from direct attack is grounded on the rule's humanitarian benefits, then they will always have reason to ask whether sticking to the rule makes sense in a given instance:

> What we want to inculcate instead is a combatant's thought that rules of IHL [international humanitarian law], and the system of values that sustain them, command categorically. Since soldiers, being human, are reflective creatures, this means that we must provide a non-instrumental argument for those rules.
> (2005: 167)

Now, as I have urged, utilitarianism itself contends that we should inculcate in combatants a blanket opposition to targeting civilians. Respect for civilian immunity should be a firm, virtually absolute part of their intuitive moral code; it is not something to be followed only on a case-by-case basis. Kutz argues, in effect, that combatants cannot cleave to that rule categorically once they understand why, on utilitarian grounds, it is so important for them to cleave to it categorically. But this is absurd. One can certainly be firmly committed to certain normative principles while at the same time understanding their consequentialist rationale and justification. Since Socrates, philosophers have stressed the importance of stepping back occasionally and critically reflecting on one's own values and commitments. To be sure, that reflection might lead one to question those values and commitments, but it might equally well lead one to affirm them. There is no reason for thinking that this is not the case here—for believing, that is, that utilitarian combatants cannot stick to the principles and moral feelings that on careful consideration they believe that they are fully justified in having.

The issue here, it is worth noting, is not moral absolutism vs. non-absolutism. These days few non-consequentialist theorists are absolutists; rather, they typically allow that any given normative principle may have to yield, in some circumstances, to rival moral considerations. Their principles are defeasible. Pose them an imaginary case (see Lefkowitz 2008: 162–3) where targeting a handful of civilians will somehow or other bring the war to an end, saving hundreds of thousands of lives, and they will target the civilians. The contention of Kutz and others is not that utilitarians acknowledge exceptions to well-justified rules, but that they are too ready to do so—so ready, in fact, that one can question whether they are really committed to the rules. This is the charge that I have tried to answer.

Allied bombing in World War II

We cannot leave the subject of non-combatant immunity to direct attack and the possibility of exceptions to it without mentioning the Allied bombing of German and Japanese cities in World War II, which intentionally targeted civilians and, indeed, killed around 800,000 of them (Grayling 2006: 5). So flagrantly did obliteration bombing of Axis cities violate the principle of discrimination and non-combatant immunity, that for some time after the war many doubted whether the received rules of war really did bar directly attacking non-combatants. However, that principle has been unambiguously reaffirmed in the Additional Geneva Protocols of 1977 as well as in the court of world opinion and, since the war, Western and most other military powers have studiously refrained from deliberately targeting civilians.

It is certainly worth studying how and why the Allies came to believe themselves compelled to attack civilians.[4] Among those reflecting on the morality of Allied policy, there are three main views: (1) the bombing policy, at least by Britain in the early part of the war, was right because it was justified on utilitarian grounds; (2) the policy was wrong despite being justified (or appearing to be justified) on utilitarian grounds; and (3) the policy was wrong on utilitarian grounds. The latter is my view. One should, of course, be wary of retrospective certainties and of judging upright and brave men and women who were engaged in a perilous struggle with an evil foe, the outcome of which was far from settled. Nevertheless, a consensus among historians holds that the terror bombing—for that is what it was and was acknowledged at the time to be—did little to damage the Axis war effort. Indeed, in hindsight the arguments used to justify the bombing, in particular that it would demoralize the other side or cause civil unrest, appear so specious that Uwe Steinhoff—a non-utilitarian—refers to them as "pseudo-utilitarian hallucinations" and goes on to charge that the bombing policy "was completely free of utilitarian logic—indeed, free from any sort of logic at all" (Steinhoff 2007: 66). Furthermore, even if there had been a utilitarian case for bombing in the early part of the war, the price that the world paid because of loss of respect for non-combatant immunity was so severe that the policy would still have been wrong.

Part of that price was the nuclear devastation of Hiroshima and Nagasaki. The culmination of the Allied bombing policy, it was made possible by a calloused indifference to civilian slaughter, which that policy had helped to bring about. President Truman and others since him have claimed that utilitarian considerations justified the bombing, however terrible, because it brought the war to a close more quickly and at a lower cost than a ground invasion of Japan would have. Most philosophers who have examined the matter dispute Truman's calculation and contend that the bombing was unnecessary (e.g., Lackey 1989: 74–8; McMahan 2009: 128–30; Rawls 1999a: 568–72, 1999b: 101–2). They believe, in particular, that given imminent Soviet entry into the war, a trial demonstration of the power of atomic weapons on some uninhabited islands would have worked just as well, especially if it had been coupled with a demand for something other than unconditional surrender. And indeed it is difficult to believe that at that point in the war no other course of action open to the Americans would have had greater expected utility. Even if this judgment can be challenged, what is certainly true is that there was no detailed examination of rival courses of action, no thorough consequentialist assessment of the options, and yet American decision-makers elected to commit two horrific war crimes. Would Truman's decision have been correct if—contrary, as I believe, to fact—any other course of action would have resulted in far more deaths and far greater loss of well-being? That is theoretically possible, but decision-makers at the time certainly lacked sufficient grounds for thinking that that was their situation.

Collateral damage

The received rules of war forbid combatants from purposely and directly attacking civilians whether the point of doing so is simply to harm them or only to weaken or in some way disadvantage the military forces of the other side. The rules, however, do not entirely forbid harming civilians. If they did, they would come close to outlawing war altogether because military operations, even if they are scrupulously directed only at combatants, frequently have negative consequences for non-combatants. They are often killed or injured or have their property damaged as an unintended or undesired side-effect of the fighting. Because of this, the rules of war have long allowed collateral or incidental harm to civilians as long as the harm done to them is proportional to the importance of the military goal being sought. Thus, the Geneva Convention forbids collateral harm to civilians if it is "excessive in relation to the concrete and direct military advantage anticipated" (Additional Protocol I, Article 57).

Non-utilitarian or non-consequentialist approaches to the ethics of war have difficulty justifying rules that allow collateral harm to civilians. After all, the civilians who are killed or harmed as a foreseeable side-effect of military operations are not participating in the fighting; they have done nothing to forfeit their right not to be injured or killed. This is obvious in the case of children (Ezorsky 1987). For this reason, some non-utilitarian theorists believe that it cannot be right to wage war if this involves harming civilians, a position that, practically speaking, is tantamount to anti-war pacifism (Holmes 1989: 183–214; Werner 2013: 43). Traditionally, however, just war theorists have held that it can be permissible for military operations to expose civilians to harm by appealing to the doctrine of double effect. It states that it is sometimes permissible to bring about as a merely foreseen consequence of one's action a harm that it would not be permissible to bring about intentionally, either as one's goal or as a means to one's goal.

More specifically, according to the doctrine of double effect, it can be permissible to act in a way that one knows will have an evil result if

1   the act one performs is aimed at a legitimate or morally good result,
2   the evil result, although foreseen, is intended neither as a means to that good result nor as desirable in itself,
3   the evil result is not disproportionate to the good result that is being sought.

Catholic theologians and others have employed double-effect reasoning in various contexts. For example, it has been used to argue that even though abortion and euthanasia are immoral because they involve killing an innocent human being, it may be permissible, on the one hand, to terminate a pregnancy if one's intention is only to save the life of the mother or, on the other, to give a terminally ill patient a lethal dose of a drug if one's intention is only to prevent the patient's suffering. In these cases, one foresees but not does not intend the death one brings about, and that is thought to make a crucial moral difference.

In the context of war, the doctrine of double effects implies that the following two situations are different in a morally important way. In the first, a pilot bombs an enemy railroad station in order to kill the civilian passengers inside (perhaps in an effort to dampen enemy morale). In the second, a pilot bombs the same station, killing the same number of civilians, in order to disrupt the transportation of troops or military goods. Although he foresees that the civilians will die, this is not his goal; it is only a side-effect of his conduct. Deontologists have frequently held, as Kant did, that to kill an innocent person is categorically forbidden; it is something we must absolutely never do under any circumstances (Anscombe 1981b). If so, then by intentionally blowing up the innocent civilians, the first pilot acts immorally even if he fights in a just war. However, because the second pilot did not intend to kill anyone, the doctrine of double effect views his conduct in a different and more positive moral light. Assuming he is performing a militarily useful maneuver, then the pilot may have done nothing wrong.

Contemporary philosophers have written a great deal about the ins and outs of the doctrine of double effect, much of it quite technical. Few of them find it satisfactory.[5] Typically, they contend that the doctrine has counterintuitive implications or that distinguishing between what one intends in performing a certain action and what one merely foresees will result from that action is problematic because it depends on how we describe the situation, which can be somewhat arbitrary (Timmons 2002: 89–93). In the case of bombing, critics are skeptical of the idea that the rightness or wrongness of killing the civilians can hang on the supposed difference between a direct and an indirect effect or on the mental state of the pilot. In their view, claiming that the deaths are unintended only obscures the pilot's moral predicament (Fisher 2011: 97). "Can anyone really think," asks Judith Thomson, "that the pilot should decide whether he may drop the bombs by looking inward for the intention with which he would be dropping them if he dropped them?" (1991: 293). For their part, utilitarians and other consequentialists believe that if the consequences are identical and all other things the same, then there is no morally significant difference between an outcome that, to use Bentham's terminology (2005: 86), I directly intend (or seek to bring about) and one that I obliquely intend (or merely anticipate will result from what I do). In determining whether an action is right or wrong, at the most basic level of analysis what matters for the consequentialist is only its expected outcome as compared to the expected outcomes of the alternative actions open to the agent.

Michael Walzer argues for a modification of the principle of double effect. On his view, it is not enough that combatants not intend the death of civilians and that any unintended deaths are commensurate with the importance of the goal. In addition, combatants must exercise due care, seeking seriously to minimize those civilian casualties even if doing so is militarily inconvenient or increases their own risk (2006b: 155–6; see also Lee 2012: 216). Walzer's proposal helpfully shifts the emphasis away from intentions to the concrete steps that combatants must take to reduce the risks to civilians. This is reflected in the "precautionary measures" prescribed by Article 57 of Additional Geneva Protocol I. It requires that combatants take "constant care" to spare the civilian population. More specifically, they must "do everything feasible to verify that the objectives to be attacked … are military objectives" and "take all feasible precautions in the choice of means and methods of attack with a view to avoiding, and in any event to minimizing, incidental loss of civilian life" and property. When selecting among military objectives, they must choose the one, "the attack on which may be expected to cause the least danger" to civilians, and refrain from any attack if the "incidental" injury or death of civilians or damage to civilian objects will be, as quoted earlier, "excessive in relation to the concrete and direct military advantage anticipated."

Nathanson (2010: 286) has encapsulated these requirements in the following two, crucially important, normative propositions:

(1) Attacks that kill or injure civilians are wrong
when the attacks that cause these harms (a) are intended to harm civilians, (b) fail to be discriminating in the choice or method of targeting, (c) are negligent, or (d) cause civilian harms that are disproportionate to the value of the military objective.

(2) Attacks that kill or injure civilians are permissible
when the harms to civilians (a) are unintended, (b) caused by a discriminate attack on a military target, (c) take place in spite of serious precautionary efforts to avoid or minimize civilian harms, and (d) are proportionate to the value of the target of the attack.

As with almost all rules, interpreting or applying Nathanson's principles in specific situations may sometimes be difficult. As H.L.A Hart remarks, "particular fact-situations do not await us already marked off from each other, and labelled as instances of the general rule." Nor, he adds, "can the rule itself step forward to claim its own instances" (1994: 126). Given the limits of language, there will inevitably be hard or penumbral cases, about which reasonable people may disagree. Nevertheless, Nathanson's two principles are clear and understandable, and in the vast majority of situations their implications are obvious and easy to follow. Even if the received rules of war did not include them, there would still be a strong utilitarian case for seeking to instill in all military personnel not only a categorical aversion to directly attacking civilians but also a strong commitment to reducing as far as possible any incidental harm to them, even if this is costly or militarily inconvenient, because of the extremely beneficial consequences, overall and in the long run, of upholding and ensuring compliance with those rules.

Some believe that in an asymmetrical conflict between a strong conventional force and a weaker unconventional force, the requirement to minimize collateral damage should be interpreted more stringently for the former than for the latter (Rodin 2006: 161–5). Others hold the reverse: that the rules should be relaxed for the stronger side because it is harder for it, than it is for the unconventional force, to minimize collateral damage (Fotion 2007: 122–3). The two positions are guided by opposed assumptions about the nature of these sorts of conflict. The first position rests on the premise that the weaker side is more likely to be in the right; otherwise, it would not risk fighting. Therefore, justice requires making it easier for it to prevail. But it seems preposterous to assume that the weaker side will generally be justified in waging war and, even if this generalization were granted, it is implausible to argue from it to the conclusion that stricter rules should always apply to conventional forces. On the other hand, if we hold that things should be made easier for the weaker side if and only if it is right to fight, then we are running together *in bello* and *ad bellum* issues, something, as we have already seen, that there are very good reasons not to do. The second position emphasizes that although it is easy for irregular rebel or guerilla forces to distinguish legitimate military targets from non-military targets, many such groups routinely and deliberately refuse to do so. Moreover, because these groups hide among civilians and fight in populated areas, in resisting them the stronger side cannot achieve a high level of compliance with the principle of civilian immunity. This line of thinking relies implicitly on an appeal to reciprocity and on the notion that the moral irresponsibility of one side lessens the responsibilities of the other. But this is contrary to the received rules of war (Roberts 2008: 237–8), and there is no compelling reason for revising them in this respect.[6]

Finally, in contrast to Nathanson's principles, which underwrite the received rules of war, consider the contention that the principle of civilian immunity in war should be interpreted as permitting only truly accidental deaths; that is, deaths that are "not only unintended but also unforeseen and reasonably unforeseeable" (McKeogh 2002: 170). This principle fits with ordinary moral thinking in most peacetime situations. Generally speaking, one cannot act in a way that one foresees will maim or kill other people, people who pose no threat to you or have done nothing to forfeit their rights, even if one is seeking a good end. That one only foresaw but did not intend the harm provides no exculpation. Without doubt, were this principle to govern warfare—were it to represent an established convention—it would reduce very considerably the harm of war. But it would do so by ruling almost all recourse to war morally out of bounds.

To this, one might rejoin, "well, so much the worse for war." In line with this sentiment, Richard Wasserstrom has written that we should not regard "as immutable the character of contemporary warfare and weaponry" but should insist, rather, "that war itself change so as to conform to the demands of morality" (1972: 19). He is right, of course, that we should not take the status quo for granted and, as I have already said, utilitarians will seek to push the received rules of war in a welfare-maximizing direction. But there are limits to what can be demanded of war in the name of morality. As I have reiterated several times, once war has broken out we are dealing with a state of affairs that is suboptimal (because alternatives superior to it were available to the belligerents) and morally undesirable (because at least one of the parties should not be fighting in the first place). We are seeking principles to govern this non-ideal state of affairs, not in a feckless effort to try to make conduct in war conform to the principles that are appropriate for us to follow in everyday life, but to try to reduce as much as we reasonably can the death and destruction that war brings. It contributes nothing to this goal to advocate principles, such as the one suggested by McKeogh, which make war almost impossible and which states and other belligerents could never be brought to accept. War cannot be legislated out of existence in this way. Nor would it be a good thing if it could. Utilitarians are not pacifists. Neither for them nor for classical just war theory is the moral goal to have rules that make war impossible, for there have almost certainly been in the past, and may well be in the future, some wars that should be fought.

Protecting civilians

The received rules of war require combatants to take all feasible precautions to avoid or reduce incidental harm to non-combatants, permitting it only if not excessive in relation to the military objective being sought. What counts as "feasible precautions" or as "excessive" admits of no general answer but will depend on the specifics of the case, and reasonable people may differ in their judgments. One must be alert, though, to the natural tendency of those in the thick of war to exaggerate the importance of a given military objective and to overlook or fail to consider seriously alternatives to it. Because it leads to tolerating greater harm to civilians than is really warranted, this tendency must be guarded against.

What is clear, though, is that adhering to the rules may require combatants to run risks that they would not need to run if the welfare of civilians did not need to be taken into account. This is as it should be. Combatants cannot jeopardize non-combatants just to make things easier or safer for themselves because it is they who, rightly or wrongly, are placing the civilians in danger, not the other way around. But how much risk must they run? This, too, is probably impossible to answer in a general way. Some have argued that when arriving at an answer in a given situation, the lives of "our" soldiers should count as much as (Hurka 2005: 64) or more than (Kasher and Yadlin 2005a: 53; 2005b: 18) the lives of "their" civilians. The partiality we feel toward our soldiers, these authors believe, is not only natural but morally justified (see also Avineri 2009). They are our fellow citizens, and we have a responsibility to avoid endangering them, a responsibility that is at least as great if not greater than our responsibility to protect foreign non-combatants.

The danger with this view is that it can easily lead to the position that "needless risks" to our troops are to be avoided and that "force protection" has priority over the safety of civilians. Against this, Paul Christopher has argued that risk to combatants does not weigh equally with risk to non-combatants because "risking one's life is part of what it means to be a soldier":

> Once we accept that it is part of the ethos of the soldier to behave courageously and to protect innocents, even at the risk of one's own life, then it becomes clear that it is the civilians' lives that must be safeguarded, not the lives of soldiers.
>
> (2004: 155)

I believe that Christopher is right about this. Strictly speaking, though, the proper argument is not, as this passage suggests, from the premise that risk taking and protecting civilians are part of what it is to be a solider to the conclusion that therefore soldiers need to place a priority on civilian safety. Rather, it is because of the importance of protecting civilians that we want soldiers to have the ethos that Christopher describes. That ethos is the conclusion, not the premise, of the argument that consequentialists favor. Nevertheless, Christopher highlights well that soldiers can reasonably be expected to accept such an ethos. They are already inculcated with a sense of duty, requiring them to risk their lives for their country and for their comrades; self-protection is not their highest obligation. This is why they can be brought to shoulder, and why it is reasonable to require them to shoulder, a duty to avoid harming civilians to the extent that this is possible, even if doing so increases the danger to them.

Combatants have a duty, then, to expose themselves to certain dangers in order to lessen the peril that non-combatants face because their assuming this duty—their adhering to this rule—helps reduce the overall harm of war. McMahan, however, rejects this consequentialist argument on the grounds that the aim of a just war "is not to limit violence overall but to limit the violation of rights" (2010b: 354). After all, he reasons, violence could often best be reduced by simply capitulating to an aggressor. This misses the point, however. The contention here is not that the reduction of violence should be the main aim of a state engaged in fighting a war that it believes to be just—that, after all, was not the point of its taking up arms—but, rather, that it is a central aim of the received rules of war. And to achieve this aim, consequentialists and others want combatants on both sides to strive diligently to protect civilians, even if this makes fighting more irksome and hazardous for them.

But even if an army cares about civilian safety, how much risk to its own soldiers should it accept so as to avoid or minimize harm to non-combatants? At what point is collateral harm to them to be considered excessive or disproportional? Now, it can happen that a proposed military operation will endanger one's own civilians. Although they will expect their armed forces to endeavor strenuously to avoid harming them, sometimes this is impossible and yet the military operation is important enough to justify proceeding anyway. This, then, points to the appropriate standard: However great a risk an army should take to avoid harming its own citizens and however much collateral harm it should tolerate when its own citizens are at stake, this is the same degree of risk it should take, and the same amount of harm it should permit, when it comes to the civilians of allied countries, of neutral countries, and also of enemy countries (cf. Margalit and Walzer 2009). I cannot claim that the received rules of war dictate this standard, for although they require "constant care" to spare civilians, they do not specify exactly what this entails. What I do claim is that utilitarians should advocate interpreting the rules this way.

Against the standard I have endorsed, it will be urged by the writers cited earlier that we cannot be expected to care as much about the civilians of enemy states as we do our own. Although that may be true, it is not quite on point. We are not favoring enemy civilians over our own civilians, but rather requiring our troops to proceed with as much care when it comes to endangering the former as they would with the latter. Nor is it unreasonable to expect our troops to do so—to understand, for instance, that protecting the children of allied countries, of neutral countries, and of enemy countries is of comparable moral importance to protecting the children of their fellow citizens. True, if one's army is on foreign territory, the civilians may be disrespectful and antipathetic, and they may have strange ways. This can make it psychologically more difficult to take risks for them. But young men and women in uniform can be brought to see that the hostile attitudes they encounter are similar to those that would be expressed by their parents and loved ones back home if the circumstances were reversed and that those attitudes provide no grounds for treating civilians callously, still less for dehumanizing them. Disregard for the other side's civilian population is one of the great dangers of war. It is made more likely by improper training and by the belief that the lives on the other side do not matter as much as the lives of our own people.

Although the rules forbidding combatants from attacking civilians and obliging them to minimize collateral harm to non-combatants are reasonably clear and clearly justified, at times combatants fail to adhere to them, exposing civilians to more harm than they should or even attacking them directly and on purpose. Sometimes these are isolated failures in a military organization that generally respects the received rules of war. However, there are military or quasi-military organizations that do not care about the Geneva principles; some of them intentionally harm or kill civilians whereas others are merely indifferent to whether their operations put them in jeopardy. Indeed, they may place greater importance on their own safety and military success than they do on the well-being of the civilians they claim to represent, for example, by engaging in military operations in populated areas. In this circumstance, it is perhaps natural to feel that it is unfair for our combatants to risk themselves to safeguard non-combatants on the other side when the enemy shows no such concern itself and, indeed, may even try to exploit our care for its civilians to its own advantage (for example, by firing rockets from inhabited locales, knowing that we will be reluctant to return fire because of the danger to bystanders). But fairness ("How come they can use human shields, and we cannot?") is not the important issue, certainly not for utilitarians. Rather, what matters is minimizing the damage of warfare by striving to protect civilians as much as we can.

Notes

1 Thus, in his memoir of the battle of Ia Drang, the first serious military engagement between U.S. and North Vietnamese forces, Harold G. Moore writes movingly:

> While those who have never known war may fail to see the logic, this story also stands as tribute to the hundreds of young men of the 320th, 33rd, and 66th Regiments of the People's Army of Vietnam who died by our hand in that place. They, too, fought and died bravely. They were a worthy enemy. We who killed them pray that their bones were recovered from that wild, desolate place where we left them, and taken home for decent and honorable burial. This is our story and theirs.
>
> (Moore and Galloway 1992: xx)

2 To my knowledge, no real combatant has ever maintained, as he charged out of the trench, as his landing craft hit the beach, or as his unit advanced across the field to encounter the enemy, that he had a right not to be fired upon, however justified he believed his cause to be.

3 For probing legal discussion of this and related matters, see Crane and Reisner (2011), Dinstein (2003), and Roberts (2003).

4 Grayling (2006) is an excellent study of the history and morality of Allied bombing. Also worth consulting are Burleigh (2011: 478–505), Garrett (2007), and Glover (1999: 69–112).

5 For a subtle and penetrating critique of the doctrine, with special attention to the example of the two bombers, see Bennett (1995: 196–225).

6 There is a parallel debate regarding armed humanitarian intervention. Some believe that the duty to minimize civilian injury should be more stringent in such interventions; others that it should be weaker (Pattison 2014: 113–15). Fuller discussion of this topic would be too much of a digression, but it is difficult to see a compelling utilitarian case for revising the received rules in either direction for this one particular type of conflict.

8

ETHICS AND THE PROFESSION OF ARMS

Even when a state is morally justified in waging war, utilitarianism imposes serious constraints on the fighting of that war. These constraints, embodied in the received rules of war, are central to the identity of the military in modern liberal democracies and other regimes that respect international law and, in particular, the law of armed conflict. An acceptance of them is part of what makes military service an honorable calling. This, and the fact that the armed forces in a decent, non-aggressive, and law-abiding society typically serve good ends, elevate participation in the modern military above mere membership in an armed group trained and prepared to engage in violence.

What are those ends? The answer might seem to be "the fighting of morally justified wars," but this is a bit too simple for two reasons. First, a state can deploy its armed forces in police actions, peace-keeping tasks, or military skirmishes short of war as well as in humanitarian operations that do not involve force or the threat of force. Fighting wars is not the only thing an army can do. Second, one of the most important goals of the armed forces is to keep the state or the country it represents secure from attack or, more broadly, to safeguard its political independence and territorial integrity, and this can often be accomplished without fighting. The very fact that a state has an army that is ready and able to defend it can have a deterrent effect. The fighting of wars is, of course, what an army is organized to do; thus, the U.S. Army says that its "mission is to fight and win our Nation's wars."[1] Still, the military performs a useful function merely by being prepared to fight.

All this is fairly evident. But in rounding out this study of the ethics of war from a utilitarian perspective, we need to look more closely at the rationale for having a standing army in the first place, at the virtues and responsibilities that military service in a modern democracy requires, and at the moral difficulties that can confront those in uniform—in particular, the challenges posed by immoral orders and wrongful wars.

Standing armies

As Chapter 5 discussed, utilitarianism upholds a right of national defense, at least for states not guilty of grave humanitarian abuses. That right, in turn, would seem to entail a right for states to possess the means necessary for defending themselves. Ultimately, though, "the costs of military forces can only be morally justified if they are related in some reasonably clear-cut way to benefits for individual human beings" (Fotion and Elfstrom 1986: 31). For utilitarians, this is elementary; a state is justified in raising, training, and supporting an army, navy, or air force only if its doing so enhances overall welfare. Although utilitarians take into account the welfare of everyone, if a state's having armed forces at its disposal maximizes expected benefit, it normally does so primarily by promoting the well-being of its own citizens.

Fotion and Elfstrom continue:

> Of all the possible justifications for maintaining a standing army, the most fundamental, and the one most readily understood as containing important benefits for particular individuals, is the argument from security. It is most basic because it refers to the very lives, freedom from attack, and access to the means of life of a people. If military forces are to be justified at all, it must ultimately be in terms of the security they provide.
>
> (1986: 32)

To be sure, states sometimes use their armed forces to protect other interests or advance ends other than security. Sometimes their doing so benefits their citizens or even humankind more generally, and sometimes it does not. States have often used their military forces in ways, both domestically and internationally, that do little or nothing to enhance the security or welfare of their citizens, let alone the well-being of everyone. Even states that are not guilty of this sometimes spend more on their militaries than their security requires, often out of a concern for national prestige, which is unlikely to benefit ordinary people. On the other hand, some states, such as Costa Rica and Andorra, have no army, and many other small states have military establishments that could not realistically hold off a determined foe. They must rely instead on diplomacy and military alliances.

It is impossible to say in general what sort of military forces states should have, how large they should be, or what sort of structure, rules, and internal culture they should have so as to maximize well-being. Those policy matters hang on the specifics of each country's situation and the environment in which it operates, and involve various, contestable empirical considerations. Anti-war pacifists would of course challenge the need for a military at all, but foregoing an army is a risky strategy, and consequentialists are unlikely to advise more than a handful of states to adopt it. Of course, in few, if any, societies are the size, structure, staffing, training, and general organization of the armed forces welfare optimal, meaning that no possible changes to them would increase net well-being. Nevertheless, of many societies we can plausibly say that they are better off with than without a standing army because of the security and other benefits it provides, even if they might profit from changes in its size, structure, organization, or internal culture.

Some may hesitate to affirm this sweeping assertion, and it certainly could be the case that the armed forces of a particular society were so likely to be used in bad ways that it would increase the welfare of all if the state were entirely divested of them and, thus, of the means of doing mischief. I doubt, however, that this is true of any but a handful of regimes. Of course, this is an empirical question, and I could be mistaken. More likely is the possibility that a state occasionally misuses its military, sending it to fight when UWP would not warrant this or deploying or threatening to deploy it in order to advance questionable foreign policy goals, but that nevertheless expected well-being would be lower if the state in question had no military at all.

Insofar as the military serves important ends and does so in a moral way, membership in that organization, especially in a democratic society that upholds certain basic rights, is a respectable, service-oriented calling. But the armed forces are not for everyone, and unless national defense or other special circumstances demand it, no one is obliged to serve in the military, still less to elect it as a career. Society needs people to follow all sorts of occupations, and within the limits set by *On Liberty*, people should be left free to pursue their own interests, aptitudes, and enthusiasms. Of course, even if it is good that a given state has armed forces at its disposal, service in them enmeshes one in a system with both good and bad features, and its day-to-day reality can sometimes disappoint or disillusion those who have chosen to enlist (which is one reason so many graduates of West Point and the other service academies leave the military at the earliest contractually permissible opportunity). But similar complaints can be lodged against many occupations.

Role responsibilities

The various social roles we occupy affect our moral obligations. In particular, in undertaking a given occupation or social role, one can acquire what philosophers call *role responsibilities*, that is, duties that are specific to and incumbent on those in that role, position, or occupation. (One can also acquire certain role-based rights.) Thus, to pick a few examples, parents, teachers, nurses, and lawyers have obligations that arise from their assuming these particular roles and that others in different roles or occupations lack. These obligations are shaped by our shared, though sometimes contested, social understandings of the nature and purpose of the role in question, and they evolve as those understandings change. Critics of utilitarianism sometimes charge that it fails to account for the individualized character of our obligations, which often grow out of the relationships we enter into, or for the partiality to clients, friends, and family that commonsense morality permits or even requires us to display. These aspects of our moral world cannot, it is alleged, be adequately accounted for in consequentialist terms. I think this charge is ill-founded. At the very least, it is clear that a consequentialist or utilitarian approach makes perfect sense when it comes to role responsibilities.

To begin with, these responsibilities reflect practices and institutions that guide people's current behavior, mold their expectations about how others will act, and shape their plans for the future. Upsetting settled patterns and expectations, upon which people have relied and around which they have organized their lives, has negative consequences. Thus, even if the roles or practices in question are suboptimal, there are utilitarian grounds for adhering to them. It will matter, of course, just how suboptimal those roles are and what both the anticipated benefits and the likely negative consequences of deviating from them will be. If a given practice, institution, or set of social roles, although less than ideal, nevertheless produces good results on balance and if the envisioned deviation from established ways will harm those whose expectations were formed by them while being unlikely to improve the practice, then there are strong grounds for adhering to one's role responsibilities. For example, even if it would be better, when it comes to civil cases, if the American legal system were less adversarial and more like the German system, this would not justify an American attorney acting as if he or she had the quite different role responsibilities of German lawyers. Likewise, in most educational systems there are fixed expectations about how grades are to be assigned; it is important for teachers to adhere to these or at least take them into account even if an altogether different grading system would be better.

This is not an argument for across-the-board conservatism. People in a given role and others as well can push in various ways for changes to established role responsibilities (whether or not consequentialist considerations favor adhering to them in the meantime). A utilitarian perspective requires critically assessing the conventional understandings of the conduct appropriate to different social roles and determining whether it is for the best that they involve the particular responsibilities they do or whether and how those responsibilities or their underlying social roles might be modified so as to increase overall social good. (For example, is it desirable that American criminal lawyers defend, as zealously as they now do, even those they know to be guilty of heinous crimes?) Asking what array of responsibilities should be associated with any given role requires asking, not what is intrinsic to the role of x, which is in any case a social construction, but rather which way of delineating it and specifying its duties would do the most good.

Here, as so often, utilitarians take an indirect approach to the promotion of well-being. They seek to determine which particular duties, the assumption of which by teachers, say, or parents, lawyers, or soldiers would best promote the good, and then to nudge social practices in that direction. If those social practices and, more specifically, their attendant roles and responsibilities are at least broadly justified from a utilitarian perspective, then people are not obliged to ask in each situation they encounter whether acting in the role-determined way will have optimal results. In the terminology employed by Rawls in an early and influential essay, utilitarians distinguish between "the justification of a practice and the justification of a particular action following under it" (1999a: 33). Assuming that utilitarianism underwrites a given practice, one does not need to show that an individual action maximizes utility, only that it is in line with the practice or role in question. This is because of the advantages of having certain established practices and, more specifically, settled social or occupational roles—with generally acknowledged duties and responsibilities—and of allowing these practices and roles to structure and coordinate people's expectations and conduct.

Brian Barry (1995: 194–5) and R.M. Hare (1999: 146) draw a related contrast, which is worth mentioning here, between first-order impartiality and second-order impartiality. The former involves impartiality as a maxim of behavior in a given area of everyday life; for example, we expect instructors to grade student exams impartially and judges to treat impartially the people appearing in their courts. In contrast, we do not expect lawyers to be impartial between clients and non-clients when handling cases or people to be impartial between friends and strangers when giving Christmas presents. Second-order impartiality, on the other hand, applies to the assessment of rules, roles, and practices. For utilitarians, it entails asking what rules, conventions, and role responsibilities it would maximize well-being for society to establish, uphold, and reinforce. For example, because of natural affection and for reasons of efficiency, utilitarians have almost always held that it is best for parents to have prime responsibility for their own children and to promote their interests as best they can, favoring them (within some limits) over other children. If this is so, however, it is not because this is self-evidently the right social arrangement but rather because of certain "psychological and sociological generalizations, obtained by empirical study of human nature in actual societies" (Sidgwick 1966: 346). In other words, impartial utilitarian assessment endorses parental partiality. Likewise, suppose, as some believe, that in criminal matters an adversarial legal system produces greater net well-being than do other legal systems. If so, then it is for the best that lawyers, again within some limits, sedulously represent the interests of their own clients rather than concerning themselves with whether in each case their doing so maximizes the well-being of all.

Duties and virtues of military personnel

The modern military is widely understood to be a profession, not least by the military itself. Whether it is or not and why and, more specifically, whether both officers and enlisted personnel are to be considered professionals are oft discussed questions, partly factual but mostly conceptual or definitional. The military meets many of the plausible criteria for being a profession (e.g., Hartle 2004: 29–41), but it differs from professions such as law and medicine, characterized historically by solo practitioners with full autonomy over their practice. Military service, by contrast, places uniformed personnel in a hierarchical organization with a clear chain of command and limits on the exercise of their independent judgment.

Which occupations are properly considered professions and the people in them professionals is a question that engages people because it elevates the social status of any occupational group to be considered a profession. Focusing on the concept of role responsibilities, however, allows us to sidestep issues about who is or is not a professional. Whether or not military service is a profession, military personnel unquestionably have distinctive role responsibilities, sometimes requiring them to endure hardships and run grave risks. These responsibilities are intimately connected to the importance that obedience, discipline, hierarchy based on rank, and organizational effectiveness all have for the armed forces. For instance, insubordination, quitting one's post, failure to repair (that is, not going to or being late to show up at one's appointed place of duty), and failure to execute an assignment if willful, negligent, or the result of culpable inefficiency are all punishable offenses in the military, crimes that have no counterpart in civilian life. Indeed, "sleeping on post," failing to do the "utmost" to "encounter the enemy," and "shamefully" surrendering are death penalty offenses, as is "cowardly conduct," which the U.S. military defines as "misbehavior motivated by fear" (Dunlap 2013: 248–9). For military personnel, these are not merely occupational obligations based on their functional importance for the organization but also moral duties insofar as that organization is necessary for the security and preservation of a decent, reasonably just society.

One's role responsibilities are often associated with specific virtues. Military personnel should, of course, have many of the same virtues that we expect any good person to have, for example, honesty, truthfulness, and consideration for others, and there are some virtues, such as diligence and cooperativeness, that help any organization to function well. In addition, though, military personnel are expected to have certain virtues, for example, physical courage, loyalty, and a willingness to sacrifice oneself for others, which we do not ordinarily expect civilians to have or, at least, not to the same degree.

Military organizations are among the most rule-governed social institutions, and the duties of military personnel are typically spelled out more explicitly than are the role responsibilities of, say, parents or teachers. Indeed, the following of rules closely and promptly is itself one of the role responsibilities upon which military organizations place great weight. Many writers stress, though, that beyond a duty to follow rules, military service, at least for officers and career soldiers, involves embracing as central to their profession certain values or virtues—such as duty, honor, and country (Hartle 2004: 57–60), selflessness, obedience, and self-mastery (Rhodes 2009: 54–9), courage, loyalty, and honesty (Coleman 2013: 40), or courage, comradeship, discipline, honor, sacrifice, and professionalism (Baker 2011: 13–29)—a commitment to which is often reinforced by the distinctive history and traditions of particular regiments or branches of service. The specific values just mentioned may seem somewhat vague, but an allegiance to them or to certain other higher ideals can undergird and strengthen one's desire to fulfill one's more specific duties and role responsibilities.

To explore this point further, consider adherence to the received rules of war, one of the vital role responsibilities of military personnel. In 1991, U.S. military authorities issued a pocket card to forces taking part in Operation Desert Storm, specifying the rules of engagement that were to govern them (Roberts and Guelff 2000: 562–3). The card lists ten restrictions on military engagement with enemy forces, including protecting hospitals, treating prisoners with respect, using booby traps appropriately, and refraining from taking war trophies. The card then states:

Remember:

1 Fight only combatants.
2 Attack only military targets.
3 Spare civilian persons and objects.
4 Restrict destruction to what your mission requires.

Although these simple instructions probably provided sufficient guidance for most situations that a U.S. combatant was likely to encounter in that war, they were obviously not intended to cover the full range of issues that soldiers might possibly face when trying to fight morally and in compliance with the received rules of war. A discussion of those issues is important, especially for officers, and should be integrated into their training and revisited throughout their careers. This connects to an important point. Instruction in the rules of war is not simply a matter of giving soldiers a list of dos and don'ts, for at least two reasons.

First, officers and to some extent enlisted personnel need to learn how to interpret and apply those rules. This involves exposing them to various hypothetical cases and encouraging them to figure out for themselves and to examine with comrades what would be the morally right course of action in those circumstances. Second, as discussed in earlier chapters, the goal is for military personnel to internalize a commitment to the received rules of war and the humanitarian values they represent. Ideally, combatants should see the rules, not as an external imposition backed up by the threat of punishment, but rather as something integral and essential to military service, properly understood. That is, the rules should be seen as reflecting a code of conduct or certain values or virtues that lie at the heart of one's military identity.

When General Douglas MacArthur (1964: 295–6) wrote that the soldier is "charged with the protection of the weak and unarmed" and that this is a "sacred trust" and "the very essence and reason for his being," he can be seen as trying to reinforce, beyond simple obedience to the rules of war, a commitment to certain values or ideals as central to the profession of arms. In a related vein, Shannon French, after a historical survey of the codes of Homeric heroes, Roman soldiers, Chinese warrior monks, the Samurai, and others, encourages today's military personnel to pick and choose "the best from among these historical and mythical warrior ideals" (French 2003: 232). This seems a bit too open-ended—after all, we want them to choose only ideals that unambiguously support fighting in accord with the received rules of war—but the underlying point is sound, namely, that it facilitates combatants fighting honorably and within the rules if they see that conduct as required by a higher ideal, code, or set of values, which is integral to military service and to which they have freely subscribed.

Oath of Office

Some writers suggest that the responsibilities of military personnel flow from the oath of service that they take (Christopher 2004: 241–2; Coleman 2013: 38–9). But it is better to see the swearing of that oath, not as creating those responsibilities, but rather as symbolizing one's conscious acceptance of them. This is for two reasons. First, whether the swearing of an oath creates a moral obligation depends on the content of the oath. From 1934 on, Wehrmacht officers were obliged to swear "unconditional obedience" to Adolf Hitler, but no pledge can morally bind one to commit atrocities. By contrast, officers in the uniformed services of the United States swear an oath to "support and defend the Constitution of the United States against all enemies" and to "faithfully discharge the duties of the[ir] office." Enlisted men and women take a slightly different oath, pledging to support and defend the Constitution and to obey the orders of their superiors. These oaths, similar to those sworn by military personnel in other modern democracies, are morally unexceptionable. Second, if perchance an officer did not swear such an oath, the person would still have the same duties as any other officer because of the role he or she has assumed. Indeed, the oath itself implies that that there are preexisting duties of office, duties that the oath acknowledges but not does create.

Serving the state or humanity?

I have emphasized the functional underpinning of one's military role responsibilities, which are defined by the needs of the organization and justified by the instrumental importance of that organization in bringing about or making possible certain good ends. I have implicitly assumed, as most writers do, that the specific ends that the military serves are determined by the state—that the state is its client—and, thus, that whether those ends are good or bad, worthy or unworthy, is a contingent matter. This may, however, be incorrect. Manuel M. Davenport has urged that

> the paramount duty … of the military professional is to promote the safety and welfare of *humanity* and this duty, according to military law, takes precedence over duties to clients, who as his fellow citizens are but a particular portion of the human race.
>
> (Davenport 1987a: 7–8)

By this, Davenport might be interpreted to mean only that the received rules of war restrain the conduct of military personnel and that in this sense the interests of humanity restrict what the military can do in service of the state. Chapters 6 and 7 developed this point, and in this passage Davenport rightly emphasizes that these humanitarian responsibilities are internal to the military role, not something external to it. This is something that even very astute commentators seem sometimes not to get quite right (e.g., Walzer 2004: 23–32). Davenport may, however, intend a stronger claim, namely, that the central role or professional responsibility of military personnel is to serve humanity, not a particular state. A passage in a subsequent essay, where Davenport restates his position, seems to support such an interpretation:

> The objective of the military organization is to exercise and manage violence to promote and preserve the safety and welfare of the human species and to do so inasmuch as possible in a manner consistent with the interests of the client-nation which sanctions this objective and the dignity and status of those who carry it out.
>
> (Davenport 1987b: 71)

This, too, is not entirely free of ambiguity. On one possible interpretation, though, Davenport is averring that the goal of the military, which in turn shapes the role responsibilities of its personnel, is to promote the safety and welfare of everyone, which it endeavors to do in a way that is compatible, if possible, with the interests of the state it represents.

It might seem that utilitarians should favor the position I am attributing to Davenport, namely, that the military should aim impartially to maximize the well-being of all, not merely to serve the interests of the state it represents. Whether this is true hinges on whether it better promotes the long-term well-being of all for the military to see its role (1) as that of serving the interests of its particular state (within the parameters set by the rules of war) or (2) as serving directly and in the first instance the well-being of everyone. In other words, is military partiality justified on utilitarian grounds analogous to the way, say, that the partiality of parents for their children or lawyers for their clients is justified? Asking whether military organizations should in general be guided by (1) or by (2) is hypothetical, to say the least, because the world is already carved into nation states, and it is difficult to see how any existing state's military could take (2) as its first-order directive, nor why any state would fund an army not guided by (1). On the other hand, if we focus on peaceful, non-aggressive democratic societies that abide by international law, then it becomes plausible to say, for reasons mentioned earlier and in Chapter 5's discussion of national defense, that their militaries may well make a greater contribution to overall human well-being precisely by focusing on providing their own society with security against external attack rather than by trying somehow to promote impartially and directly the good of all states and all peoples. If so, then second-order impartiality underwrites their first-order partiality.

Furthermore, the principle of civilian control of the military entails answer (1) because it holds that the military is to serve its civilian masters and carry out as diligently as it can the missions assigned to it. I say more about civilian control later, but although the principle is not beyond question, it is so central to democratic practice that there would have to be very strong arguments for abandoning it—even if, contrary to what historical experience suggests, military organizations were particularly adept at determining when violence would, in Davenport's words, best "promote and preserve the safety and welfare of the human species." For

utilitarians, of course, the civilians who control the military should endeavor con-
scientiously to wage war when and only when UWP permits or requires this. This
they sometimes flagrantly fail to do. Nevertheless, in a well-ordered democratic
society, it is almost certainly for the best that decisions about war and peace rest
with public officials rather than with the military, even if we suppose that the military desired only to maximize the well-being of all.

Alleged limitations of a utilitarian approach

Some writers balk at a utilitarian or consequentialist approach to the virtues and
role responsibilities we want those in uniform to have. French (2003: 7), in particular, contends that even though this approach correctly highlights that the "unique
demands of military service ... require special virtues or moral commitments," it
falls short for three interrelated reasons.

First, by linking "the motive for ethical behavior to military effectiveness," a
functional or instrumental approach does not by itself "provide reasons for the
warrior to behave well when bad behavior does not seem to have a negative
impact on the function of the military" (French 2003: 7). In the same vein, J. Carl
Ficarrotta, although acknowledging the aptness of a functional approach, writes
that it fails to give "the military professional ... special reasons to be 'good' through
and through," that is, to be moral "outside the military context" (Ficarrotta 2008:
53). For example, it gives the military officer no special reason to be charitable or
to refrain from lying to a spouse or cheating on income tax. Second, even within
a military context, the functional approach has limits, French argues. Because it
rests on generalizations that may not always hold true, it cannot condemn military
personnel for bad behavior as long as it "does not in fact cause them to fail to
function effectively in their specific martial roles" (French 2003: 8). Sometimes,
failing to act in a way in which it is generally important for military personnel to
act will have no bad consequences. Third, French argues that the consequentialist
approach considers warriors "only as a means to an end, namely, the protecting of
the nation" (2003: 9). Rather, she wants to emphasize the importance for soldiers
themselves of adhering to a moral code because "accepting certain constraints as a
moral duty, even when it is inconvenient or inefficient to do so, allows warriors
to hold on to their humanity while experiencing the horror of war." The code
grounds them, keeping the individual combatant from "becoming a monster in his
or her own eyes" (2003: 10).

Let us consider these arguments in turn. First, French and Ficarrotta are correct
that there are limits to what a functional or role-based argument can justify. That
should not surprise us, however. Any instrumentalist or consequentialist role-based
defense of certain virtues or responsibilities will not justify duties or mandate conduct that is not relevant to that role. This is unproblematic. One's moral obligations
in the non-military spheres of one's life would simply be grounded elsewhere. It
has been held, however, that, unlike other occupations, at which a morally deficient person might excel, a "bad man cannot be ... a good sailor, or soldier, or

airman" (Hackett 1979: 124–5). This implies that a good military professional must be a good person in all other ways, which strikes me as implausible. Human beings are complicated, and it certainly seems possible for a person to be loyal to comrades, honest in dealing with superiors and subordinates, and courageous in battle and yet be disloyal, dishonest, or cowardly in other contexts. Psychologists have long established that character traits which common sense assumes to be unified and constant are far from invariant. For example, those who are rigidly honest in one context may cheat in another.[2] On the other hand, if Hackett's thesis were correct and character traits less mutable than they probably are, then moral obligations that appear non-military in character (such as paying child support) would be part of one's military role responsibilities.[3]

Turning to the second argument, it is true that a functionally oriented, consequentialist account of role responsibilities rests on generalizations. It contends that certain types of conduct are important for an efficient and effective military organization but not that each and every instance of the desired type of conduct promotes organizational efficiency or that every particular instance of the non-desired type of conduct will have bad organizational effects. But that does not matter. Courage in battle is a valuable trait for infantrymen to have, for obvious reasons, even if some instances of cowardice do no harm and not every display of courage benefits the organization. The instrumentalist or consequentialist approach seeks to justify one's internalizing certain values and developing certain dispositions of character. Thus, for instance, courage under fire is to be valued for its own sake, as part of what it is to be a soldier, and its exercise should be more or less automatic, not something that hinges on one's calculating whether acting courageously in the given circumstances would best promote overall utility.

French's third contention—that the functional case for the military virtues we have been discussing treats the bearers of those virtues only as means to some social end—makes little sense. We consider many traits or dispositions to be virtues precisely because of the good effects for others of our having them; kindness and generosity are examples. But this does not imply that in being kind or generous (to the appropriate degree and in the appropriate way) a person is only being used as an instrument for promoting social well-being. Moralists have long insisted that exercising generosity and other virtues can enrich one's own life. In line with this, French highlights the importance for combatants themselves of having internalized the values utilitarians want them to have and of seeing themselves as governed by a code, a code that requires allegiance to the rules of war and that thus distinguishes them from killers and makes their calling an honorable one. This is an important point. Adherence to such a code, as French is right to argue, allows combatants to remain morally whole and psychologically undamaged. It is important, not just for others, but also for their own sake. Nevertheless, we want combatants to strive to protect civilians and to be willing to do so at some risk to themselves primarily because this disposition benefits non-combatants. That it also benefits the combatants themselves, as French maintains, is important and makes inculcating that disposition easier, but it is ultimately a happy side-effect.

Obeying orders

Military organizations are almost always strongly hierarchical, with subordinates required to obey the orders of superiors promptly, fully, and basically without question. The military places a much higher premium on obedience than do most other organizations because its smooth and efficient running hinges on people following, routinely and unhesitatingly, the commands of their superiors. This is obviously of great moment in wartime. The military historian John Keegan once wrote that his colleagues at Sandhurst who had seen combat "understood in their bones that only the habit of obedience and the automatic performance of orders make an army work and spare life that would be lost by prevarication or dispute" (Keegan 1998: x–xi). But dispositions necessary in wartime must be cultivated in peacetime. As the U.S. Supreme Court has put it: "The inescapable demands of military discipline and obedience to orders cannot be taught on battlefields; the habit of immediate compliance with military procedures and orders must be virtually reflex, with no time for debate or reflection" (Dunlap 2013: 249).

Obedience is not, however, an unqualified moral virtue. Although we want adults to be able to cooperate with others and to work together in common projects, we expect them to think for themselves and to use their own judgment. Indeed, the very concept of moral agency implies that one cannot escape deciding certain questions for oneself. However, in a military context the occupational virtue of obedience to orders has a moral dimension because of its instrumental value in making it possible for the organization to achieve its good ends.

A trait that it is generally morally desirable for people to have can be exercised in an inappropriate way, in the service of an unsuitable object, or without due regard for other pertinent moral factors. This leads some writers to deny that the trait displayed in such a situation is a virtue (so that a bank robber cannot genuinely display the virtue of courage or an SS officer that of loyalty), but whatever view one takes of this linguistic issue, the phenomenon itself is real. A trait, characteristic, or motivation that it is generally good for people to have or that it is valuable for them to have in a certain organizational or other contexts can be turned toward a bad end—for example, when one obeys the immoral orders of a superior officer.

The military code of contemporary states requires those in uniform to obey all lawful orders. This represents a change from earlier days, when military personnel were expected to obey all orders, period—a change due in part to the Nuremburg trials. They established the principle that it is no defense against a war-crimes charge that one was merely following orders. Not only is one not obliged to follow orders commanding such crimes, but also one has a duty to refuse them and can be punished for failing to do so. Furthermore, in a modern military organization, the chain of command is rule governed. Those who give orders to those below them in the hierarchy are themselves subject to the orders of those higher up, and there are restrictions on who can order whom, and what they can order them to do. An order could be unlawful because of its content (for example, ordering a subordinate to purloin civilian property) or the order could be unlawful because the ordered action, although morally neutral or even good (for example, contributing money to a charity), lies outside the legitimate authority of the superior to command.

Because the military codes of most modern military organizations incorporate the Geneva principles or similar humanitarian standards, an order violating them would be unlawful; hence, one would not be required to obey it. It is not an easy thing, of course, for an enlisted person or a junior officer to refuse to obey an order on the grounds that it is unlawful. Doing so goes against his or her training and the whole culture of the organization, and the person's disobedience is likely to bring disagreeable personal consequences even if it is ultimately vindicated. Moreover, whether an order is lawful can sometimes hinge on recondite legal questions beyond the competence of most military personnel.[4] This and the belief that one's superiors probably have a better grasp of the overall situation may well make enlisted personnel, in particular, reluctant to refuse orders unless their illegality or immorality is blatant.

The phrase "lawful orders" is ambiguous. It might mean orders that are consistent with the rules and regulations of the military organization in question, orders that adhere to international law, or orders that respect some higher moral law. Usually, though, it is one or both of the first two things that people have in mind when they speak of orders as lawful or unlawful. As I have said, obvious war crimes, such as killing prisoners, are not only immoral but also unlawful. On the other hand, orders could be morally questionable without being unlawful. For example, one might believe that the foreseeable collateral consequences to civilians of a proposed military action would be so severe that, given the nature of the objective, carrying it out would be wrong despite being permitted by international law and the military's own rules of engagement.

More often, I suspect, soldiers will encounter orders they believe to be not so much immoral as ill-considered, militarily unsound, or excessively dangerous. Normally such orders are to be carried out despite one's misgivings. Subordinates are not encouraged to challenge their superiors or question their judgment, especially not in the heat of battle, although there is often more give-and-take in small units, even in combat, than civilians may imagine. Sometimes, though, it may be appropriate to seek clarification of orders to understand their implications and the intentions of one's superior in issuing them. If done respectfully and in the right circumstances, this is often considered permissible. In any case, the military holds superiors responsible for the orders they issue, not the subordinates who implement them. Still, the latter sometimes balk at carrying out orders that are wrongheaded, ill-informed, or fail to grasp the realities of the situation, often finding creative ways short of direct refusal to avoid following them.

Military organizations differ in the initiative they permit or encourage subalterns to exercise and in how much latitude they grant them in carrying out the intention, as opposed to the letter, of a given order. Sometimes company- or field-grade officers may be prepared to deviate from orders they consider seriously misguided, hoping that their divagation will ultimately be viewed as justified, if not in the eyes of their immediate superior, then by those in higher authority. Or they can ask to have the order in writing in order to make it clear to higher authorities that they disagree with it. Faced with standing orders that they find objectionable, they can sometimes obtain transfer to a different unit.

What is important to bring out is that military officers often experience these situations as a clash of military responsibilities, responsibilities that are simultaneously moral, professional, and legal (in the sense of being required by the military code of conduct). On the one hand, they have a duty to obey their superiors. On the other, they have duties to their subordinates (for instance, not to endanger them needlessly); they have various duties to the organization as whole, including the obligation to contribute as effectively as possible to the achievement of its goals; and they have a duty to adhere to the ethical code they have been taught. For them, it is not always or even usually a conflict between legal obligations on the one hand and moral responsibilities on the other hand or between military obligations and non-military obligations. There are moral and professional responsibilities on both sides, moral and professional reasons for obedience as well as for disobedience, and all these considerations connect to their role responsibilities.

Conflicts that many describe (e.g., Hare 1999: 173–4; Walzer 2004: 23–32) as being between one's military responsibilities (for example, to obey an order or respect the chain of command) and one's non-military humanitarian obligations (for example, to protect civilians) are often better seen as a conflict of responsibilities that are, or should be, internal to the military role itself, properly understood. Consider the famous case of Hugh Thompson, Jr., the helicopter officer who rescued a number of civilians from massacre at My Lai, at one point ordering his subordinates to fire on American troops if necessary to prevent them from murdering fleeing Vietnamese villagers. Stopping the slaughter and bringing the men of another unit under control can be seen as a military duty, not just an exogenous humanitarian duty, even though Thompson was acting outside the chain of command and outside his assigned duties.

Whether the conflicting obligations that uniformed personnel sometimes face are best seen as internal to the military role or as being between their military and human responsibilities, what are they to do when the rules and principles that should normally govern their actions are at odds? For most non-consequentialists these days, the answer remains essentially the same as Ross (1930) gave. We must rely on our intuitions, weighing and comparing our conflicting prima facie duties as best we can in order to decide which one, in the given circumstances, is the most stringent. For utilitarians like me, on the other hand, when rules and principles that are justified on utilitarian grounds clash, then one must be prepared to transcend the intuitive moral precepts that ordinarily and appropriately regulate our conduct and reason in a directly utilitarian way, assessing the likely outcomes of alternative courses of action and choosing that with the greatest expected well-being. Of course, one does not have to think twice about lying to a murderer in order to save a friend's life. Because the everyday obligation to tell the truth has obvious limits, it is not necessary to leave the realm of intuitive moral reasoning to reach this conclusion. Moreover, utilitarians will want people to internalize different moral principles at different levels of strength so that, for example, they will feel much, much greater reluctance to kill somebody or to allow somebody to be killed than they will to tell a lie. In other cases, however, a clash of everyday or first-order principles cannot be resolved at that level. We must ascend to direct utilitarian calculation. This can be challenging, but there is no alternative because the nature of the case is such that we cannot rely on the relatively simple rules that cover most day-to-day situations.

In disobeying an order one believes wrong, one may nevertheless commit an offense and make oneself liable to punishment. That possibility is one of many consequences that utilitarian calculation would have to take into account, and it may tip the balance in favor of obedience. But then, again, it may not. Circumstances are easily imaginable where the consequences of obeying an unsatisfactory order are so serious as to swamp the personal consequences of disobedience. However, even if a soldier correctly believes that disobedience is justified, his commanders may nevertheless be legally and even morally justified in rebuking or punishing him. This will depend on the circumstances, of course, but they have an obligation to uphold military discipline and, in particular, to reinforce the importance of following lawful orders (Hare 1999: 172).

This may seem paradoxical, but there are good grounds for reinforcing the general duty of adhering to orders, and, ex hypothesi, the order in question is lawful. Let us assume, further, that it would be impractical or inadvisable to adjust the current set of rules and regulations so as to remove one's legal obligation to obey orders of that sort (possibly because doing so would defy easy codification). We are not, in other words, dealing with a situation that should be an explicitly recognized exception to the general duty to obey orders. Given this, utilitarian commanders might reasonably believe that punishing a deviation from the rule in order to bolster the general observance of orders is the best course of conduct open to them, even if they regard the individual as right not to have complied. Of course, the punishment might be mild or a mere formality, or the authorities might instead judge it best to turn a blind eye to the whole episode. What course of action they should take will, naturally, hang on the consequences of the options open to them. The point, though, is that because of their institutional role, those higher up the chain of command confront a different set of choices—different alternatives with different consequences—than were faced by the person deciding whether to obey or refuse to obey the original order.

Serving in wrongful wars

In Chapter 7, I maintained that the rules of war, quite properly, apply equally to combatants on both sides of a conflict, regardless of whether their side is morally justified in waging war. Those rules hold combatants responsible for their conduct during a war but not for whether their side is right to fight in the first place. At the same time, though, I acknowledged the plausibility of the principle that if a given war is wrong, then it cannot be right for anyone to fight that war. I must now say more about these matters.

To begin with, the above principle, although colorable, is imprecise. UWP pertains only to states. It provides the criterion of when their waging war would be morally right or wrong. But from what it is right or wrong for a state to do, we cannot immediately infer what it would be right or wrong for an individual to do. Some non-consequentialists acknowledge this, and for a reason with which utilitarians concur, namely, that "the relevant alternatives available to a government waging a war differ systematically from the relevant alternatives available to civilians, combatants, and other governments, etc., who might contribute to that war" (Bazargan 2011: 513).

To be sure, for utilitarians it is broadly true that if one's nation is considering embarking on a war of "unscrupulous aggression" or, indeed, is already fighting one, then one must use whatever "moral and intellectual influence he may possess" to prevent or halt the war (Sidgwick 1998a: 52). There are two reasons for this. The first is that one's individual protest, even if it cannot by itself stop the war, may contribute to accomplishing this goal. The expected good of opposing the war, say, by writing a letter to the editor, speaking at a rally, or arguing against it among colleagues may be greater than that of anything else one could do, even if there is only a very, very small chance that one's opposition will play a decisive role in forestalling or mitigating the harm. As Derek Parfit has argued in detail, in doing their calculations it is a mistake for consequentialists to ignore small chances and small effects as well as the cumulative effects of sets of acts (Parfit 1984: 67–86). Second, utilitarians want people to embrace certain elementary principles of justice, and standing up for those principles helps reinforce attitudes and dispositions that conduce greatly to well-being. Speaking out against an immoral war reflects a commitment to principles that utilitarians want people to have and, in turn, helps reinforce that commitment in oneself and others.

Implicit in Sidgwick's remark, however, are two caveats. First, he acknowledges, as quoted at the beginning of Chapter 6, that we cannot say in general how far one go should in opposing the war; this will depend on the particular circumstances. With a lot at stake, there could presumably be a utilitarian case for going beyond purely intellectual or moral suasion to civil disobedience or other more intransigent forms of opposition. On the other hand, an individual might conceivably be placed in circumstances where the net results of expressing even the most circumspect criticism of the war would be suboptimal. This cannot be ruled out, but it is a somewhat fanciful scenario. Moreover, as I have said, utilitarians will obviously want people to stand by the convictions that it is desirable for them to have in the first place even if this requires, as Sidgwick writes, "facing unpopularity" (1998a: 52). Second, in the passage in question, Sidgwick has in view an aggressive war that is manifestly immoral, but in many cases the morality of a state's waging war may not be open-and-shut. Reasonable people may disagree about whether UWP justifies fighting or not. If so, that increases the desirability of defenders and opponents of the war continuing to debate it, but it should also induce in them some epistemic modesty, weakening the case for either side to take extra-legal steps in support of or in opposition to the war.

Should one enlist in an army that is waging a war that one believes UWP condemns? Only in far-fetched circumstances—perhaps it is the only way of supporting one's elderly and infirm mother—might utilitarian calculation endorse this. For one thing, utilitarians will want people to internalize and to follow the principle of avoiding participation in unjust collective ventures, even if non-enlistment, just by itself, makes little difference. This is because of the good that widespread inculcation of this disposition does. The case becomes more difficult if we imagine someone who is already in the armed forces when the war breaks out. In that case, he or she may have conflicting responsibilities. Furthermore, the person may risk punishment for criticizing the war, for shirking his or her contribution to it, or for refusing flatly to participate in it. In some cases, the price one would pay for overtly opposing or flagrantly resisting involvement in the war might not be warranted by the relatively minor contribution it would make to stopping it.

Let us pursue this further, focusing in particular on commissioned and non-commissioned officers. Assume that although now embarked on a morally unjustified war, their state is a basically just and democratic one. In these circumstances, some writers believe that officers have a duty to fight a war they think is morally wrong. Paul Christopher writes:

> When the American people hire, train, equip, and support a professional officer corps, they expect them to be responsive to an elected authority regarding *when they should do the job for which they have been hired, trained, and equipped* ... A refusal to go [to fight] when called upon constitutes an abandonment of the oath of office, the profession of arms, and the soldiers who depend on their officers for competent leadership—it is a betrayal of the national trust.
>
> (2004: 241–2)

As he sees it, officership entails a commitment to certain principles; these include abiding by the *ad bellum* decisions of the appropriate political authorities and being willing to fight wars that are what he calls "formally just," that is, authorized according to established constitutional procedures. For him, the key notion is civilian control of the military. Even resignation in protest he finds problematic because it constitutes a public statement indicating disapproval of the decision civilian leaders have made.

Christopher buttresses his argument with the contention that "we often never know objectively and with any degree of certainty which side in a war is just, even in retrospect" (2004: 240). Hence, formal justice is enough: "It is as close to objective justice," he writes, "as we know how to get" (2004: 241). This skepticism seems too extreme. Impartial observers often have compelling grounds for affirming that a given war is or is not morally right. Furthermore, given the number of morally unjustified wars that states have waged, a general presumption that formally just wars, that is wars that came about according to established political procedures, will also be substantively just is untenable. However, as Estlund (2007) has argued (but cf. McMahan 2009: 68–70), judgments about the rightness of waging war made by a democratic system that enjoys robust public debate and seeks to wage only morally justified wars, although fallible, carry epistemic weight. Under these conditions, military personnel can plausibly be said to have a role-based duty to fight as directed even if the judgment of the authorities is mistaken—as long as it is not too unreasonable given the available facts.

Military officers in a democracy accept that they have a responsibility to fight when and where directed. Few if any of them would prefer it otherwise. Indeed, since Huntington's classic work (1957), those who study the military have concurred that this responsibility and, more generally, an acceptance of civilian control over decisions about war and peace are at the heart of the modern American military's professional identity. Role responsibilities, however, are not set in stone. Wolfendale (2009), for one, thinks that if the military is a profession, then officers should be seen as having a duty to act in accord with the "guiding ideals," "moral values," and "moral commitments" of their profession and, therefore, a responsibility to refuse to participate in wrongful wars. Accordingly, questions of *jus ad bellum* "form a legitimate part of the military's professional jurisdiction" (Wolfendale 2009: 131). But Wolfendale never says explicitly what these ideals, values, and commitments are or how or why they entail that officers have *ad bellum* responsibilities. The underlying idea seems to be that professionals should permit their services to be used only in morally acceptable ways. But whether it is morally unacceptable for officers in a democracy always to fight as directed—whether doing so would be contrary to the ideals and values of their profession—is precisely the issue. One could, of course, dodge Wolfendale's argument by refusing to accord military officers the status of professionals just because they are and should be subordinate to superiors in a hierarchical system. But the more telling point is that her contention that their status as professionals, if that is what they are, entails their having veto power over the civilian decision to wage war bumps up against the fact that the military's understanding of its professional identity—of its values, commitments, and guiding ideals—entails the very opposite conclusion. Wolfendale has not shown that the armed forces are mistaken to believe that military professionalism requires subordination to civilian authorities in matters of basic military and foreign policy.

From a utilitarian perspective, one cannot argue validly from the general nature of professionalism to a conclusion about the role responsibilities of military officers. The issue, rather, is whether it would be good for those responsibilities to be other than they are and, in particular, whether it would have good results if officers believed that they had an obligation as military professionals to refuse to fight wars that fail to satisfy UWP. George R. Lucas, Jr., argues that for a military organization to permit this sort of dissent is infeasible and "fundamentally opposed to [its] very structure, purpose, and function" (Lucas 2009: 152–5). Those with little military experience sometimes pooh-pooh these sorts of concerns. They seem to believe either that the armed forces could function perfectly well without their characteristic emphasis on discipline and hierarchy or that it would not be a bad thing if they were unable effectively to prosecute immoral wars because their personnel refused to participate in them. In practice, though, assigning officers a professional duty to refuse to participate in immoral wars is equivalent to assigning them a duty to refuse to participate in wars they judge to be immoral. Yet there is no reason for assuming that their moral beliefs will be more reliable than those of civilian leaders. Furthermore, even if a given war fails to satisfy UWP, it is far from clear that the refusal of some officers to fight, let alone the breaking down of military structures because of widespread insubordination, will typically have desirable results, either in the short or long term, especially if the other side also lacks sufficient justification for fighting or if the war, while failing to satisfy UWP, will do more good than harm. Furthermore, circumstances can change. For example, some of those who thought that it was wrong of the United States to invade Iraq in 2003 came to believe a few years later that it would be morally irresponsible of it simply to withdraw.[5] Should a hypothetical officer who refused to deploy in 2003 rejoin the contest a few years later?

Even more important is the argument, which I have touched on several times, that charging military officers with a professional duty to refuse to fight wars they disagree with on moral grounds subverts civilian control of the military. A democratic society can hardly welcome the officer class having the final say over the decision to wage or continue waging war. Rather, it is our political leaders and ultimately ordinary citizens who are responsible for seeing that their states fight only morally justified wars; we should not rely on the officer class, still less on enlisted personnel, to ensure that.[6] For one thing, as I have said, it cannot be assumed that military officers are likely to make sounder moral judgments about war and peace than are civilian leaders. And if military officers have a professional veto over war, then it is hard to see why it should be exercised only on purely moral grounds as opposed to prudential or other professional grounds or, indeed, why it should be restricted to the morality or professional wisdom of the war as a whole rather than being extended to major strategic decisions during the course of the war, which civilian leaders normally decide now. Furthermore, assigning officers a duty to refuse participation in wars or campaigns they disagree with on moral or other professional grounds could lead to abuse, specifically, to their refusing to participate, or threatening to do so, from organizational self-interest or for partisan political reasons.

Finally, there is what Cheyney Ryan calls the "sovereignty symmetry problem": "If soldiers are obliged to refuse a war they regard as unjust, are they also obliged to *initiate* a war they regard as *just*—when this too means ignoring their government's orders?" (Ryan 2008: 148). The prospect of the armed forces starting or extending wars on their own initiative is scary. In theory, though, Ryan's problem is surmountable. From a utilitarian perspective, if getting officers to assume an obligation to refuse unjust wars would have good results whereas their accepting an obligation to initiate just wars would not, then the role responsibilities of military officer should simply be asymmetrical in this respect. The question is whether this is sustainable in practice or whether officers who believed they have a duty not to fight wars contrary to UWP, whatever their government says, would tend naturally to believe that they had a duty to fight wars that UWP approves, such as certain humanitarian interventions, but which the polity has declined to undertake.

I have been arguing that the role responsibilities of officers should not be revised to include a professional duty to refuse to fight wars that a democratic state reasonably (though possibly erroneously) believes are right to fight. Even if this is correct, some other related changes to military policy or culture might have beneficial results. For example, it would probably be good if high military leaders saw themselves as having a firm duty to guide their civilian superiors—the leaders they are advising—away from grave military or moral errors and were even prepared to resign over serious disagreements (Cook 2008; Whetham 2011: 74; see also Gabriel 1987: 111). Without damaging organizational effectiveness or undermining civilian control, the military might make room for greater discussion of *ad bellum* issues in the ranks and possibly permit military officers to engage in public, non-partisan discourse over them (Fotion and Elfstrom 1986: 88–91). Many think, too, that it would have beneficial consequences to accommodate as far as possible selective conscientious objection by serving officers, with reassignment to other duties as opposed to court martial or dishonorable discharge (McMahan 2009: 97–100; Robinson 2009; see also Ellner et al. 2014). This, however, would be an individual right based on personal conscience as opposed to a professional duty to refuse to fight (Lucas 2009: 148). Whether these or other changes, which fall short of modifying the basic role responsibility of officers to fight as directed, would have good consequences deserves further, empirically and historically informed discussion.

Mention of conscientious objection reminds us that military officers are also men and women. They are moral agents, and their military role does not shelter them from responsibility for the choices they make. They have moral duties in addition to their professional role responsibilities. Faced with having to fight in an aggressive war that is patently immoral and causing enormous harm, those ordinary duties could trump their responsibilities as military officers. The latter have moral weight, but they are defeasible. Consider, in this light, Christopher's contention that an officer's refusal to fight is an abandonment of the soldiers who depend on him for competent leadership. In some cases, I have just suggested, an officer might be morally justified in declining to participate in an egregiously immoral war; if so, then it follows that he is justified in abdicating his ordinary professional role and its incumbent obligations. Assuming his doing so does not endanger those in his command (for example, by quitting in the middle of battle), they cannot claim to have a right that he continue to fight until the end of the war.

To be sure, an officer's role responsibilities are not to be put aside lightly. When the morality of the war is controversial and people one respects disagree with one's judgment that it is wrong, then an officer should probably defer to his military superiors and, ultimately, to civilian authorities and carry out the assignment. This is because of the importance of officers' adhering to their role-based legal, moral, and professional responsibilities in a democratic society with civilian control of the military. Nevertheless, those responsibilities will not always eclipse other moral considerations.

What exactly are officers to do when their role-based moral responsibilities collide with the broad, non-role-based obligation, which everyone has, to oppose, and to refrain from participating in, seriously and undeniably immoral wars? There is no simple answer to this question. One must weigh the expected value of the consequences of carrying on with one's military duties while remaining silent about one's moral reservations and compare it to the likely results of a variety of other actions. These include speaking against the war to one's comrades; criticizing it in public forums; requesting a transfer; resigning from military service or seeking re-classification and discharge as a conscientious objector; flatly refusing to deploy; or deploying but participating as little as one can in the fighting or even actively undermining the war effort in order to mitigate the harm that is being done. What the best course of action is will depend entirely on the particularities of the situation. Continuing to carry out one's military duties as usual might conceivably be the best option; on the other hand, drastic circumstances could call for extreme steps.

To reiterate, in this sort of situation where important intuitive or prima facie moral principles collide, utilitarians insist that one must think through as concretely as possible the consequences of the different courses of action open to one. Among those consequences, it is worth emphasizing, is the personal price, in particular, the risk of court martial and possible incarceration, that an officer would incur by refusing to participate in the war. Utilitarianism requires taking one's own interests into account along with those of others; it does not necessarily dictate self-sacrifice. The good that would come from opposing the war in certain ways might not justify the cost to oneself. More moderate displays of opposition to the war might have greater expected benefit. Utilitarians, however, are unlikely to blame those who sacrifice more than utilitarianism says they should in order to oppose a war that UWP implies is profoundly wrong. Altruistic conduct, and more specifically the determination to act morally with little regard for oneself, are such admirable dispositions that utilitarians hesitate to criticize their exercise in the rare cases where they lead one to excessive sacrifice. Nor, on the other hand, are utilitarians likely to blame officers who, after conscientious utilitarian reflection, remain at their posts even if it turns out that they should have done more to oppose the war. These are difficult calculations to make, and in this situation little or no good is likely to come from censuring those who made a sincere effort to do what is right.

Notes

1 See the U.S. Army's Mission Statement at: www.army.mil/info/organization.
2 For more on these matters, see Doris (2002).
3 Even if the Hackett thesis is false (as I think), there may be good utilitarian grounds for military organizations to act as if it was not and to tell recruits that part of being a good soldier, sailor, or marine is paying your taxes, giving to charities, respecting your spouse, etc.

4 Consider, for example, J. Joseph Miller's argument that any orders to invade Iraq in 2003 were illegal because they violated the United Nations Charter and, hence, the U.S. Constitution (Miller 2004). This is not a question, it seems to me, about which we can reasonably expect ordinary people, including soldiers and sailors, to have an informed legal opinion, still less to be able to counter the arguments of the government's own lawyers.

5 For a critique of the invasion from a utilitarian perspective, see Gruzalski (2006).

6 Lucas (2009: 156–8) chides academics for foisting on ordinary soldiers the responsibility for stopping wars that they (the academics) failed to convince their fellow citizens were wrong.

CONCLUSION

Chapter 8 discussed the role responsibilities of military officers. Among these are the obligations they have to those who serve under them, including the duty not to waste their lives. The latter seems obvious and is, indeed, required by the principle of proportionality, but history supplies ample examples of generals who spent the lives of their men with profligacy. For a variety of reasons, however, military leaders in modern democracies are very alert to potential casualties, and there is great—possibly too great (Cook 2004: 92; Whetham 2011: 21–2)—emphasis on so-called force protection. Indeed, officers sometimes say that their job is to bring their people home safely. This cannot be taken literally, of course. War obliges commanders to order troops into combat, often in circumstances that guarantee that at least some of them will perish.

Officers have a responsibility to preserve as best they can not only the lives and but also the humanity of those they lead (French 2009). Modern military organizations are increasingly sensitive to the various psychological wounds that exposure to combat can cause. The nature of war is such that even when it is fought justly, combatants inevitably violate the norms of civilian life; they operate in a psychologically alien terrain and do things that are far beyond normal bounds, things they may later find difficult to live with. Furthermore, there are the "moral injuries" to self and character caused by "perpetrating, failing to prevent, or bearing witness to acts that transgress deeply held moral beliefs and expectations," injuries that can impair the future well-being of combatants (Shay 2013: 303). How can combatants avoid moral injury? How can they experience the horrors of war and yet retain their moral bearings and humanity? Finding satisfactory answers to these questions is no simple matter, but a few things are clear.

To begin with, officers must consistently reinforce what the military organization as a whole should be teaching, namely, the centrality to military identity of adherence to the received rules of war. Moreover, they must exemplify these professional values themselves. Among other things, they must refrain from dehumanizing both the enemy they are fighting and the civilians who get caught up in the contest, teaching those in their command always to respect the dignity and humanity of the people they encounter. They should, furthermore, avoid as best they can placing young men and women in morally risky situations, that is, in situations in which—as a result of inadequate training, deficient leadership, or ill-considered or unrealistic orders—fear, desperation, or too great an emphasis on success of the mission can lead them to violate the received rules of war and the principles of *jus in bello* that should be at the core of their professional identity and sense of self. Insofar, however, as both officers and enlisted men and women understand the moral basis of the rules they are to follow, the less difficult it will be for them to retain their moral and psychological balance even in the most extreme and terrifying circumstances, thus preserving themselves from damage to their psyche and character. This book has endeavored to contribute to that understanding.

To spare young men and women from moral and psychological injury, it helps if they believe that they are fighting in a morally justified war. This makes it easier to return to civilian life proud of what they have done. Few things are more corrosive than knowledge that one fought and possibly killed in a cause that lacked moral legitimacy, even if one fought honorably and within the rules of war. Chapter 8 maintained that officers are not professionally responsible for ensuring that their subordinates fight only in justified wars. That, rather, is a responsibility, directly, of our political leaders and, indirectly, of all of us, especially in a democracy. This responsibility is more likely to be fulfilled if people think clearly about the morality of war and understand exactly when it is right to wage it and when it is not, and why. This book has endeavored to bring us closer to that understanding, too.

Specifically, this book has developed and defended a utilitarian response to the two central ethical questions posed by war, namely: When is it right to fight? And what are the moral limits on how war may be fought? Utilitarianism entails the principle (UWP) that it is morally right for a state to wage war if and only if no other course of action open to it has greater expected well-being. This is a demanding criterion, one that states have often failed to meet. Nevertheless, even non-utilitarians should find the core idea compelling: States should not resort to arms unless they have no better option, that is, no option that better promotes the long-term well-being of all. Of course, determining whether waging a given war satisfies UWP can be tough. To some extent, this difficulty can be mitigated in practice, first, by using the familiar *ad bellum* rules of just war theory to guide discussion and, second, by recognizing and respecting a right of national defense. That right entails that states are prima facie justified in using necessary and proportionate force to ward off armed attack without having to show that their doing so maximizes well-being. Undoubtedly, controversial cases will remain. But UWP productively focuses debate where it belongs—on the impact that different policies are likely to have on the lives of real human beings.

Even if a state is morally justified in waging war, there are moral constraints on how that war may be fought. In particular, utilitarianism staunchly supports what I called the received rules of war, which comprise the positive law of armed conflict along with the principles of necessity, proportionality, and discrimination and non-combatant immunity. It requires states and those who fight for them to adhere firmly to those rules, while at the same time it seeks to refine or modify the received rules so as to make them as welfare-promoting as possible. Moreover, or so I argued, only a consequentialist account satisfactorily explains why those rules have the moral force they do. I also contended that these rules are not (as the *ad bellum* principles of just war theory are for utilitarians) mere guidelines or rules of thumb. Rather, utilitarians want combatants to have internalized a firm, virtually absolute moral commitment to them. Those rules—not direct act-utilitarian calculation—should govern their conduct during war.

Much of the argument and analysis of this book sails against the tide of recent philosophical work on the ethics of war, which is largely non-consequentialist in character. I have given some reasons for thinking that despite its philosophical sophistication, moral seriousness, and many valuable insights, much of contemporary just war theorizing is deficient because it lacks theoretical underpinning, resting instead on appeals to our moral intuitions, intuitions that tend to reflect everyday life in peacetime. This is one reason why philosophers are at loggerheads over some central questions in the ethics of war. But even if well-founded, this complaint hardly establishes the viability or moral attractiveness of a utilitarian approach to war. Readers must judge that for themselves based on their assessment of the particular answers that the theory proffers to the central questions in this field. It is worth reiterating, though, that adopting a utilitarian approach to the ethics of war does not require embracing utilitarianism as one's overall normative theory. Utilitarianism, of course, entails utilitarian answers to the ethical questions posed by war, but those answers stand independent of the general theory and can and, I believe, should be accepted even by those who favor some other basic account of right and wrong or who find no general normative theory completely satisfactory. This is because of the distinctive appeal, when it comes to questions of war, of a consequentialist procedure, especially one that emphasizes, as utilitarianism does, the moral centrality of human well-being.

By the same token, this book has not sought to defend utilitarianism across the board or to address all possible objections to it. It has, furthermore, skirted a number of theoretical matters that divide contemporary utilitarians and that a full treatment of the theory would have to address. In particular, it has said little about the meaning of well-being, not entering into the debate over how best to conceptualize it—does it, for instance, consist, as many believe, solely in having one's preferences fulfilled? These and other questions that are important for utilitarianism and for moral theory generally are tangential to the more applied goals of this book, the arguments of which are compatible with a number of different answers to them. On the other hand, if this book has succeeded in advancing plausible and perhaps compelling answers to the basic ethical questions of war, this will redound to the credit of utilitarianism, enhancing its claim to be considered a cogent and defensible general account of right and wrong. At the same time, by elaborating a utilitarian approach to the ethical questions associated with war, the present study sheds fresh light on the theory itself and, in this way, represents a modest contribution not just to the ethics of war but also to the consequentialist tradition in ethics and to moral philosophy more generally.

Much more, of course, could be said about a number of the issues that I have dealt with. No one is more conscious of this than I am, nor of various matters that this work leaves unaddressed. Progress in philosophy, though real, takes time, and only in recent years have philosophers written much about the ethics of war, and little of that from a utilitarian perspective. If this book contributes fruitfully to the growing discussion of the moral questions raised by war and certainly if it inspires others to pursue further and in more detail consequentialist or utilitarian answers to those questions, then it will have accomplished something.

REFERENCES

Adams, M.C.C. (1994) *The Best War Ever: America and World War II*, Baltimore, MD: Johns Hopkins University Press.

Alexander, L. and Sherwin, E. (2008) *Demystifying Legal Reasoning*, Cambridge: Cambridge University Press.

Altman, A. and Wellman, C.H. (2008) "From humanitarian intervention to assassination: human rights and political violence," *Ethics*, 118(2): 228–57.

Andrić, V. (2013) "Objective consequentialism and the licensing dilemma," *Philosophical Studies*, 162(3): 547–66.

Ang, J.M.S. (2013) "Fighting the humanitarian war: justifications and limitations," in F. Allhoff, N.G. Evans, and A. Henschke (eds) *Routledge Handbook of Ethics and War: Just War Theory in the Twenty-First Century*, New York: Routledge.

Anscombe, G.E.M. (1981a) "Mr. Truman's degree," *Ethics, Religion and Politics (Collected Philosophical Papers, Vol. 3)*, Minneapolis: University of Minnesota Press.

—— (1981b) "War and murder," *Ethics, Religion and Politics (Collected Philosophical Papers, Vol. 3)*, Minneapolis: University of Minnesota Press.

Appiah, K.A. (2008) *Experiments in Ethics*, Cambridge, MA: Harvard University Press.

Austin, J. (1995) *The Province of Jurisprudence Determined*, ed. W.E. Rumble, Cambridge: Cambridge University Press.

Avineri, S. (2009) "'Israel: civilians and combatants': an exchange," *New York Review of Books*, 56(13): 74.

Ayer, A.J. (1985) "The scope of reason," *Dialetica*, 39(4): 265–77.

Baker, D.-P. (2011) *Just Warriors, Inc.: The Ethics of Privatized Force*, London: Continuum.

Barry, B. (1995) *Justice as Impartiality*, Oxford: Oxford University Press.

Bazargan, S. (2011) "The permissibility of aiding and abetting unjust wars," *Journal of Moral Philosophy*, 8(4): 513–29.

—— (2014) "Varieties of contingent pacifism in war," in H. Frowe and G. Lang (eds) *How We Fight*, Oxford: Oxford University Press.

Bellamy, A.J. (2006) *Just Wars: From Cicero to Iraq*, Cambridge: Polity Press.

—— (2015) "The responsibility to protect turns ten," *Ethics and International Affairs*, 29(2): 161–85.

Bennett, J. (1995) *The Act Itself*, Oxford: Oxford University Press.

Bentham, J. (1843a) "Principles of international law," in J. Bowring (ed.) *The Works of Jeremy Bentham, Vol. 2*, Edinburgh: William Tait.

—— (1843b) "Memoirs and correspondence," in J. Bowring (ed.) *The Works of Jeremy Bentham, Vol. 10*, Edinburgh: William Tait.

—— (2005) *An Introduction to the Principles of Morals and Legislation*, ed. J.H. Burns and H.L.A. Hart, Oxford: Oxford University Press.

Besser-Jones, L. (2005) "Just war theory, legitimate authority, and the 'war' on terror," in T. Shanahan (ed.) *Philosophy 9/11: Thinking about the War on Terrorism*, LaSalle, IL: Open Court.

Betts, R.K. (2003) "Striking first: a history of thankfully lost opportunities," *Ethics and International Affairs*, 17(1): 17–24.

Biggar, N. (2007) "Between development and doubt: the recent career of just war doctrine in British churches," in C. Reed and D. Ryall (eds) *The Price of Peace: Just War in the Twenty-First Century*, Cambridge: Cambridge University Press.

Brandt, R.B. (1972) "Utilitarianism and the rules of war," *Philosophy and Public Affairs*, 1(2): 145–65.

—— (1979) *A Theory of the Good and the Right*, Oxford: Oxford University Press.

—— (1992) *Morality, Utilitarianism, and Rights*, Cambridge: Cambridge University Press.

Brink, D.O. (2014) "Principles and intuitions in ethics: historical and contemporary perspectives," *Ethics*, 124(4): 665–94.

Buchanan, A. and Keohane, R.O. (2004) "The preventive use of force: a cosmopolitan institutional proposal," *Ethics and International Affairs*, 18(1): 1–22.

Bulley, D. (2010) "The politics of ethical foreign policy: a responsibility to protect whom?" *European Journal of International Relations*, 16(3): 441–61.

Burleigh, M. (2011) *Moral Combat: Good and Evil in World War II*, New York: HarperCollins.

Christopher, P. (2004) *The Ethics of War and Peace: An Introduction to Legal and Moral Issues*, 3rd edn, Upper Saddle River, NJ: Prentice Hall.

Coates, A.J. (1997) *The Ethics of War*, Manchester: Manchester University Press.

Cohen, M. (1974) "Morality and the law of war," in V. Held, S. Morgenbesser, and T. Nagel (eds) *Philosophy, Morality, and International Affairs*, New York: Oxford University Press.

Coleman, S. (2013) *Military Ethics: An Introduction with Case Studies*, New York: Oxford University Press.

Conway, S. (1989) "Bentham on peace and war," *Utilitas*, 1(1): 82–101.

Cook, M.L. (2004) *The Moral Warrior: Ethics and Service in the U.S. Military*, Albany, NY: SUNY Press.

—— (2008) "Revolt of the generals: a case study in professional ethics," *Parameters*, 38(1): 4–15.

Coppieters, B. and Fotion, N. (eds) (2002) *Moral Constraints on War: Principles and Cases*, Lanham, MD: Lexington.

Crane, D.M. and Reisner, D. (2011) "'Jousting at windmills': the laws of armed conflict in an age of terror—state actors and nonstate elements," in W.C. Banks (ed.) *New Battlefields/Old Laws: Critical Debates on Asymmetric Warfare*, New York: Columbia University Press.

Crawford, N.C. (2007) "The false promise of preventive war: the 'new security consensus' and a more insecure world," in H. Shue and D. Rodin (eds) *Preemption: Military Action and Moral Justification*, Oxford: Oxford University Press.

Davenport, M.M. (1987a) "Professionals or hired guns? Loyalties are the difference," in M. Watkin, K. Wenker, and J. Kempf (eds) *Military Ethics*, Washington, DC: National Defense University Press.

—— (1987b) "Ethics and the military organization," in M. Watkin, K. Wenker, and J. Kempf (eds) *Military Ethics*, Washington, DC: National Defense University Press.

Dill, J. and Shue, H. (2012) "Limiting the killing in war: military necessity and the St. Petersburg assumption," *Ethics and International Affairs*, 26(3): 311–33.

Dinstein, Y. (2003) "Unlawful combatancy," in F.L. Borch and P.S. Wilson (eds) *International Law and the War on Terror (International Law Studies, Vol. 79)*, Newport, RI: Naval War College.

Dipert, R.R. (2006) "Preventive war and the epistemological dimension of the morality of war," *Journal of Military Ethics*, 5(1): 32–54.

Dobos, N. (2008) "Rebellion, humanitarian intervention, and the prudential constraints on war," *Journal of Military Ethics*, 7(2): 102–15.

Doris, J.M. (2002) *Lack of Character: Personality and Moral Behavior*, Cambridge: Cambridge University Press.

Dower, N. (2009) *The Ethics of War and Peace*, Cambridge: Polity Press.

Downes, A.B. (2008) *Targeting Civilians in War*, Ithaca, NY: Cornell University Press.

Doyle, M.W. (2014) "Law, ethics, and the responsibility to protect," in D.E. Scheid (ed.) *The Ethics of Armed Humanitarian Intervention*, Cambridge: Cambridge University Press.

Dunlap Jr., C.J. (2013) "Military justice," in D.M. Kennedy (ed.) *The Modern American Military*, New York: Oxford University Press.

Dworkin, R. (1977) *Taking Rights Seriously*, Cambridge, MA: Harvard University Press.

Eckert, A.E. (2009) "National defense and state personality," *Journal of International Political Theory*, 5(2): 161–76.

Ellner, A., Robinson, P., and Whetham, D. (eds) (2014) *When Soldiers Say No: Selective Conscientious Objection in the Modern Military*, Farnham: Ashgate.

Elshtain, J.B. (2003) *Just War Against Terror: The Burden of American Power in a Violent World*, New York: Basic Books.

Estlund, D. (2007) "On the following of orders in an unjust war," *Journal of Political Philosophy*, 15(2): 213–34.

Ezorsky, G. (1987) "War and innocence," *Public Affairs Quarterly*, 1(2): 111–16.

Fabre, C. (2009) "Guns, food, and liability to attack in war," *Ethics*, 120(1): 36–63.

—— (2012) *Cosmopolitan War*, Oxford: Oxford University Press.

Fabre, C. and Lazar, S. (eds) (2014) *The Morality of Defensive War*, Oxford: Oxford University Press.

Feldman, F. (2006) "Actual utility, the objection from impracticality, and the move to expected utility," *Philosophical Studies*, 129(1): 49–79.

Fiala, A. (2008) *The Just War Myth*, Lanham, MD: Rowman & Littlefield.

—— (2010) "Pacifism," *Stanford Encyclopedia of Philosophy*, online at http://plato.stanford. edu.

Ficarrotta, J.C. (2008) "A higher moral standard for the military," in G.R. Lucas, Jr. and W.R. Rubel (eds) *Ethics and the Military Profession: The Moral Foundations of Leadership*, Boston, MA: Pearson Custom Publishing.

Fisher, D. (2011) *Morality and War: Can War be Just in the Twenty-First Century?* Oxford: Oxford University Press.

Fletcher, G.P. and Ohlin, J.D. (2008) *Defending Humanity: When Force is Justified and Why*, Oxford: Oxford University Press.

Fotion, N. (2007) *War and Ethics: A New Just War Theory*, London: Continuum.

Fotion, N. and Elfstrom, C. (1986) *Military Ethics: Guidelines for Peace and War*, London: Routledge & Kegan Paul.

French, S.E. (2003) *The Code of the Warrior: Exploring Warrior Values Past and Present*, Lanham, MD: Rowman & Littlefield.

—— (2009) "Sergeant Davis's stern charge: the obligation of officers to preserve the humanity of their troops," *Journal of Military Ethics*, 8(2): 116–26.

Frowe, H. (2011) *The Ethics of War and Peace: An Introduction*, London and New York: Routledge.

Frowe, H. and Lang, G. (2014) "Introduction," in H. Frowe and G. Lang (eds) *How We Fight*, Oxford: Oxford University Press.

Fullinwider, R.K. (1975) "War and innocence," *Philosophy and Public Affairs*, 5(1): 90–7.

Gabriel, R.A. (1987) "Legitimate avenues of military protest in a democratic society," in M. Watkin, K. Wenker, and J. Kempf (eds) *Military Ethics*, Washington, DC: National Defense University Press.

Garrett, S.A. (2007) "Airpower and non-combatant immunity: the road to Dresden," in I. Primoratz (ed.) *Civilian Immunity in War*, Oxford: Oxford University Press.

Glover, J. (1999) *Humanity: A Moral History of the Twentieth Century*, New Haven, CN: Yale University Press.

Godwin, W. (1971) *Enquiry Concerning Political Justice*, ed. K.C. Carter, Oxford: Oxford University Press.

Goodin, R.E. (1995) *Utilitarianism as a Public Philosophy*, Cambridge: Cambridge University Press.

Grayling, A.C. (2006) *Among the Dead Cities: The History and Moral Legacy of the WWII Bombing of Civilians in Germany and Japan*, New York: Walker.

Green, J.D. (2014) "Beyond point-and-shoot morality: why cognitive (neuro)science matters for ethics," *Ethics*, 124(4): 695–726.

Green, M. (1992) "War, innocence, and theories of sovereignty," *Social Theory and Practice*, 18(1): 39–62.

Gross, M.L. (2010) *Moral Dilemmas of Modern Warfare: Torture, Assassination, and Blackmail in an Age of Asymmetric Conflict*, Cambridge: Cambridge University Press.

—— (2015) *The Ethics of Insurgency: A Critical Guide to Just Guerrilla Warfare*, Cambridge: Cambridge University Press.

Gruzalski, B. (2006) "Some implications of utilitarianism for practical ethics: the case against the military response to terrorism," in H.R. West (ed.) *The Blackwell Guide to Mill's Utilitarianism*, Oxford: Blackwell.

Guthrie, G. and Quinlan, M. (2007) *Just War: The Just War Tradition: Ethics in Modern Warfare*, New York: Walker.

Hackett, J.W. (1979) "The military in service of the state," in M.M. Wakin (ed.) *War, Morality, and the Military Profession*, Boulder, CO: Westview.

Haines, S. (2014) "Humanitarian intervention: genocide, crimes against humanity and the use of force," in G. Kassimeris and J. Buckley (eds) *The Ashgate Research Companion to Modern Warfare*, Farnham: Ashgate.

Hampshire, S. (1970) "Russell, radicalism, and reason," *New York Review of Books*, 15(6): 4–6.

—— (1978) "Morality and pessimism," in S. Hampshire (ed.) *Public and Private Morality*, Cambridge: Cambridge University Press.

Hanson, V.D. (2009) *The Western Way of War: Infantry Battle in Classical Greece*, 2nd edn, Berkeley: University of California Press.

Hardin, R. (1988) *Morality within the Limits of Reason*, Chicago, IL: University of Chicago Press.

Hare, R.M. (1963) *Freedom and Reason*, New York: Oxford University Press.

—— (1972) "Rules of war and moral reasoning," *Philosophy and Public Affairs*, 1(2): 166–81.

—— (1979) "What is wrong with slavery?" *Philosophy and Public Affairs*, 8(2): 103–21.

—— (1981) *Moral Thinking: Its Level, Method, and Point*, Oxford: Oxford University Press.

—— (1999) *Objective Prescriptions and Other Essays*, Oxford: Oxford University Press.

Harsanyi, J.C. (1976) *Essays in Ethics, Social Behavior, and Scientific Explanation*, Dordrecht: Reidel.

—— (1982) "Morality and the theory of rational behavior," in A. Sen and B. Williams (eds) *Utilitarianism and Beyond*, Cambridge: Cambridge University Press.

Hart, H.L.A. (1994) *The Concept of Law*, 2nd edn, Oxford: Oxford University Press.

Hartle, A.E. (2004) *Moral Issues in Military Decision Making*, 2nd edn, Lawrence: University Press of Kansas.

Hedges, C. (2002) *War is a Force that Gives us Meaning*, New York: Public Affairs.

Heinze, E.A. (2005) "Commonsense morality and the consequentialist ethics of humanitarian intervention," *Journal of Military Ethics*, 4(3): 168–82.

—— (2009) *Waging Humanitarian War: The Ethics, Law, and Politics of Humanitarian Intervention*, Albany: State University of New York Press.

Held, V. (2004) "Terrorism and war," *Journal of Ethics*, 8(1): 59–75.

Holmes, R.L. (1989) *On War and Morality*, Princeton, NJ: Princeton University Press.

Hooker, B. (2000) *Ideal Code, Real World*, Oxford: Oxford University Press.

Howard, M. (ed.) (1979) *Restraints on War: Studies in the Limitation of Armed Conflict*, Oxford: Oxford University Press.

Howard, M., Andreopoulos, G.J., and Shulman, M.R. (eds) (1994) *The Laws of War: Constraints on Warfare in the Western World*, New Haven, CN: Yale University Press.

Howard-Snyder, F. (2011) "Doing vs. allowing harm," *Stanford Encyclopedia of Philosophy*, online at http://plato.stanford.edu.

Huntington, S.P. (1957) *The Soldier and the State: The Theory and Politics of Civil–Military Relations*, Cambridge, MA: Harvard University Press.

Hurka, T. (2005) "Proportionality in the morality of war," *Philosophy and Public Affairs*, 33(1): 34–66.

—— (2007) "Liability and just cause," *Ethics and International Affairs*, 21(2): 199–218.

Johnson, J.T. (1981) *Just War Tradition and the Restraint of War: A Moral and Historical Inquiry*, Princeton, NJ: Princeton University Press.

—— (1999) *Morality and Contemporary Warfare*, New Haven, CN: Yale University Press.

—— (2000) "Maintaining the protection of non-combatants," *Journal of Peace Research*, 37(4): 421–48.

—— (2005) *The War to Oust Saddam Hussein*, Lanham, MD: Rowman & Littlefield.

—— (2011) *Ethics and the Use of Force: Just War in Historical Perspective*, Farnham: Ashgate.

Kagan, S. (1989) *The Limits of Morality*, Oxford: Oxford University Press.

—— (2000) "Evaluative focal points," in B. Hooker, E. Mason, and D.E. Miller (eds) *Morality, Rules and Consequences: A Critical Reader*, Edinburgh: Edinburgh University Press.

Kamm, F.M. (2012) *The Moral Target: Aiming at Right Conduct in War and Other Conflicts*, Oxford: Oxford University Press.

Kaplow, L. and Shavell, S. (2002) *Fairness versus Welfare*, Cambridge, MA: Harvard University Press.

Kasher, A. and Yadlin, A. (2005a) "Assassination and preventive killing," *SAIS Review of International Affairs*, 25(1): 41–57.

—— (2005b) "Military ethics of fighting terror: an Israeli perspective," *Journal of Military Ethics*, 4(1): 3–32.

Keegan, J. (1998) *War and Our World*, New York: Random House.

Kuperman, A. (2009) "Rethinking the responsibility to protect," *Whitehead Journal of Diplomacy and International Relations*, 10(1): 33–43.

Kutz, C. (2005) "The difference uniforms make: collective violence in criminal law and war," *Philosophy and Public Affairs*, 33(2): 148–80.

Lackey, D.P. (1989) *The Ethics of War and Peace*, Upper Saddle River, NJ: Prentice Hall.

Lango, J.W. (2014) *The Ethics of Armed Conflict: A Cosmopolitan Just War Theory*, Edinburgh: Edinburgh University Press.

Lazar, S. (2014) "National defence, self-defence, and the problem of political aggression," in C. Fabre and S. Lazar (eds) *The Morality of Defensive War*, Oxford: Oxford University Press.

Lee, S.P. (2012) *Ethics and War: An Introduction*, Cambridge: Cambridge University Press.

Lefkowitz, D. (2008) "Collateral damage," in L. May (ed.) *War: Essays in Political Philosophy*, Cambridge: Cambridge University Press.

Luban, D. (1980) "Just war and human rights," *Philosophy and Public Affairs*, 9(2): 160–81.

—— (2004) "Preventive war," *Philosophy and Public Affairs*, 32(3): 207–48.

Lucas Jr., G.R. (2003) "From *jus ad bellum* to *jus ad pacem*: re-thinking just-war criteria for the use of military force for humanitarian ends," in D.K. Chatterjee and D.E. Scheid (eds) *Ethics and Foreign Intervention*, Cambridge: Cambridge University Press.

—— (2009) "Advice and dissent: 'the uniform perspective,'" *Journal of Military Ethics*, 8(2): 141–61.

—— (2013) "The case for preventive war," in D.K. Chatterjee (ed.) *The Ethics of Preventive War*, Cambridge: Cambridge University Press.

—— (2014) "Revisiting armed humanitarian intervention: a 25-year retrospective," in D.E. Scheid (ed.) *The Ethics of Armed Humanitarian Intervention*, Cambridge: Cambridge University Press.

MacArthur, D. (1964) *Reminiscences*, New York: McGraw-Hill.

McKeogh, C. (2002) *Innocent Civilians: The Morality of Killing in War*, Basingstoke: Palgrave Macmillan.

McMahan, J. (2006) "The ethics of killing in war," *Philosophia*, 34(1): 23–41.

—— (2009) *Killing in War*, Oxford: Oxford University Press.

—— (2010a) "Laws of war," in S. Besson and J. Tasioulas (eds) *The Philosophy of International Law*, Oxford: Oxford University Press.

—— (2010b) "The just distribution of harm between combatants and noncombatants," *Philosophy and Public Affairs*, 38(4): 342–79.

—— (2012) "Individual liability in war: a response to Fabre, Leveringhaus, and Tadros," *Utilitas*, 24(2): 278–99.

McMahan, J. and McKim, R. (1993) "The just war and the Gulf War," *Canadian Journal of Philosophy*, 23(4): 501–41.

Mapel, D.R. (2007) "The right of national defense," *International Studies Perspectives*, 8(1): 1–15.

Margalit, A. and Walzer, M. (2009) "Israel: civilians and combatants," *New York Review of Books*, 56(8): 21–2.

Mavrodes, G.I. (1975) "Conventions and the morality of war," *Philosophy and Public Affairs*, 4(2): 117–31.

May, L. (2007) *War Crimes and Just War*, New York: Cambridge University Press.

Meggle, G. (2003) "Is this war good? An ethical commentary," in A. Jokic (ed.) *Humanitarian Intervention: Moral and Philosophical Issues*, Peterborough, ON: Broadview.

Merton, T. (1993) *Henry's Wars and Shakespeare's Laws: Perspectives on the Law of War in the Later Middle Ages*, Oxford: Oxford University Press.

Mill, J. (1808) *Commerce Defended: An Answer to the Arguments by which Mr. Spence, Mr. Corbett, and Others, Have Attempted to Prove that Commerce is not a Source of National Wealth*, London: C. and R. Baldwin.

—— (1825) "Law of nations," reprinted from the *Supplement* to the *Encyclopedia Britannica*, London: J. Innis.

Mill, J.S. (1969a) "Bentham," in J.M. Robson (ed.) *The Collected Works of John Stuart Mill, Vol. 10: Essays on Ethics, Religion and Society*, Toronto: University of Toronto Press.

—— (1969b) "Whewell on moral philosophy," in J.M. Robson (ed.) *The Collected Works of John Stuart Mill, Vol. 10: Essays on Ethics, Religion and Society*, Toronto: University of Toronto Press.

—— (1969c) "Utilitarianism," in J.M. Robson (ed.) *The Collected Works of John Stuart Mill, Vol. 10: Essays on Ethics, Religion and Society*, Toronto: University of Toronto Press.

—— (1972a) *The Collected Works of John Stuart Mill, Vol. 15: The Later Letters of John Stuart Mill, 1849–1873*, Part II, ed. F.E. Mineka and D.N. Lindley, Toronto: University of Toronto Press.

—— (1972b) *The Collected Works of John Stuart Mill, Vol. 16: The Later Letters of John Stuart Mill, 1849–1873*, Part III, ed. F.E. Mineka and D.N. Lindley, Toronto: University of Toronto Press.

—— (1974) *The Collected Works of John Stuart Mill, Vol. 8: A System of Logic, Ratiocinative and Inductive, Part 2*, ed. J.M. Robson, Toronto: University of Toronto Press.

—— (1977) "On liberty," in J.M. Robson (ed.) *The Collected Works of John Stuart Mill, Vol. 18: Essays on Politics and Society, Part 1*, Toronto: University of Toronto Press.

—— (1981) *The Collected Works of John Stuart Mill, Vol. 1: Autobiography and Literary Essays*, ed. J.M. Robson and J. Stillinger, Toronto: University of Toronto Press.

—— (1984a) "A few words on non-intervention," in J.M. Robson (ed.) *The Collected Works of John Stuart Mill, Vol. 21: Essays on Equality, Law, and Education*, Toronto: University of Toronto Press.

—— (1984b) "The contest in America," in J.M. Robson (ed.) *The Collected Works of John Stuart Mill, Vol. 21: Essays on Equality, Law, and Education*, Toronto: University of Toronto Press.

Miller, J.J. (2004) "*Jus ad bellum* and an officer's moral obligations: invincible ignorance, the Constitution, and Iraq," *Social Theory and Practice*, 30(4): 457–84.

Miller, R.W. (2010) "Crossing borders to fight injustice: the ethics of humanitarian intervention," in R. Wertheimer (ed.) *Empowering our Military Conscience: Transforming Just War Theory and Military Moral Education*, Farnham: Ashgate.

Moore, G.E. (1968) *Principia Ethica*, Cambridge: Cambridge University Press.

—— (2005) *Ethics*, ed. W.H. Shaw, Oxford: Oxford University Press.

Moore, H.G. and Galloway, J.L. (1992) *We Were Soldiers Once … and Young: Ia Drang—the Battle That Changed the War in Vietnam*, New York: Random House.

Moseley, A. (2009) "Just war theory," *Internet Encyclopedia of Philosophy*, online at http://www.iep.utm.edu.

Nagel, T. (1972) "War and massacre," *Philosophy and Public Affairs*, 1(2): 123–44.

Nathanson, S. (2010) *Terrorism and the Ethics of War*, Cambridge: Cambridge University Press.

—— (2012) "Are attacks on civilians always wrong?" in D.W. Lovell and I. Primoratz (eds) *Protecting Civilians During Violent Conflict: Theoretical and Practical Issues for the 21st Century*, Farnham: Ashgate.

—— (2013) "Are preventive wars always wrong?" in D.K. Chatterjee (ed.) *The Ethics of Preventive War*, Cambridge: Cambridge University Press.

Norcross, A. (2008) "Off her trolley? Francis Kamm and the metaphysics of morality," *Utilitas*, 20(1): 65–80.

Norman, R. (1995) *Ethics, Killing and War*, Cambridge: Cambridge University Press.

Nozick, R. (1974) *Anarchy, State, and Utopia*, New York: Basic Books.

Orend, B. (2005) "War," *Stanford Encyclopedia of Philosophy*, online at http://plato.stanford.edu.

—— (2006) *The Morality of War*, Peterborough, ON: Broadview.

Paley, W. (2002) *The Principles of Moral and Political Philosophy*, Indianapolis, IN: Liberty Fund.

Parfit, D. (1984) *Reasons and Persons*, Oxford: Oxford University Press.

Pattison, J. (2010) *Humanitarian Intervention and the Responsibility to Protect: Who Should Intervene?* Oxford: Oxford University Press.

—— (2014) "Bombing the beneficiaries: the distribution of the costs of the responsibility to protect and humanitarian intervention," in D.E. Scheid (ed.) *The Ethics of Armed Humanitarian Intervention*, Cambridge: Cambridge University Press.

Pettit, P. (1991) "Consequentialism," in P. Singer (ed.) *A Companion to Ethics*, Oxford: Blackwell.

Pettit, P. and Smith, M. (2000) "Global consequentialism," in B. Hooker, E. Mason, and D.E. Miller (eds) *Morality, Rules and Consequences: A Critical Reader*, Edinburgh: Edinburgh University Press.

Pojman, L.P. (2000) *Life and Death: Grappling with the Moral Dilemmas of Our Times*, 2nd edn, Belmont, CA: Wadsworth.

Portmore, D.W. (2001) "Can an act-consequentialist theory be agent relative?" *American Philosophical Quarterly*, 38(4): 363–77.

Primoratz, I. (2007) "Civilian immunity in war: its ground, scope, and weight," in I. Primoratz (ed.) *Civilian Immunity in War*, Oxford: Oxford University Press.

Quinn, M. (2014) "Bentham on mensuration: calculation and moral reasoning," *Utilitas*, 26(1): 61–104.

Rachels, J. (2003) *The Elements of Moral Philosophy*, 4th edn, New York: McGraw-Hill.

Railton, P. (1988) "Alienation, consequentialism, and the demands of morality," *Philosophy and Public Affairs*, 13(2): 134–71.

Rawls, J. (1971) *A Theory of Justice*, Cambridge, MA: Harvard University Press.

—— (1999a) *Collected Papers*, ed. S. Freeman, Cambridge, MA: Harvard University Press.

—— (1999b) *The Law of Peoples*, Cambridge, MA: Harvard University Press.

Regan, R.J. (2103) *Just War: Principles and Cases*, 2nd edn, Washington, DC: Catholic University of America Press.

Reichberg, G.M., Syse, H., and Begby, E. (eds) (2006) *The Ethics of War: Classic and Contemporary Readings*, Oxford: Blackwell.

Rhodes, B. (2009) *An Introduction to Military Ethics: A Reference Handbook*, Santa Barbara, CA: Praeger.

Roberts, A. (2003) "The laws of war in the war on terror," in F.L Borch and P.S. Wilson (eds) *International Law and the War on Terror (International Law Studies, Vol. 79)*, Newport, RI: Naval War College.

—— (2008) "The principle of equal application of the laws of war," in D. Rodin and H. Shue (eds) *Just and Unjust Warriors: The Moral and Legal Status of Soldiers*, Oxford: Oxford University Press.

Roberts, A. and Guelff, R. (eds) (2000) *Documents on the Laws of War*, 3rd edn, Oxford: Oxford University Press.

Robinson, P. (2009) "Integrity and selective conscientious objection," *Journal of Military Ethics*, 8(1): 34–47.

Rodin, D. (2002) *War and Self-Defense*, Oxford: Oxford University Press.

—— (2006) "The ethics of asymmetric warfare," in R. Sorabji and D. Rodin (eds) *The Ethics of War: Shared Problems in Different Traditions*, Farnham: Ashgate.

—— (2007) "The problem with prevention," in H. Shue and D. Rodin (eds) *Preemption: Military Action and Moral Justification*, Oxford: Oxford University Press.

—— (2008) "The moral inequality of soldiers: why *jus in bello* asymmetry is half right," in D. Rodin and H. Shue (eds) *Just and Unjust Warriors: The Moral and Legal Status of Soldiers*, Oxford: Oxford University Press.

—— (2014) "The myth of national self-defence," in C. Fabre and S. Lazar (eds) *The Morality of Defensive War*, Oxford: Oxford University Press.

Roff, H.M. (2009) "Response to Pattison: whose responsibility to protect?" *Journal of Military Ethics*, 8(1): 79–85.

Ross, W.D. (1930) *The Right and the Good*, Oxford: Oxford University Press.

Russell, B. (1915) "The ethics of war," *International Journal of Ethics*, 25(2): 127–42.

—— (1943–4) "The future of pacifism," *The American Scholar*, 13(1): 7–10.

—— (2009) "The elements of ethics," in B. Russell (ed.) *Philosophical Essays*, Abingdon: Routledge.

Ruys, T. (2010) *"Armed Attack" and Article 51 of the UN Charter: Evolutions in Customary Law and Practice*, Cambridge: Cambridge University Press.

Ryan, C. (2008) "Moral equality, victimhood, and the sovereignty symmetry problem," in D. Rodin and H. Shue (eds) *Just and Unjust Warriors: The Moral and Legal Status of Soldiers*, Oxford: Oxford University Press.

—— (2013) "Pacifism, just war, and self-defense," *Philosophia*, 41(4): 977–1005.

Sartorius, R. (1972) "Individual conduct and social norms: a utilitarian account," *Ethics*, 82(3): 200–18.

Schauer, F. (1991) *Playing by the Rules: A Philosophical Examination of Rule-Based Decision-Making in Law and Life*, Oxford: Oxford University Press.

Shaver, R. (2004) "The appeal of utilitarianism," *Utilitas*, 16(3): 235–50.

Shaw, W.H. (1993) "On the paradox of deontology," in J. Heil (ed.) *Rationality, Morality, and Self-Interests: Essays Honoring Mark Carl Overvold*, Boulder, CO: Westview.

—— (1999) *Contemporary Ethics: Taking Account of Utilitarianism*, Oxford: Blackwell.

Shay, J. (2013) "Casualties," in D.M. Kennedy (ed.) *The Modern American Military*, New York: Oxford University Press.

Shue, H. (2008) "Do we need a 'morality of war'?" in D. Rodin and H. Shue (eds) *Just and Unjust Warriors: The Moral and Legal Status of Soldiers*, Oxford: Oxford University Press.

—— (2010) "Laws of war," in S. Besson and J. Tasioulas (eds) *The Philosophy of International Law*, Oxford: Oxford University Press.

Shue, H. and Wippman, D. (2002) "Limiting attacks on dual-use facilities performing indispensable civilian functions," *Cornell International Law Journal*, 35(3): 559–79.

Sidgwick, H. (1908) *The Elements of Politics*, 3rd edn, London: Macmillan.

—— (1966) *The Methods of Ethics*, 7th edn, New York: Dover.

—— (1998a) "The morality of strife," *Practical Ethics: A Collection of Addresses and Essays*, ed. S. Bok, New York: Oxford University Press.

—— (1998b) "Public morality," *Practical Ethics: A Collection of Addresses and Essays*, ed. S. Bok, New York: Oxford University Press.

Singer, P. (2005) "Ethics and intuitions," *Journal of Ethics*, 9(3/4): 331–52.

Sinnott-Armstrong, W. (2007) "Preventive war: what is it good for?" in H. Shue and D. Rodin (eds) *Preemption: Military Action and Moral Justification*, Oxford: Oxford University Press.

Smart, J.J.C. (1973) "An outline of a system of utilitarian ethics," in J.J.C. Smart and B. Williams, *Utilitarianism: For and Against*, Cambridge: Cambridge University Press.

Steinhoff, U. (2007) *On the Ethics of War and Terrorism*, Oxford: Oxford University Press.

Taylor, H. (1988) "War and peace," in J.M. Robson and B.L. Kinzer (eds) *The Collected Works of John Stuart Mill, Vol. 19: Public and Parliamentary Speeches, Part II*, Toronto: University of Toronto Press.

Tesón, F.R. (2006) "Eight principles for humanitarian intervention," *Journal of Military Ethics*, 5(2): 93–113.

Thomson, J.J. (1991) "Self-defense," *Philosophy and Public Affairs*, 20(4): 283–310.

—— (2001) *Goodness and Advice*, Princeton, NJ: Princeton University Press.

Thucydides (1996) *The Landmark Thucydides: A Comprehensive Guide to the Peloponnesian War*, ed. R.B. Strassler, New York: Touchstone.

Timmons, M. (2002) *Moral Theory: An Introduction*, Lanham, MD: Rowman & Littlefield.

Varouxakis, G. (2013) *Liberty Abroad: J. S. Mill on International Relations*, Cambridge: Cambridge University Press.

Vaughn, L. (2010) *Contemporary Moral Arguments: Readings in Ethical Issues*, New York: Oxford University Press.

Walzer, M. (2004) *Arguing about War*, New Haven, CN: Yale University Press.

—— (2006a) "Response to McMahan's paper," *Philosophia*, 34(1): 43–5.

—— (2006b) *Just and Unjust Wars*, 4th edn, New York: Basic Books.

Wasserstrom, R. (1972) "The laws of war," *The Monist*, 56(1): 1–19.

—— (1974) "The responsibility of the individual for war crimes," in V. Held, S. Morgenbesser, and T. Nagel (eds) *Philosophy, Morality, and International Affairs*, New York: Oxford University Press.

Waters, C.P.M and Green, J.A. (2010) "International law: military force and armed conflict," in G. Kassimeris and J. Buckley (eds) *The Ashgate Research Companion to Modern Warfare*, Farnham: Ashgate.

Werner, R. (2013) "Just war theory: going to war and collective self-deception," in F. Allhoff, N.G. Evans, and A. Henschke (eds) *Routledge Handbook of Ethics and War: Just War Theory in the Twenty-First Century*, New York: Routledge.

Whetham, D. (2009) *Just Wars and Moral Victories: Surprise, Deception, and the Normative Framework of European War in the Later Middle Ages*, Leiden and Boston: Brill.

—— (2011) "The just war tradition: a pragmatic compromise," in D. Whetham (ed.) *Ethics, Law and Military Operations*, Basingstoke: Palgrave Macmillan.

Whitham, W. (2014) "A reconsideration of John Stuart Mill's account of political violence," *Utilitas*, 26(4): 409–31.

Whitman, J.P. (1993) "Utilitarianism and the laws of land warfare," *Public Affairs Quarterly*, 7(3): 261–75.

—— (2006–7) "Just war theory and the war on terrorism: a utilitarian perspective," *Public Integrity*, 9(1): 23–43.

Wilkins, B. (2003) "Humanitarian intervention: some doubts," in A. Jokic (ed.) *Humanitarian Intervention: Moral and Philosophical Issues*, Peterborough, ON: Broadview.

Williams, G. (1989) "J. S. Mill and political violence," *Utilitas*, 1(1): 102–11.

Wolfendale, J. (2009) "Professional integrity and disobedience in the military," *Journal of Military Ethics*, 8(2): 127–40.

Yasukawa, R. (1991) "James Mill on peace and war," *Utilitas*, 3(2): 179–97.

Zimmerman, M.J. (2008) *Living with Uncertainty: The Moral Significance of Ignorance*, Cambridge: Cambridge University Press.

Zupan, D.S. (2004) *War, Morality, and Autonomy: An Investigation in Just War Theory*, Farnham: Ashgate.

INDEX

CPSIA information can be obtained
at www.ICGtesting.com
Printed in the USA
BVHW040202030122
625347BV00010B/606